The Practical Guide to Information Design

The Practical Guide to Information Design

by Ronnie Lipton

John Wiley & Sons, Inc.

Library of Congress Cataloging-in-Publication Data:

Lipton, Ronnie.
   The practical guide to information design / by Ronnie Lipton.
      p. cm.
   Includes bibliographical references and index.

   ISBN-13 978-0-471-66295-2
   ISBN-10 0-471-66295-X (cloth)

   1. Commercial art—Technique.
   2. Graphic arts—Technique.
   3. Communication in design.
   I. Title.
NC1001.L58 2005
741.6—dc22

                        2005023408

Printed in the United States of America

10 9 8 7 6 5 4 3 2 1

Contents

Acknowledgments

It took many villages to make this book. Special thanks to:

Jessica Fagerhaugh, Tim Kenney, and Patrick Mirza for pivotal editing and kickstarting, even house calls. Thanks to Jeff Young for the same, plus photos, tech help, regular meals (did I say *love*?), and the benefit of the encyclopedia in his head. And thanks to four brilliant final-chapter reviewers who are responsible for improving this book beyond description, but not for any errors or inconsistencies that remain because I didn't have time to fix them: Ginny Redish (also for frequently sharing her abundant wisdom, hospitality, library, and referrals), Stephen Kosslyn (also for his insightful tours inside the eye and brain), Alex W. White (also for contributing so much to the type chapter, including type samples), and Jan V. White, clarity king (also for inspiring and guiding me over decades, and for handing me one of his unpublished—always perfect—articles).

Also, thanks to Kim Farcot for ongoing support and help and all-around sweetness; to Nigel Holmes, Nathan Shedroff, and Alina Wheeler for each referring enough friends to fill ten books (to Alina also for ongoing support and connecting me with her editor, now mine); to Margaret Cummins; to Robin Landa and Elizabeth Resnick for generously responding to my cold calls and sharing their book-business smarts; to Stefan Bucher for always brilliant brainstorming; to Tom Piwowar, Nanda Piwowar, and Ron Northrip for keeping my computer updated and happy for the duration (also to Tom for provocative debates); to Petra Algerova and Wally Burns for smart, thorough help with research (to Petra also for countless other book-support services and much-needed distractions); to Conrad Taylor for enlightening and entertaining calls and letters.

Many thanks, too, to those who generously contributed

. . . time, insights, and artwork: Aries Arditi; Carolyn Bagin; Ellie Barber; Burkey Belser; Sudhir Bhatia; Roger Black; Ken Carbone; Patrick Cavanagh; Dan Chen; Michael Chesman; Allen Coté; Kelley Dragonette; Lea Eiseman; Bob Erickson; Ann Firth; Felicia Garrett; Maria Giudice with Renee Anderson, Laura Haertling, and Clancy Nolan; John Grimwade; Peter Haack; Carla Hall with Kate Dautrich; Lars Harmsen; Gordon Hoeft; Nigel Holmes; Tony Julien; Joel Katz (who even redrew—in full color—three versions of a discarded preliminary sketch for this book); Stephen Kosslyn; Sanjay Koyani; Steve Krug; Jake Lefebure; Dave Merrill; Paul Mijksenaar; Dennis Powell; Whitney Quesenbery; Angelo Ragaza; Ginny Redish; Margaret Saliba; Phil Sawyer; Steven Schattman; Irene Jackson Schon; Eric Seidman; Nathan Shedroff; Bill Simmons; Jerry Snider; Sharon Stark; Marc Stoiber; Mark Sylvester; Greg Thomas; Colin Wheildon; Alex W. White; Jan V. White; and Richard Saul Wurman.

. . . research, syllabi, student exercises, and lesson plans: Carol Barnum, Gordon Drummond, Dave Farkas, and Karla Kitalong.

. . . artwork: Carol Anderson, Dieter Braun, Bill Cahan, Jeanie Comstock, Sean Culhane, Gary Drake, Jaimey Easler, Marian Emr, Britt Fagerheim, Kelly Groff, Dan Hoffman, Mirko Ilić, Noah Iliinsky, George Jones, Robin Latham, Dan Levin, Isaac Mizrahi, Eileen Rinkus, Melanie Sasse, Laurie Sims, Michael Stone, George Tscherny, Barbara Tversky, Deb Unger, Jill Wachter, Sam Wilson, and Penny Wright.

. . . additional help: Claire Duggart, Linda Jorgensen, Bruce Martin, James Reston Jr., Patti Schwartz, Deb Tompkins, and Virginia Von Fremd.

And many thanks always to Mark Beach, a most generous and understanding mentor/teacher; Les Greenberg, like Mark a printing genius; Gus Miller, the art teacher who taught me to see; Vincent Palumbo, master stone carver, master life teacher; Polly Pattison, newsletter-design and people-connecting maven; Ed Peskowitz, writing guru and benefactor; Fred Showker, longtime design buddy and tech adviser; and Jeff Young, Shirley and Nat Lipton, and Millie Young.

Introduction

Thank you for picking up this copy of *The Practical Guide to Information Design*. And congratulations on your interest in information design, because it's a field whose mission is helping people. Information design is the study and practice of bringing clarity and comprehensibility to visual materials that are meant to direct, teach, explain, or otherwise inform. It's both a discipline and a lifelong learning opportunity.

Effective information design accomplishes a lot:

- It helps people navigate and understand the increasingly complex world of facts, figures, directions, and demands.

- It helps people finish a task, solve a problem, or meet a need.

- It minimizes or eliminates frustrations.

- It begins and ends with understanding the people who will use the content and making sure that the content and its presentation and delivery serve them.

This book's goal is to help you design effectively for your audiences. It's to show you how to present content that's so clear and understandable, its viewers can perceive and comprehend it without having to think about navigational issues such as:

- "Where should I look first? Where do I look next?"

- "What kind of information is this?"

- "Where am I in this content (beginning, middle, end)?"

- "Why can't I understand this?"

Some information designers would add "simplicity" to the definition in the first paragraph on page 1. But others in the field argue that simplicity advocates are simply dumbing down information. There's no end to the opinions on this subject; many information designers seem to like nothing better than a good debate.

To simplify or not to simplify: well, it depends—on the audience, content, context, environment, materials, and other factors you'll learn about that affect perception and comprehension. Instead of signing on to either camp for life, let those factors determine your designs in each project. It's often best to simplify as much as you can while fully serving the audience's needs. It's *always* best to avoid simplifying to the point of insulting the audience's intelligence. This book will show you how to let knowledge of your audience guide you.

In fact, as most information designers will tell you only half jokingly, "it depends" is the answer to most information-design questions. (Can it be an accident that "it depends" shares an acronym with "information design"? Probably not.)

or content issues such as:

- "What's the point here?"
- "Why I should care about it?"
- "Why is it telling me everything except what I want to know?"

Your audiences are most likely to perceive and comprehend direction if you make sure you've covered the following elements:

- The concept fits into the right context for the audience. By learning what the audience already knows, you can link the new information to that preexisting knowledge in a logical way. And you'll present the right amount of information, not more or less than the audience needs.

- The concept's design offers no obstacles to perception and understanding. For example, it's free of distracting clutter, so it offers a clear path to reading and comprehension.

- The design uses meaningful nonverbal clues that enhance understanding, such as grouping related information and separating the unrelated.

Information design applies to a huge range of projects, including Web sites, forms, manuals, maps, publications, signs, slides, instructions, packages, equipment displays and keypads, commercials, menus, and more. To begin the process of connecting with your audiences, pay attention to yourself as an audience member. Notice and evaluate your reaction to the information that reaches you on a daily basis. The more you become aware of how information design works in your world, the more adept you'll become at creating it.

You might learn the most about how information design works by examining examples that *don't* work for you. You've experienced their inherent frustration if you've ever:

- tried to fill out an incomprehensible tax form or insurance application

- had to build or install something despite an instruction manual that failed to instruct properly

- been late for an appointment because highway signs on your route showed up too late for you to act upon them

- almost missed a plane because you couldn't find the departure time or gate or flight number on your boarding pass

• squinted in vain in a dimly lit basement at a too-small laundry-care label

(Such examples also will help you explain your field of work or study to those for whom it's not yet a household word. For that purpose, you won't find many examples that are higher-profile than the impact of Florida's poorly designed butterfly ballot on the 2000 U.S. presidential election.)

Another example of design that often doesn't work is informational kiosks in corporate lobbies, says Nathan Shedroff, information designer and author of *Experience Design*. Despite beautiful graphics and wonderful soundtracks, many kiosks became obsolete because their designers considered only the newcomer who would engage the kiosk just once or twice to learn about the corporation. They ignored the security guard or receptionist who would be forced to hear that soundtrack hour after hour, day after day. So, Shedroff says, it didn't take long for the forced listener to unplug the speakers or the whole system.

These examples illustrate the need to examine the audience, tasks, and environment before you make decisions about type, contrast, material, comprehensibility, and much more. They teach the importance of asking the right questions and making sure the design reflects the answers.

Let's consider that laundry-care label. To design a useful one, ideally you'd begin to understand the audience's needs by observing some typical audience members: people who check the label before they wash or dry the garment. Or at least you'd want to talk to them to find out what their needs are. For example:

• "How do you do laundry? Please describe your process."

• "Do you sort clothes first?" "If so, where?"

• "How often do you read the labels while you do the laundry?"

• "When do you read the labels?"

• "Where do you wash clothes?"

• "Please describe the surroundings." (After hearing the answer, you might also need to ask about lighting levels and whether there's a surface for placing clothes while hunting for and reading labels.)

• "Where do you expect to find the label in the garment?"

• "Have you ever had trouble reading a laundry care label?" (If yes, "What was the problem?")

- "About how long do you tend to keep clothes?"
- "Do labels tend to stay attached and legible as long as you keep clothes?"
- "About how often do you do laundry?"
- "How old are your washer and dryer? What are their conditions?"

Answers to such questions should lead you to understand the depth of the design problem. (You might also benefit from information such as how many washings an average garment endures, but you'll probably need to go to a laundry association for that info.) More than just putting the required words and symbols on a piece of cloth, your goal becomes how those words, symbols, and cloth can best serve the audience.

For example, some audience members have complained that thin labels flop around too much when wet to read easily, so let's look at thicker label material. But the label can't be so thick or stiff that it could irritate skin, another complaint heard in interviews. The label should attach where the audience expects to find it. And from the first day through multiple wearings and washings:

- the label must stay on
- the label's printing must not fade
- type and symbols must be big and contrasting enough to be legible even in dim light

More examples of information design's value

Instructions, directions, and other forms of information design must respect and anticipate the needs of the people using them, as shown in this scenario from Burkey Belser of Greenfield Belser Ltd., a design firm in Washington, D.C.

The elevator doors are about to close on a pregnant woman. You rush to the controls to open them, but you can't decipher the icons on the buttons to find the right one in time. Maybe the correct button has two triangles on their sides pointing away from a vertical line. You take too long under pressure of the "deadline" to find out you want *that* button and not the one with triangles pointing toward the vertical line.

Belser also cites a related scenario: You punch the wrong button for your floor. Because there's no "undo" button, all you can do is

This elevator keypad's icon represents the button for closing the doors.

This icon's on the one for opening the doors.

But could you make the correct choice in a pinch?

apologize or be embarrassed if you've scheduled an unneeded stop. By failing to anticipate what could go wrong, the designers of the elevator keypad failed to be helpful.

Airplane tickets fail to be helpful because of what they leave out. "Typically they will tell you when the plane departs, but not when it arrives," Belser says. Why *don't* tickets fill in the info gaps? "For most airlines, a ticket falls into the category of a form, an office supply," he notes, so it's not designed as something that's more highly valued.

With unhelpful, unclear manuals and other forms of instructions, companies regularly lose the opportunity to endear themselves to customers. "Wouldn't you have a loyal customer if everything you sent was easy to assemble, understand, install? You'd create a whole different relationship with that customer," Belser says.

These examples lead to this conclusion: *Effective information design shifts the focus from what we want to say to what the audience wants and needs, and how the audience wants and needs it.*

All that and more: What's in the book for you

To help you become a better information designer, whatever your background, this book demonstrates how to create materials that will serve both your audience and the organization that provides them. You'll see the process illustrated by examples and explanations from the world's most effective information designers. You'll find out how and what these designers learned about their audiences, and how that knowledge informed their designs. Every example connects to a principle for you to practice.

The book groups into three main sections: audience, word design, and picture design. It begins by showing how people are alike in how we perceive, based on our shared physiology and the corresponding principles of cognitive psychology (Chapter 1, "How humans [almost] universally perceive"). It goes on to show how we differ—how our individual cultures, experiences, needs, and preferences affect our responses to visual information (Chapter 2, "Usability and how to achieve it"). Both chapters show how an understanding of the audience should affect your designs.

In Sections II and III you'll find detailed guidelines and examples to help you convey information clearly in a variety of formats to a variety of audiences. Section II, for example, will show you how to make audience-serving decisions about type, layout, writing, and color.

Section III focuses on pictures: photos, illustrations, drawings, and information graphics such as graphs, charts, and maps.

You can read the chapters in any order, according to your needs and interests. So move from chapter to chapter in sequence, favor what attracts you most, or cherry-pick the examples that relate to an assignment that's on your desk right now.

You'll also find a list of the best sources of additional information in the information-design field. So, for example, if you specialize in Web design, you'll benefit from supplementing this book with one or more sources on the format. (Also note that understanding other formats besides your specialty will inform and improve the ones you design most often.)

Speaking of sources, much of what you'll find in the book is based on research. Even more comes from the practical experience and observations of information designers (including me). That's a valuable combination to adopt in your information design work: Balance research with the intuition you'll develop with experience. And learn to question any statement that begins with the words "research shows" to see whether it really applies to the situation at hand. Don't assume it does. (See page 7.)

Is this book for you?

This book *is* for you if you:

- design information (whether or not you're trained in graphic design, illustration, and/or writing)
- hire designers
- must convince a supervisor or management team of information design's value
- study or teach information design

You'll find exercises throughout the book to help you start thinking and making decisions like an information designer. In addition, you can use most of the illustrations in the book as an exercise: Analyze the design, maybe test it by showing it to people who aren't information designers, and see if you can improve it. You'll also find several additional exercises online at www.wiley.com/go/informationdesign.

Awareness building: An exercise for life

Become more aware of how you read and comprehend by becoming more aware of information design around you as you travel

⟫ Where Research's Value Ends

Information-design research studies often include test participants who are more motivated to perform than typical readers or Web site browsers. (It's what Janice Redish calls a "zero-friction" test.) First, participants agree to take part. Next, many of them aim to please or do well on the test, so their performance doesn't reflect how they'd react to the material "off-stage" (if they'd even see it there).

Whether and how much the test approximates reality, in fact, are the big questions. Whenever you hear outside research cited as if it applies universally, look at the details to find out how and whether the test situation applies to your own, or if it even supports its conclusions. For example, *Type & Layout,* a book by Colin Wheildon, tested some of the great-debate issues of type and design, such as justified type columns versus flush-left/ragged-right ones. Although the book begins with pages of validations for the research methodology from impeccable sources, it comes to misguided and flawed conclusions, including this one: that people comprehend information delivered in justified columns better than in ragged-right ones. "Almost twice as many readers understand totally justified text than text set ragged right," the author/researcher writes.

"How could that be?" I asked Wheildon on the phone in 1995. Justification, especially if not expertly

done, creates inconsistent word spaces from line to line, and it demands a constantly shifting reading pace. The technology in place at the time of his research explained the discrepancy: Although the book was released in the United States in the 1990s, it presented research conducted in the mid-1980s. Its type samples came from the kind of phototypesetting machines in use before the personal-computer era.

So? Those old phototypesetters could easily nuance the word spaces in justified type to look as consistent as in ragged right.* But with a personal computer, the feat's time-consuming and tougher to repeat, especially by nontypographers, for whom flush-left/ragged-right is more forgiving. Prove it yourself. Pick up almost any recent newsletter with justified columns and you're likely to see wordspace gaps you can drive a truck through. The narrower the column, the less consistency you'll see in word spaces.

So because the tested type samples were of a better quality than what readers typically see these days, Wheildon's conclusion doesn't generally apply. In our conversation, the author acknowledged that the typesetting quality could skew the findings.

Technological differences don't account for other findings, such as serif versus sans serif (his results favor serif). But those have been challenged in credible articles by Ole Lund, Kathleen

Tinkel, and others who fault, among other things, Wheildon's choice of test typefaces. For a controlled—and fair—comparison, the sans serif and serif faces should be similar in every aspect except the absence or presence of serifs, such as the pair Aries Arditi of the Lighthouse Institute designed for his own legibility tests. (His results showed insignificant differences between the two faces' legibility; you'll see more about this in Chapter 3.)

Point is, even "scientific" tests can reach conclusions that don't apply to your situations, yet they bear almost the weight of law in a designer's or client's desire to follow them. And even studies that warn readers about limitations can take on inapplicable influence when they're misquoted or quoted out of context in books, articles, and lectures. Years after *Type & Layout*'s U.S. release, you might still run into the pro-justified-column "evidence" being expressed with almost religious fervor. But you'll know better.

You'll find some research that *is* applicable, though, if you don't adopt a policy of ignoring it. Instead, always question it and look for differences between the tested participants and material and your situation. Then test findings using your own material with people who represent your audience. (You'll find plenty about testing in Chapter 2 and case studies throughout the book.)

---

*But consistently spaced justified columns are *not* impossible, and personal computers are no excuse, information designer

Conrad Taylor told me in an e-mail. Taylor added that he has written articles since the late 1980s on how to adjust let-

ter and word spaces in justified columns of type. Yet few text producers on deadline have the time or interest to do so.

through the day. Take note of posters, signs, packaging, fliers—every visual platform for words or pictures. For example, what's around you now? You might find an Exit or No Smoking sign; a menu from your local lunch place; information on your computer monitor and keypad; book covers; and a label on your water bottle, soda can, or candy bar.

From this day forward, collect samples of information design you find every day. Here's how to work with each sample:

Step 1: What is it?

Take physical inventory of the product in your hands:

- What's the product made of? Paper? Plastic? Light, as in a Web site? Metal, as in a soda can?
- What's its rough size? Letter size? A couple of inches?
- How many pages (if any) are there?
- What's its rough weight?
- What's its finish? For example, if it's paper, is it uncoated or coated? If it's coated, is it glossy or dull?
- What's its opacity? Can you see through it? If so, does what's on the back interfere with what's on the front?
- How many colors are there (if any), and what are they?
- How many columns of type does it have (if any)?
- What are the other design elements (if any)?
- What does the type (if any) look like?
- How many illustrations are there (if any)? What do they look like? Do they have anything in common in terms of style?

Also notice how tough it is to start with the inventory and to hold off on critiquing the piece. You'll get to that in the next steps. But starting with the inventory will help you notice the physical parts that make up the whole, so you'll expand your repertoire of design elements. And you'll become aware of the effects of individual elements on the impact of the piece.

Step 2: Who's the audience?

If the product is a publication, notice how long it took you to find out who the audience is. You shouldn't need much time; if the audience isn't obvious, it's the fault of the piece. But why does it need to be obvious for, say, a newsletter with which the audience is already familiar? It's because every issue of most periodicals, even established ones, attract at least some newcomers.

Step 3: Evaluate as a viewer/reader

Look at the product as a member of the audience, not as an information designer.

- What was your first impression?
- What works for you and what doesn't?
- Which design decisions ease reading, navigating, and understanding the piece?
- Which ones interfere with them?
- Does the design adhere to information design principles (that you'll learn more about in coming chapters), such as:
  - consistency (is there a design style sheet at work—for example, does one headline look like another?)
  - proximity (does the amount of space between elements reflect the relationship between the elements?)
  - chunking (are related elements grouped and separated from others to make them digestible, instead of dauntingly unbroken?)
  - alignment (does every element line up with some other one?)
  - hierarchy (does the most important information look most important—placed at the top, bigger, bolder, or emphasized in some other way?)
  - structure (is the information presented in a sequence that will make sense to the audience?)
  - balance and eye flow (is there a clear starting place, and do the type and layout choices support the movement of your eye through the material?)
  - clarity (is the writing clear and concise, free of unnecessary jargon or undefined terms, and at the right level for the audience?)

Step 4: Redesign

First put yourself in the place of the sample's designer to look for any possible reasons for the decisions the designer made. Next think about

Tinkering with terminology (with apologies to Miles A. Tinker)

Information designers tend to be a talkative, even argumentative lot. If you use the word *readability* to mean type that can be clearly read, but you're talking with someone who calls the same thing *legibility,* you'll spark a debate that could go on for years.

In his book *Legibility of Print,* Miles A. Tinker, a type-clarity researcher, devotes a page to the history of the terms: The confusion began when *readability* became the label for formulas that measure reading comprehension by the length of words, sentences, and paragraphs used in test samples.

To add to the confusion, some people still use *readability* to refer to the legibility of a lot of text, and *legibility* for the recognizability of short phrases and single words, such as an illuminated Exit sign.

This book uses *legibility* to refer to type's clarity with regard to:

- typography (including typeface, size, column width, spacing)
- color and contrast

- production and material quality
- environmental conditions (room lighting and temperature, noise level, etc.)

This book uses *readability* to refer to:

- the text's construction (including the length of words, sentences, and paragraphs—what's measured by readability formulas)
- the reader's reading skill
- the reader's interest, attention, and comfort levels

The book might also use *clarity* or *understanding* to refer to both. You'll get the meaning reinforced by the context along with the term.

A final note: Although researchers can and do test clarity of reading separate from clarity of the presentation, avoid seeing the two as separate in the materials that go to the audience. That's because audience members see them as one. They make a quick decision to read based on the entire package as it's presented in time and space.

how you would improve upon the sample. Finding the flaws is useful, but redesigning brings you the exercise's full benefits. Redesign in your mind, in notes and sketches, or on the computer. Do so with the understanding that most designs can improve with more adherence to principles of good design and knowledge of the audience.

To explain the value of information design, you also could do the exercise with a group of colleagues or students. Ask each person to present an evaluation of two found information design pieces; one that he or she finds effective and one not effective. Lead the group in discussing the evaluation—for example, do group members agree with

On these carousel animals, certain details show up only for the benefit of the audience.
Photographer: Ronnie Lipton.

On the side the audience doesn't see, those details go missing.

the presenter's evaluation, and if not, why not?—and in brainstorming ways to improve both pieces.

From the audience's perspective

On many carousels, carved and painted details such as horse manes appear only on one side of the animal, the side seen from the perspective of observers and potential customers. Let that carousel—and this book—remind you to consider the audience's perspective when you design.

Section I: audience

≪

Identifying
the Audience

CHAPTER 1

How humans (almost) universally perceive

PART 1: Perception principles

The first step in designing for your audience and its needs is to find out what makes people alike. How do most humans—those with normally functioning eyes and brains—perceive and comprehend information? Basic principles of cognitive psychology apply. Perhaps chief among them is our selective attention.

"The mind is not a camera," writes Stephen Kosslyn in his book *Graph Design for the Eye and Mind*. Although the camera captures everything within its frame, the mind captures only what it chooses to, especially in a crowded "frame" or scene. So what any two minds choose to capture in a given scene will vary. But you can learn to predict and, to an extent, control what they view in the "scenes" you design if you create and arrange their elements in line with inherent human behavior:

We humans look for and recognize patterns, and we expect them to mean something. We also notice interruptions in pattern, and expect *those* to mean something different from the consistent elements. We see what's bigger, bolder, or brighter as more important than what's smaller, lighter, or duller. And we look for order and unity, even trying to impose them where they don't exist. Anything that lacks order in visual displays tends to make us uncomfortable. So we mentally group individual parts to form a whole. (You might say we seek relationships among visual elements in much the same way as we seek relationships with other people.)

For example, you can see that parts-as-a-whole principle in facing pages of a magazine or newsletter with two or more articles that begin with a drop cap. Readers notice when the caps spell out a word, as in the illustration on the next page. Readers especially notice when the

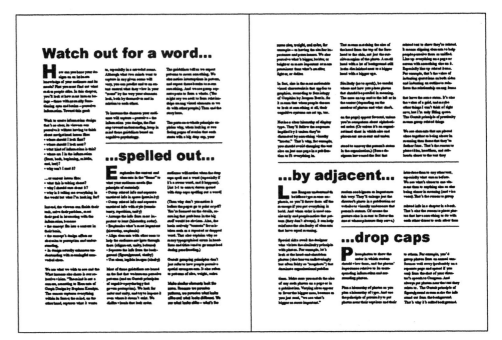

Our perceptual systems combine parts into a whole, which is why we combine drop caps into words when they let us.

caps spell out a swear word. It happens more than you'd expect, so make sure you check before you send off the pages.

You might wonder why the designer, editor, or proofreader didn't notice and remove the unintended word before the audience could see it. It's probably because each person focused more on the details than on the big picture. It's also why many typographical errors in headlines and titles go unnoticed during proofreading. The mind also tends to actively "correct" for mistakes such as a repeated or dropped word. So it's also hard to spot a small supporting word (such as *the*) at the end of one line that repeats at the start of the next line in the column.

Basic principles translate into guidelines for designing content your audience members can perceive, which they must do before they can comprehend it:

• Limit the content and elements in the design to what your audience needs; don't include everything you know (the principle of restraint).

• Group related information to show it *is* related, and separate unrelated info.

  • Use space. Physically move the informational elements together or apart (the principle of *proximity*).

- Use style—the size, face, style, color, and shape of elements—to show their relationships with other elements. Match related elements and contrast unrelated ones (the principle of *similarity;* also *consistency* and *repetition*).

- Emphasize what's most important (the principles of *hierarchy* and *emphasis*).

- Arrange information from most important to least (the principle of *hierarchy* or *sequence*).

- Align elements with others to help the audience navigate through them (the principles of *alignment, unity,* and *balance*).

- Make the content stand out clearly from the background (the principles of *figure/ground* and *clarity*).

- Use clear and legible images (the principle of *clarity*).

Gestalt principles of perception

Some of the principles about how parts relate to the whole come from the movement of psychology known as Gestalt, which is German for "form." Gestalt practitioners including Max Wertheimer, Wolfgang Köhler, and Kurt Koffka began applying the ideas to human visual perception in the early part of the last century. Here are some of their principles and how I've interpreted—even sometimes stretched—them into practical information-design guidelines.

THE GESTALT PRINCIPLE OF SIMILARITY:
Make equal elements look equal

What Gestalt psychologists really meant by the similarity principle is that we humans tend to group similar elements into one perceptual unit. But in order to group similar elements, we must be able to recognize their similarity. Our ability to perceive patterns means we can discern obvious similarities and differences. We regard elements that *look* alike—such as article subheads that share a typeface, style, size, and color, for example—as *being* alike, having the same level of importance. So it only makes sense to emphasize similarities and differences with your design.

In much the same way, we regard elements that are obviously bigger as being more important, and those that are obviously smaller as being less important. In fact, size is the most noticeable graphic trait, writes Jacques Bertin in his book *Semiology of Graphics*. So people understand the different levels of importance implied by a size hierarchy of elements unless something visually "louder" distracts us. Defy those natural laws—by, say, reducing one section of type to fit the page—and you could confuse readers, who expect changes to mean more than a lack of space.

And when people see bold type, they tend to recognize its emphasis, an understanding you'll defeat by boldfacing everything. When they notice color that's used consistently, the pattern can help to reinforce the element's meaning.

The guideline also applies to photos, with risks to the designer who violates it. Consider the head-and-shoulders photos (also known as "mug shots") that are so common in publications. Make the size of any such photos on a page or (two-page) spread identical. If you don't, the size difference could imply that the people in the photos have different levels of importance. Match the size of the head from the top of the forehead to the chin, not just the size of the frame. A small head in a big frame will look less significant than a bigger adjacent head even in a slightly smaller frame.

Also watch where you place photos of equal importance. Depending on the number of photos and what else is on the page, the photos at top left or center might look favored. Even arranging photos by alphabetical order of the people's names can't compete with the stronger nonverbal impression. But top-down placement does work for a photographic organizational chart in which position conveys each person's relative status. And, like it or not, some designers use the size-equals-importance code to enlarge just the director's photo, visually underscoring that person's status (and trying to flatter the one at whose pleasure they serve).

But do use size and placement to show the order in which readers should view photos. And use them to show how the photos rank with each other and relate to corresponding content. Plan a hierarchy of photos—from most to least important—as you do a hierarchy of type.

The similarity principle also extends to alignment. Align every element with something else in the frame to help viewers see the elements in the unified context of the whole. In particular, align related elements to emphasize their relationship and their contrast with other elements. Consider aligned contact info on a business card or an indented quotation within flush text. In both examples, grouped alignment reinforces the difference between two categories of type.

Similar alignment explains the value of a grid. That's a framework of invisible vertical and horizontal lines designed for placing type and images and reserving unfilled space similarly from page to page or project to project. A well-planned grid anticipates and accommodates the range of elements in the project while avoiding monotony. Adherence to a grid gives projects a sense of order and unity, and helps readers find things.

Pages designed without a grid tend to draw the eye from the content to the chaos. Think of the last slide show you saw in which the titles bounced with each new slide. Lack of alignment also annoys audiences of other forms of design, maybe most when they know something's wrong but not what it is.

THE GESTALT PRINCIPLE OF PROXIMITY:
Group related things

The principle states that we group elements that are close in space as a single perceptual unit. Here again, let's stretch the idea: We expect elements that are close in space to be more related than those farther away in space. So, for example, place:

- titles, headlines, and subheads closer to the text they introduce than to any other text, especially what comes before. For example, reduced space under the subhead above shows its connection to this paragraph; extra space above the subhead shows its separation from the paragraph above it.

- related photos closer to each other than to unrelated ones. For example, you'd group photos from an annual conference well away from the shot of your director addressing Congress.

- photos near the text they relate to

- captions near the photos they describe (close without touching)

THE GESTALT PRINCIPLE OF FIGURE/GROUND:
Make the content stand out from the background

We separate what we see into foreground (figure—for our purposes, the content) and background (ground). In information design, never ask the audience to work at telling them apart. Make the content prominently emerge from (contrast with) its background, and keep the background in the background, never intruding.

Now you see one thing, now you see another, but you can't focus on the vase and the faces in profile—or any foreground and background—at the same time. (Notice something else: the vase appears symmetrical despite inconsistent profiles. That's because we perceive the power of the whole over its parts before focusing on the details if we choose to. And here, perhaps the ambiguity of a focal point—the vase or the faces—further interferes with gathering details.) *Adapted from Edgar Rubin's concept/drawing.*

Low or no contrast, on the other hand, blurs the distinction between figure and ground. Edgar Rubin, a psychologist who studied figure/ground relationships, created the famous image of a vase within two human facial profiles. Looking at its re-creation, what do you see first, the faces or the vase? Notice that you can't focus on them both at once. To see the second one, you must shift your focus. So because it's impossible to focus on both figure and ground—or type and background—at the same time, make it easy for the audience to focus on the type by playing down the background. (Escher's drawings, which also blur the divisions between figure and ground, are fascinating, but nothing to mimic in information design.)

EXERCISE: Make your own version of Rubin's vase using silhouettes of someone you know. Display the image near your work area to remind you to keep content clearly in the foreground and backgrounds clearly in the background.

You can achieve the essential design principle of contrast with:

- *size.* Make type big enough to stand out from the background. (What if you want to discourage people from reading the "fine print"? Reconsider using fine print whenever readers need the info buried in it; they're on to that trick.)

- *"color."* Black type on a white background gives the highest, most comfortable contrast for sustained text reading. On the other hand, in many cases the same combination reversed (white type on a black background) emphasizes the background over the type. For graphics, favor cool, deep colors as a background for warm, bright colors. On signs, black on yellow is the best-projecting combination. (If you live in the United States, you've probably noticed a fluorescent yellow-green gradually replacing nonfluorescent yellow-orange on Pedestrian Crossing and other signs.)

- *weight.* Make type heavy enough to be visible. Especially on low-visibility surfaces, typefaces with uniform stroke widths tend to achieve more contrast between figure and ground than those built from thick and thin strokes. (But avoid going so bold with type, especially in small sizes, that the enclosed space in the characters, such as the loop in the lowercase *e,* start to fill in.)

• *quiet, solid backgrounds.* Understate your design's background because a loud one competes with reading the way loud background music competes with conversation.

Also avoid the temptation to put text on a shifting background such as a photo or a gradient screen, which makes reading as tough as listening to an inconsistent cell-phone signal. An evenly screened background also lowers contrast, as does heavily textured or colorful paper.

AN EXAMPLE OF GOOD CONTRAST

Consider the environment in which you'll deliver your message. High-contrast colors and type weight help make the poster in Color Plate 1 stand out against other messages on a subway car's cluttered walls. Although most of the background reverses, text is big, limited, and visible enough to hold its own, especially with its powerful uniform strokes. You might *see* the green against the black first, but you're more likely to *read* the higher-contrast bold white main info.

In the green panel on the left side of the poster, the color's brightness still takes a backseat to the black-outlined white images. With more and weaker (reversed or serif) type, it also would pose more of a reading challenge. But despite its reversing, the white paragraph on the black panel transmits more easily than it might have because of its bigger point size and limited words. Still, if you squint, you can see the background intruding on the shape of each letter.

MORE FIGURE/GROUND RELATIVES

Other principles work with contrast to affect the perception of figure/ground. What's bigger or bolder appears to be more in the foreground than what's smaller or lighter (hierarchy). It also tends to appear closer to the viewer. Contrast's primary design partner is emphasis: making the most important elements in the foreground stand out from the rest. Every information design project, page, or view needs a focal point, an emphasis, an obvious place for the reader to start.

The principle of balance (see sidebar on pages 22–24) and the use of empty space also play into figure/ground. Extra space between elements tends to draw the reader's eye to where you don't want it—the background. So leave just enough space between elements to frame them, but not so much as to distract from them. And use more space to frame pages than individual elements. That way, the elements won't seem to be pulled off the page; the frame will look strong enough to enclose them.

≫ Instilling a sense of proportion and balance: 'Golden' layout tips

We can look much earlier than the Gestalt psychologists for another principle of perception, expressed as "we perceive most what pleases us." Form follows function in information design, but that doesn't mean we should *ignore* form. Strive for pleasing form, which can enhance the information-gathering experience for the audience.

What's pleasing? According to early architects, it's the golden mean: about 0.618, not far from a 2:3 (about .667) ratio.* You can see it in such classic constructions as Egyptian pyramids, the Parthenon, and Stonehenge, and in nature. Le Corbusier, a Swiss architect, developed the "moduler," a measurement system he applied to architecture and sometimes to graphic design based on the golden proportions found in the human body.

But we're talking about information design, not buildings. Here's how you might apply it.

In a line divided in two according to the golden mean, the proportion of the smaller part to the bigger part equals the proportion of the bigger part to the whole line. So, to divide an 11-inch line according to the golden ratio, multiply 11 by .618.

You'll get 6.798. Round it off to 6.8 to make it easier to work with, then mark off that point on the 11-inch line, leaving a shorter section of 4.2.

The golden ratio is reinforced by

Here's an 11-pica line divided into classic proportions, about 6.8 and 4.2. The proportion of the smaller section to the bigger one equals the proportion of the bigger one to the whole line.

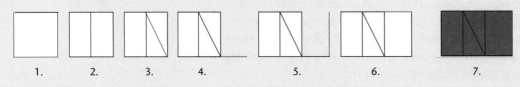

1.　　2.　　3.　　4.　　　　5.　　　　6.　　　　　　7.

How to draw a rectangle that conforms to classic proportions (without math):
1. Draw a square.
2. Divide the square in half with a vertical line.
3. Draw a line from the top of that vertical to one of the lower corners of the square.
4. Draw a line of the same length as the diagonal from the square's midpoint along the square's baseline. It will extend beyond the square.
5. Draw a vertical line from the end of that extended line to the top of the square.
6. Connect the top of the vertical to the square.
7. The rectangle made from that extension to the original left edge of the square (the dark area) represents a golden proportion.

You can also make a golden rectangle within the golden rectangle.
1. Draw a diagonal line between corners of the golden rectangle.
2. Where the diagonal intersects the vertical of the original square, draw a horizontal line to the edge of the rectangle that was extended beyond the square.
3. Next draw a diagonal from the outside bottom corner of the original square to the upper corner of the golden rectangle.
4. Run a vertical line from the intersection of that diagonal and the horizontal line to the bottom of the first golden rectangle to make another one.
5. More lines created by the diagonals form more golden rectangles within these.
Adapted from The Grid, *by Allen Hurlbutt.*

1.

2.

3.

4.

5.

* Also known as the "golden section," "golden ratio," or "golden proportion." However, Japanese architects preferred the 1:2 proportion, designing buildings based on the ratio found in tatami mats.

the Fibonacci sequence, a number series found by a thirteenth-century mathematician who sought to predict the reproductive patterns of rabbits.

Each number in the sequence comes from by adding the two numbers before it: 0, 1, 1, 2, 3, 5, 8, 13, 21, 34, 55. And dividing any two neighbors beyond 2 in the sequence, you get close to 1.618 or .618 (depending on which you divide into which).

The pattern is found throughout nature (in the number of leaves in a cluster or on a branch, in petals in a flower), in classical musical compositions, and in architecture.

Possibilities for a typical layout? Here's one based on an 8½-by-11-inch sheet. Although those dimensions don't correspond to the golden proportion, they still can inspire page layout.*

Another related, simpler way of dividing up space pleasingly is favored by photographers (see first diagram on page 24): The rule of thirds, based on the 2:3 (.667) proportion, divides a space, such as a page or a photo, equally into nine rectangles—three rows of three columns. Use one or more of the four intersection points as the focal point or points of the visual.

Or (more closely related to the golden ratio), divide the space into thirteen segments (each way, width and height) and put the focal point at the eighth segment (counting from the left or right, top or bottom).

Or draw a diagonal line from one corner to another, then draw a line perpendicular to the diagonal from each of the other corners. Use either of the intersection points for the focus.

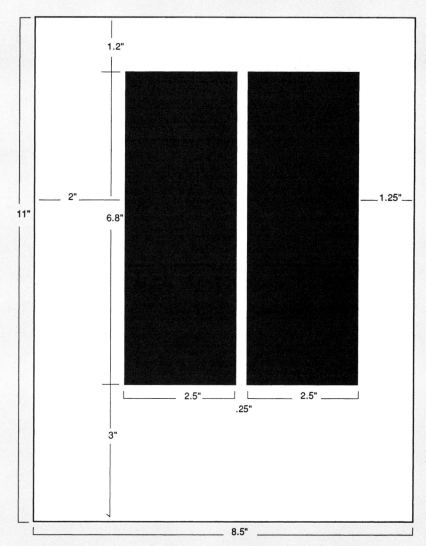

How would you divide a letter-sized sheet into pleasing columns according to the golden ratio? Divide its width to find the amount of space for columns: 8.5 x .618 = about 5.25 inches.

So you can make two 2.5-inch columns and add that extra quarter inch to the space between them. (You also could make three columns of 1.6 inches each with .125 inch between them, but they would be too narrow for the space.) Divide the 3.25-inch remaining space in the same way, which the ratio turns into 2 inches on one side and 1.25 inches on the other.

How long should the columns be on the page? 11 inches x .618 = 6.8 inches, with the remaining 4.2 inches for top and bottom margin, divided into 3-inch and 1.2-inch portions. Figured this way, the basic page doesn't conform to the golden portion, but the relationship of the columns and the space does.

---

* *Universal Principles of Design* pointed out that its own approximate 17-by-10-inch spreads (consisting of two facing pages of 8½-by-10 inches each) roughly correspond to the golden ratio.

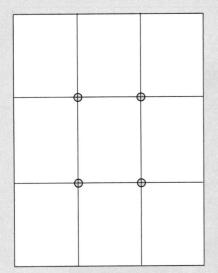

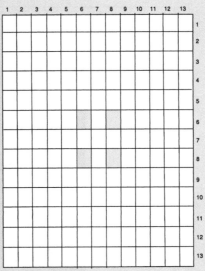

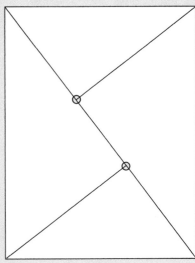

The rule of thirds, based on a 2:3 proportion, places the focal point at one of the intersection points.

A 13-square grid is another way of dividing up a page, with the focal point at the eighth square (counting from the left or right, top or bottom).

Still another way. Here again, the color marks the best options for the focal point.

THE GESTALT PRINCIPLE OF PRÄGNANZ:
Simplify (appropriately) and give context
We look for the simplest possible explanation in any visual based on its—and our—surroundings. But that's too much work to ask of your audience members, so simplify for them, at least as much as it makes sense to do.

Adding principles of adult learning, we also look for context. When we see something new, we look for existing mental niches to file it in. Use that idea to choose and present content based on what's familiar to your audience. Content should begin where the audience's knowledge leaves off, and you should connect the two. And design should favor conventions, such as putting a Web site's logo in the upper right or changing the color of a visited link.

THE GESTALT PRINCIPLE OF COMMON FATE:
Viewers notice direction
We group lines and shapes that seem to be heading in the same direction. For example, on a bar graph, bars above zero are seen as one group, those below zero as another.

THE GESTALT PRINCIPLES OF CLOSURE AND GOOD CONTINUATION:
Viewers fill in visual gaps
Closure is when we mentally fill in any gaps in regular objects, such as circles, so we'll tend to complete a broken circle. Good continuation means that we group things that are on the same line or a curve. For example, we understand the graduated climb or decline of bars in a graph, and we expect the variation in graduated screens to mean something.

Let's go beyond the Gestalt meanings to show how continuation-like elements can help to unify projects. For example, a thick bar at the top of every page encourages horizontal movement—continuation, so to speak—through a print publication. In a Web site, a matching menu bar and logo in the same spots on every page form an implied connection and a path between pages. Those elements also impose continuity.

What's first and topmost, and why it matters
We also tend to see what comes first, such as what's at the top on a filled printed page as more important than what comes after. So on a manual or newsletter page, for example, put the headline or title

What comes first is often most important, but not always, as on this poster, where what's bigger and bolder—and closer to optically centered—gets the attention. *Concept: Partner 2010. Design firm: Magma [Büro für Gestaltung]. Client: City of Karlsruhe. Art director: Ulrich Weiß. Designers: Sandra Augstein, Axel Brinkmann.*

and the most important story first, where readers expect to find it. (Size, weight, or format can trump this placement, as in the case of the illustration on page 25. Although the title comes after secondary info, its size and weight—but also its more central location in a sparse page—identifies it as the priority.)

Faced with a text-packed page, people whose native language reads left to right tend to start at the upper left. Then we make our way as quickly as we can to the lower right of the page or spread in a kind of backwards N-shape. So place text along that natural eye path, because text generally takes the most motivation and effort for readers to follow. Save the lesser-traveled paths of the upper right and lower left corners for artwork, for which readers are more likely to go out of their way.

The upper-left starting spot also seems to apply to news Web sites, according to the 2004 Eyetrack III study by the Poynter Institute, the Estlow Center for Journalism and New Media at the University of Denver, and Eyetools. Although eye flow varies by what's on the page, the researchers found, eyes tend to start at the upper left before venturing to the right, then down. Eyes go first to big headlines and favored text, not photos. (But on a *printed* newspaper page, eyes stop first on the photos, according to the first Eyetrack study fourteen years earlier, which looked only at printed newspapers.)

But findings differ because tests do (more proof of the risks in trying to apply other people's tests to your situations). Janice Redish and others have found evidence of what's been called "banner blindness" in Web site viewers. She cites findings from eye-tracking studies and her own usability tests that show that people tend to enter toward the upper middle of a page, where they expect the content to begin. Why not left middle? There we expect to see "colored stuff (maybe ads or photos) that isn't content," she says. The apparent contradiction might stem from different types of Web sites studied: news sites versus sites readers enter to do a task, such as download a passport application or register for a class.

SEQUENTIAL EXCEPTIONS

In listings (linear series of words or phrases), sometimes the obvious beginning isn't necessarily the most important. Let the needs or interest of the audience guide you. Take newspaper wedding anniversary announcements. A sequential numerical order would start with the first-year anniversaries. But you could argue that enduring marriages—

> I hope eye flow problems explain how I missed prominent visual symbolism in an English-subtitled Czech film. While discussing the film, I realized I'd watched at a comparatively superficial level. I contend I missed the deeper meaning while reading long subtitles while my friends—native Czech-speakers—could focus fully on the scene. Even worse, say some opera fans, are that art form's *sur*titles.

or a celebrating couple's fame—are the biggest news, worthy of higher billing.

Also note that what comes earlier in a list isn't necessarily as memorable as what comes later. Hearing a list that's too long to recall entirely, we're more likely to recall the first items (the "primacy effect") and the last items (the "recency effect") in the series than those in the middle. We'll probably react the same way to a list we read, unless we stop to focus on portions out of sequence. Make long lists more memorable and meaningful by shortening or subdividing lists under logical subcategories and putting the most important stuff at the beginning or end.

The only ways to organize

In his books *Information Anxiety* and *Information Anxiety 2,* Richard Saul Wurman identified the only ways information can be organized, themselves organized into the acronym LATCH:

- Location

- Alphabet

- Time

- Category

- Hierarchy* (or "continuum," as he called it in the first, pre-acronym edition)

What's most important—what will help the audience get what they need from the information—should drive how you choose to portray it. For example, you could list cities and towns of any country by:

- location, under their states, provinces, or regions (which also might be organized geographically—say, from north to south—or alphabetically). Order by location might be most useful to tourists, travel agents, politicians, marketers, and demographers.

- alphabetical order. Useful to people who know only the place's name.

- the date when each was founded or incorporated. Useful to historians.

- category: city or a town, predominant political or religious affiliation of its population, major industry, and the like. Each delineation helps people sort out areas relevant to their interests.

- hierarchy: comparative size of population, economic status, land mass, height above sea level, and so on. Useful to students, economists, and demographers.

---

* also known as "order," "sequence," "structure," or "rank."

Consider organization's role in this task: You need to find the name and address of a restaurant you've been to only once. The print phone book's alphabetical listings don't help because they are too long to scan through. The answer lies in either location or cuisine (category) listings.

Also consider city guidebooks, which traditionally list attractions by their category, such as monuments, museums, restaurants, clubs, and shops. Wurman questioned that form of organization, finding it more useful to organize by neighborhood (location), as he did in his "Access" city guide series.

The LATCH organization also applies to graphics, not just words, even though most of the categories can be expressed verbally or numerically. For example, a used-car advertiser might arrange the cars' photos by:

- country of origin or current home (location)
- manufacturer and model name (alphabetical)
- date of origin (time)
- type (sports car, sedan, sport utility vehicle, or truck; convertible or hardtop; two- or four-door) (category)
- size, mileage, condition (hierarchy)

EXERCISE: What's the organization method or methods in each of these examples? For each, also consider if an extra method might help the audience, and if so, how.

- Train schedule
- Course catalog
- Shoe catalog
- Web site map
- History museum floor plan
- Bike trail map
- Road signs
- Magazine's table of contents
- Book's index
- Ruler in a convenience store or bank to record a robber's height
- Bar chart to measure sales by store by month over six months

---

What we remember (all we recall)

We keep four chunks of information in short-term memory at a time.* Retention and accuracy decrease as the number of chunks increases. Test it yourself: See whether and for how long you can recall a new phone number without writing it down. And unless you commit that phone number to long-term memory, you'll quickly replace it with the next contender for the space. (A TV spot for a breath mint built its premise on the limits of short-term memory: A woman writes her phone number in her breath's mist on a subway car window for a man she likes, but he misses the message because he doesn't have a pen and paper, unlike men around him, who eagerly take notes.)

Content that's grouped into logical subdivisions aids both perception and retention. That's why an office equipment catalog would group all lamps under one heading and all chairs under another, maybe with subsets under each category (desk or floor lamps, chairs with arms or wheels).

Another possible aid to retention is color in or near emphasized items. Just realize that type in color might have less contrast—and thus less legibility—than black type. Putting color near the type adds the memory-enhancing benefit of color without sacrificing legibility.

Also use well-placed, adequate space and contrast to help readers recall the content. It follows that the same clutter in the frame or prominence of the background that keeps readers from focusing on something will also keep them from remembering it.

More about context and applying principles

We perceive and understand best what's individually familiar to us. Use that fact to choose formats you know are familiar to your audience, similar to familiar ones, or obvious enough to be clear. For example, it might help if the audience has seen pie charts before and understands the relationships inherent in them. But the image of a circle and its divisions is universal. And the idea that what's bigger means more is also universal. So it's also fair to expect the audience to understand that a bigger slice means a bigger percentage. Same with bar charts, in which taller bars mean more of something. And the principles of similarity and proximity contribute the understanding that there's a relationship among the bars or the pie slices. That's a lot of information conveyed without words.

We also universally perceive what looks clear and well organized, adhering to all the perception principles discussed above plus salience: People expect a change in style to signal a change in meaning.

---

* Some researchers say as many as seven chunks, others as few as three.

Although this watch has long hands for minutes, in this case the longer hands and the prominence given to minutes over hours in the outer circle make sense. It's a recent Russian "Poljot" chronograph based on a design for Luftwaffe pilots in World War II. On watches such as this, minutes get the emphasis because pilots must calculate in seconds and minutes, not hours. *Photographer/Watch's owner: Jeff Young.*

EXERCISE (a variation on the Introduction's "Exercise for life"): As you notice designs around you throughout your day, consider what makes sense intuitively versus what relies on acquired knowledge. For example, you had to learn that the shortest hand on a watch or clock points to hours, the longer hand to minutes, and the longest to seconds, because it's not intuitive. Intuitive—but mechanically impractical—design would have matched hand length to time-period length. (More intuitively, hands for longer periods usually are thicker than those for shorter ones.)

PART 2: Body/mind basics: How the eye/brain sees, perceives, reads

What happens physiologically when we look at an image? In a nutshell, light delivers images and colors to the brain through nerve cells in the retina of the eye. To get to the retina, at the back of the eye, images and colors travel through various layers. They include substances (such as the cornea, iris, pupil, lens, and gel-like humors) that control the amount of entering light or aid focus.

We read, recognize faces, and see color with a spot on the retina called the fovea.* It's the place in the eye that provides the sharpest vision.

Two kinds of nerve cells live in the retina: rods and cones. Rods control our ability to see (and read and drive) in low light. Cones control our color and detail vision. Photosensitive chemicals in the rods and cones cause an electrical reaction that sends seen images through optic nerves to the brain's cerebral cortex (where we also think, learn, and remember).

How we perceive words: The eye/brain case for legible type

We don't read letter by letter, or even necessarily, word by word. Instead, the eye moves through text in a series of eye jumps (or saccades), stops (or fixations), and backtracking steps (regressions, which account for 10–15 percent of our reading time). Each saccade covers seven to nine letters of text, according to "The Science of Word Recognition," by Kevin Larson of Microsoft. Reading happens when we fixate, which we do near the middle of a word. A typical fixation takes in three or four letters on either side of it, so it includes the word and maybe any small familiar words next to it. During a fixation, we also plan our next stopping point.

---

* In fact, a scientist might use the phrase "foveate on" to mean "focus on," because the part of the eye that close-focuses on details such as words is the fovea.

The implications: Support a consistent, comprehensible reading (jumping) pace with consistent, legible type, especially using appropriate contrast and word and line spacing.

How we perceive color

The retina contains three types of cones, each most sensitive to light in a different wavelength, according to Stephen Kosslyn, author of *Graph Design for the Eye and Mind* and other books about cognitive psychology and visual perception. As he and Robin Rosenberg write in *Fundamentals of Psychology: The Brain, the Person, the World:* "One type of cone is most responsive to light in the wavelength seen as [a yellow-orange], another to light in the wavelength seen as green, and another in the wavelength seen as violet." The cone types combine to help us see the range of visible color (similar to the way only three colors produce many more colors on a computer monitor).

Wavelength, a color's position on the visible spectrum, relates to color temperature. Red (a warm color, along with orange and yellow) has the longest wavelength; blue (a cool color, along with green and violet) has one of the shortest wavelengths.

The different wavelengths focus on different points around the retina, actually changing the shape of the lens. Long-wavelength red focuses behind the retina, rounding the lens and making the red look closer and bigger, according to *Color Perception in Art,* by Faber Birren. (It's also known to raise blood pressure.) Blue's shorter wavelength makes it focus in front of the retina, flattening the lens and making the color look farther away and smaller. So, for reasons of perception, red tends to work best in foregrounds, and blue's best in backgrounds.

But although yellow is the most luminous and most reflective color, it won't stand out against white unless the yellow has plenty of red in it. Every design quality is relative, as the Gestalt psychologists also found. Changing one part of its environment causes everything to change, so watch the relationships among the elements in your design.

Look to colors' positions on the spectrum (translated into the color wheel you probably first saw in grade school), for clues to combining colors effectively in design. For example, use adjacent colors—such as red and orange—as adjacent colors in a design for harmony, or to show dimension. But don't use them when you want a strong contrast between elements. For contrast, you might pair red with yellow, but neither with their immediate neighbor, orange.

To avoid a distracting shimmering effect, also avoid pairing longest-wavelength red with shortest-wavelength blue in equal intensities. The eye can't focus on two such different wavelengths at once, Kosslyn writes. But you can pair the two without inducing shimmering if you put another color between them. (See Color Plate 2.)

A similar shimmering effect comes from pairing so-called complementary colors, those opposite each other on the color wheel: red/green, yellow/purple, orange/blue. (A student of mine wondered aloud whether so many reds with greens before Christmas is really what's behind the stress associated with the holiday.)

To avoid shimmering, put another color between potentially incompatible pairs. If you want to put them next to each other, use different intensities. In fact, it's best to avoid the same intensity between any two colors that meet, or it might be tough for the audience to distinguish the boundary between them. But if you're designing a cereal box, Kosslyn says, you might want that shimmering color interaction to call attention to it from a packed retail shelf.

Red/green pairs, in particular, pose another problem: To color-blind people (about 8 percent of males and about 0.4 percent of females), the two colors look the same, so the colors can't convey any information. Red/green is the most common color deficiency among color-blind people. Most can discern other colors, so a more accurate term for the deficiency might be "red/green-blind." (See Color Plate 3.)

How we perceive symbols

Communicating nonverbally to avoid language or reading barriers is a worthy goal. Unfortunately, it's also an elusive one, as you know if you or your audience has ever misunderstood a Web icon, a garment's cleaning tag, pictogram assembly instructions, or any other attempt at a universal message.

Otto Neurath's utopian dream of a universal language is not much closer to reality than in 1936, when he offered his Isotypes system of symbols, or in 1972, when Henry Dreyfuss included that system and others in his book *The Symbol Sourcebook*. But Neurath's vision lives on as the inspiration for international symbols on signs and packaging.

The Dreyfuss book is engaging, even useful if you don't assume the symbols in it are universal. If you look up the book, see how many of them you can figure out without looking at the captions. Some of the symbols are so "totally unclear, even I don't understand them," such as the ones "for full or empty things," says Paul Mijksenaar, founder of

Bureau Mijksenaar, a design firm that specializes in wayfinding systems and icons; a professor at Delft University of Technology; and the author of books on visual information.

Some symbols are used and understood almost universally. Those include curves or ramps that get larger to show a loudspeaker's increasing volume. Even more familiar to most people is the red diagonal to say that "something is closed or not available or shouldn't be done or is forbidden," Mijksenaar says. (For the latter, by the way, the slash properly runs from upper left to lower right, like the diagonal stroke in "N," as in "NO." See below.)

But the very use of the word *language*—whether it refers to a verbal language or a pictorial one—suggests something that has to be learned, "because that's the characteristic of a language. It's a man-made thing. Even an arrow is a man-made thing" whose meaning must be learned, Mijksenaar says. Until people in some remote tribes were regularly exposed to arrows in graphic and product design, they understood the symbols only as representing things to shoot with bows.

Among the symbols proposed for a utopian nonverbal language in Henry Dreyfuss's book are these two. If you don't know what they mean, the symbols—and the language itself—don't work. The Symbol Sourcebook *by Henry Dreyfuss.*

These symbols, in wider use today than the ones above, might be clearer . . . or are they?

BORROWING VERSUS CREATING SYMBOLS

If your project will include symbols—whether to replace or supplement language—see what symbols are on hand before you plan something new. Bureau Mijksenaar looks for any applicable standards, including international (such as ISO), national (AIGA [American Institute of Graphic Artists] or DOT [Department of Transportation]), local, and industry. Standards have the advantages of familiarity and testing.

If the team members must start from scratch, they must develop a way to help the audience to learn the symbols. That might include putting the pictogram's meaning on every map, folder, or application that includes it.

A circle and a slash, in red, warn drivers to leave their car someplace else.

Use the direction of the diagonal stroke in the "N" in "No" to remind you which way to draw the slash when you design warning signs.

But even using established symbols won't guarantee your audience will understand them. Test them while there's still time to change or label any symbols that aren't clear. Neither will using "associative" colors guarantee understanding, Mijksenaar says. For example, red connotes warning and fire, so it's often used on signs to signal danger. But it's used almost as often for other kinds of signs just because it's noticeable. And even when the message is danger, is it an escape route or a caution to keep out? The meaning then depends on the words.

Any symbol that needs explaining won't fit some cases, such as emergency or road signs whose meaning must project instantly. And for messages that do lend themselves to a nonverbal treatment, only a limited number of truly universal symbols apply. Those include human, animal, or environmental symbols such as water and the sun. One of the most familiar uses of human symbols is on restroom doors, but in fact those symbols might be confusing if they weren't so familiar. Because they use only an article of clothing to distinguish the genders, the symbols could give pause to a woman wearing pants or to a man in a kilt or caftan.

CLARITY'S A BIGGER CHALLENGE IN SMALL SIZES
A Web site and stationery for a consulting firm, shown on this page, use natural pairs to suggest the firm's synergy with viewers. Designed to run small, icons must be clear enough to be *read* small, so too much detail can defeat the purpose. These contain more detail than typical,

Symbols need to be instantly identifiable . . . are these pairs? They appear throughout a corporate identity system and a Web site to show synergy . . .

. . . and sometimes, as on this Web page, the opposite of synergy. *Design firm: Design Army for Scott & Yandura. Creative director/ Designer: Pum Lefebure. Illustrator/Account manager: Jake Lefebure. Programmer: Todd Lyda*

but probably not so much that viewers can't identify them. (Can you identify the icon pairs?)

Separate icons on the home page introduce the theme and relate—more or less—to the menu options (the least successful relationship being the robot to illustrate "who we are"). On other pages, the options move upward to a menu bar, with the current page name made appropriately bold.

SYMBOLS FIGHT CHAOS

The power of traffic lights as a universal symbol became clear in the aftermath of Hurricane Isabel in 2003. With the signals out, people turning left at the intersection and those going straight felt equally entitled to the right of way (judging from the yelling and honking). In the absence of a universally mutually understood governing code—red, yellow, and green lights—anarchy reigned.

MORE SYMBOLIC EXAMPLES

(See also Color Plates 4, 5, and 6.)

Speaking of symbols and arrows, here's a design that uses shape and color not just to inform, but to inform *on*. The plastic card is designed to stick to boxes that contain delicate items. The shipper activates it by pulling out a clear plastic "gate" and sends the package on its way. *Manufacturer: Index Packaging.*

When the activated package label's arrowhead stays white, it shows the package was handled with care.

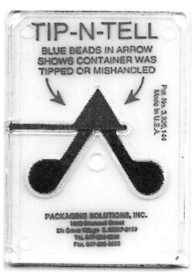

Mishandling turns the arrowhead blue.

Most of an accompanying warning label goes on the package to explain the system; the bottom part goes on the bill of lading to direct people to the package label. It all prints in red, to reinforce the warning message. *Exercise:* Legibility and clarity suffer on the type inside the arrow. Analyze the problems, and improve it.

This Canadian magazine ad, the best in a series, uses symbols to simply and humorously convey the product's purpose and new color. The symbols also contrast with typical ads for such products that show people who look in need or relieved. Are the Stop/Play symbols universal, or at least universal enough to be clear to constipated Canadians?

Although the agency didn't test them, it assumed "enough homogeneity in the audience that it could appreciate popular cultural symbols in Canada," says Marc Stoiber, who conceived the ads. *Agency: Grey WorldWide Toronto. Client: Novartis. Product: Ex-Lax. Creative director: Marc Stoiber. Writers: Matt Bielby, Sam Cerullo. Art directors: Sam Cerullo, Matt Bielby. Photographer: Shin Sugino. Agency print producer: Chris Penny. Agency account supervisors: Brad Cressman, Laurie Sloan.*

EXERCISE: Collect at least six in-use symbols that are likely to communicate to people of almost any culture and language.

EXERCISE: Create one or two symbols to communicate something useful to people of almost any culture or language, then test them. Show them to a range of people to see how the viewers interpret the symbol. Make corrections, retest, and record your process.

EXERCISE: Design two sets of restroom symbols: one for a separate room for each gender, the other for a unisex room.

CHAPTER 2

Usability
and how to achieve it

Usable information design certainly incorporates how most people perceive and comprehend. But it's best known for taking audience concern to a deeper level—examining how each particular audience varies from others and within itself—and designing accordingly.

An understanding of usability, and how you achieve it in your designs, begins with its multilayered definition. The word itself— dissected into *use ability*—provides a clue, but leaves out the essential parts: the people and their experience. *Usability is the ability of an object or system to be used with satisfaction by the people in the environment and context the object or system is intended for.*

Let's focus on satisfaction for a moment. Being *able* to fill out an insurance form or get an online boarding pass doesn't mean the experience was *satisfying*. By designing an experience for your audience members that's as satisfying as it is functional, you'll improve their day and probably earn their loyalty.

Usability combines useful content with a presentation and format that lets the audience easily, even intuitively, navigate and understand it. And although you might hear the term *usability* used most commonly with Web sites, it's hardly limited to them. Consider the audience's experience in every project you design.

To ensure your projects are usable, strive to design information that encompasses what Whitney Quesenbery of Whitney Interactive Design refers to as the "five *E*'s of usability." Make your design:

1. *effective*. Can audience members—users—complete their task?

2. *efficient*. Can they complete the task with a reasonable amount of time and effort?

3. *engaging*. Is working on the task satisfying, maybe even pleasant?

>> *Users* is not a dirty word. Yet to some information designers and writers, using the word to describe the audience is proof that you don't know—or respect—the audience. As Edward Tufte and others have quipped, the only other industry that calls its customers "users" is illegal drugs. That's funny, but quite beside the point.

Using the word *users* for Web site visitors (and any other information-design audience) helps to remind the people who develop, design, maintain, or approve the site why the audience tends to visit: to *do* something, such as to get info or sign up for something, not just to casually observe. People who recognize that fact work to help their audience members with their tasks. By using a term to describe the audience that focuses on those tasks, they show the utmost respect for their audience. What's more, the term is the natural counterpart to *usability*.**

Of course you'll want to make your terminology more specific if and when you can. For example, you might call people who click one link *applicants,* and those who click another one *shoppers*. And, as you'll see later in this chapter, as you continue your research into audience members, you'll also need to add knowledge of the audience members that goes well beyond a label. Learning who they are and what drives them will help you enhance their experience when they engage with your content far more than arguing about labels will.

---

* Well, we could coin the term *audienceability*. (That idea should give information-design and usability bloggers hundreds of hours of debating enjoyment.)

4. *error tolerant.* Does the design help users avoid and recover from mistakes?

5. *easy to learn.* Is the design based on what users (see the sidebar to the left) already know? And are elements used consistently to reinforce what users learned when starting the task?

Keep the list in mind when you encounter, design, or research any task-oriented visual information. Why research? Usability rarely happens on its own. To know what users will find effective, efficient, engaging, error tolerant, and easy to learn, it helps a lot to know the users, their environment, and their context (abilities, background, knowledge, habits, and preferences), then design with that knowledge.

Research basics: Getting to the heart of the audience

This chapter—and the book—includes case studies that used a wide range of techniques you might use to find out about your audience. They fall into these major categories:

* Find out all you can from your clients:
  * Interview the people who give you the project.
  * Talk to people who have regular direct contact with the audience in person, by phone, or online. That might include customer service or sales reps, clerks, registrars, bookkeepers, and so on. Ask your clients to arrange access to them.
  * Look at the clients' logs of the audience's phone calls, e-mails, Web site paths, and search engine entries. (If the clients aren't keeping and using these logs, urge them to start. You might help them to design a system for capturing this valuable intelligence.)

* Do or commission your own research. For example:
  * Interview audience members in person (one-on-one or in a focus group), by phone, or online.
  * Conduct a survey (in print or online).
  * Observe audience members working with your materials and those of other companies.

* Look at outside research about the audience.

Interview your clients and their colleagues

Whenever you get a design project, always ask your clients for a detailed description of the audience members and their needs. Here are some essential questions to start with:

- Why are these people in a position to interact with the design? What need, problem, or question brought them to it? What's their task? Even if the answers seem obvious to you before you ask for them, they might show you a flaw in your assumptions early on.
- What else do audience members see on the topic from other sources?
- What else do they see from the client? (Look at the proposed project in the context of other materials to see whether it would make sense to combine, redesign, or eliminate some.)
- What does the audience already know?
- What problems or challenges does the audience have?

Educate your clients

Clients who haven't looked at the audience might not be able to answer all of those questions. Or you might have to explain why you're even asking. If so, consider it worth the effort to train your clients in the value of research and serving the audience members' needs, not just the clients'. Consider it a long-term process; you can use this book and its case studies as support.

You also might need to educate your own team members, suggests Sanjay Koyani, a senior usability engineer at the U.S. Department of Health and Human Services. Teach them not just about the need for testing but also its goal: "making sure we have a deep understanding of the users, their priorities, and our measures of success," rather than just that the site works on the servers.

When designer Paul Mijksenaar recommends that clients test their designs with the audience, "most of the clients say, 'Well, you are the expert, you should know'" what's right without research, he says. "We *can* say if the details are too complex," he notes, but not "how people behave or the meaning of the sign . . . we can't foresee how people will react to a new element."

What to learn about your audience and why

Learning the audience starts with knowing their demographic categories, such as age, gender, education, income, and marital status—information that's relatively easy to get secondhand. But it also means delving deeper into the audience's psychographics, such as attitudes, ambitions, habits, preferences, skills, and details of daily life. Psychographic info is tougher to get at, but it's worth the effort.

Knowing how your audience members think, act, and feel will tell how they're alike and different from each other and from other audiences. It will:

- keep the focus on what the audience needs instead of on what the client wants to tell them. (And any utterance of "What do we want to tell them?" should always trigger the better question "Why should they care?")

- serve as a benchmark for every content and design decision

- help to eliminate or minimize the effects of different agendas within the team that can derail a project

- help you and your colleagues think about and speak to the audience as individuals (instead of as "you guys," as an insurance rep's voice-mail message addressed callers: "If you guys are calling for claims forms . . . ," which seems to reflect the rep's lack of concern for her audience)

But words alone won't convince the audience you care. No one's fooled by a utility company's assurance that "your call is important to us," especially when it repeats during a long wait on hold. Although this example is not visual, it falls under information design because it's part of the audience's information-seeking experience. Consider the whole picture to give your audience a consistently positive one.

Research will also help you:

- anticipate what will work for the audience members

- avoid alienating them

- develop empathy for them

- connect with them

- do your part to make life easier for the people you serve

How to learn about your audience from your audience
Research techniques include:
- interviewing the audience
  - one-on-one or in groups
  - in person or on the phone
  - print or online surveys

- testing the audience
  - Create project-related tasks for audience members.

- Observe them doing the task.

- Ask them to tell you what they're doing as they do it.

- Interview them after the task about their experience.

- Test before you design—perhaps using an existing similar project—and during and after design.

For a step-by-step walk through testing for one project, see—and do—the swim schedule project on pages 42–60.

Testing tips . . . and limits

Tests don't have to be expensive or complicated. In fact, it's better to keep them low-cost and simple to encourage more testing, according to *Don't Make Me Think* by Steve Krug, who focuses on Web testing. Ask people to do typical tasks you set for them, or, he suggests, you might let them set their own tasks. You also can show people rough sketches and ask for reactions.

Krug notes that there's a limit to what testing will do for your project. It won't tell you what everyone wants, because there is no "average Web user." Krug's observation of test participants over the years confirmed that individual Web use behavior is both unique and idiosyncratic. Good design allows for such diverse behavior.

According to Krug's commonsense approach to testing:

- Test early because it's harder to change things at the end. Before you design anything, test with sites of organizations that are similar to yours.

- Test often, even if it means using participants who don't represent the audience in some ways for some of the tests. For example, if you're designing a Web site for realtors, you could test navigation throughout the design process with nonrealtors who have Web skills that are similar to your audience's in between tests with the actual audience. (Janice Redish also believes in frequent tests, even with only a few people, but only with people who represent your key audiences. But, she says, "most Web sites are meant for the public, and it's not too hard to find the public.")

- Test inexpensively. Testing can be informal; it doesn't need a lab or scientists.

- Test after making changes.

- Videotape tests. (*Continues on page 61*)

How a swim schedule became more usable

Let's analyze, test, and redesign a typical information-design project you might find in your neighborhood. It's a swim center's schedule, meant to answer a simple question for the audience: "When can I swim laps at this place?" But the answer isn't always so simple or quick to find.

- Scheduling is complicated. Swim teams and classes fill some or all of the sixteen lap lanes at various, inconsistent times every day.
- The pools are different. Eight of the lap lanes are in a shallow pool; the other eight are in a deeper one.
- The schedule design is hard to use.

Of these three issues, the only one we can change is the design. Let's test it.

To find out whether the schedule is effective and whether we can improve it, we'll use four techniques:

- *Usability testing* with the audience
- *Analyzing the design*
- *Interviewing staff members* who take swimmers' questions about the schedule
- *Interviewing the audience* (before you design)

You'll do an exercise that will include the first two techniques. Then we'll discuss the other two, which are where you'd start in an actual information-design project.

Usability testing: Get inside the experience of the test participant

In an actual test, the test participant would do a task, and the facilitator would observe it. But to give you a taste of the experience just for this exercise, you'll perform both roles. So while you do the task you're about to get, notice everywhere your eye falls and in what order: Where do you look first? What do you *see* first? What's next, and next after that? How much time did you spend getting oriented? And how many times does your eye glance at the schedule without finding what you're looking for?

If you met any obstacles, however brief, on the way to your answer, identify them and take notes. Avoid judging your comprehension pace; just observe it. (And if you still think the answer took too long to find, blame the design, not yourself. Also avoid assuming that if you got the answer quickly, everyone else will . . . and avoid questioning the intelligence of those who don't.)

Here's the task: Find the current time and day on the schedule. See whether you could swim laps now at the swim center.

Usability testing: Test others

Now give yourself the essential "other" perspective, because you can't assume other people's experiences will match yours. In an actual project you get from a client, you'll test only other people. For this part of the test exercise, follow these steps:

1. Enlarge the schedule to 8½ by 11 inches on a photocopier or scanner. (That's its original size; we've had to reduce it to fit the page.) Make six copies.

2. Find six test participants from your town, neighborhood, office, or classes. To represent the swim center's diverse audience, choose a range of ages, genders, cultures, and educational levels.

3. Test one participant at a time, alone, so you can focus on each participant as he or she does the task. Ask each person to assume the same posture (for example, standing or sitting, holding swimming equipment or not. (If this were not an exercise, you could have looked to your preliminary research to tell you how most people use the schedule). Then give each person the schedule and ask the same question: "Can you swim now?"

4. Sit where you can observe both the person and the schedule.

5. Observe each participant's process in finding the answer. Capture the process with written notes, or with audio- or videotape if you have the equipment and if participants sign a permission form. To help you cover each participant consistently, you might draw up a form with spaces for the various categories you'll look at, such as:

- comments, questions, and answers. Ask the participant to talk you through his or her process. If the participant grows silent, ask "What are you doing (or looking at) now?" or "What's going on now?"
- sounds, such as grunts, groans, cheers, sighs
- eye flow

MONTGOMERY COUNTY DEPARTMENT OF RECREATION - AQUATIC SECTION

MONTGOMERY AQUATIC CENTER
AT NORTH BETHESDA
5900 Executive Boulevard, North Bethesda, MD 20852 • 301-468-4211

LAP LANE AVAILABILITY
Nov. 15, 2004 - Feb. 26, 2005

A.M.	MONDAY	TUESDAY	WEDNESDAY	THURSDAY	FRIDAY	SATURDAY	SUNDAY	A.M.
6:00	8 LANES SHALLOW							6:00
7:00	8 LANES SHALLOW / 8 LANES DEEP							7:00
8:00						8 SHALLOW / 8 DEEP		8:00
9:00	8 SHALLOW / 2 DEEP	3 SHALLOW / 8 DEEP	8 SHALLOW / 2 DEEP	3 SHALLOW / 8 DEEP	8 SHALLOW / 2 DEEP	8 SHALLOW		9:00
10:00		8 SHALLOW / 8 DEEP		8 SHALLOW / 8 DEEP				10:00
	3 SHALLOW	8 SHALLOW / 3 DEEP	3 SHALLOW	8 SHALLOW / 3 DEEP	3 SHALLOW			
11:00		8 SHALLOW / 8 DEEP		8 SHALLOW / 8 DEEP				11:00
	8 DEEP		8 DEEP		8 DEEP			
12:00 NOON		3 SHALLOW		3 SHALLOW				12:00 NOON
	4 SHALLOW / 8 DEEP		4 SHALLOW / 8 DEEP		4 SHALLOW / 8 DEEP			
1:00	4 SHALLOW / 4 DEEP	3 SHALLOW / 4 DEEP	4 SHALLOW / 4 DEEP	3 SHALLOW / 4 DEEP	4 SHALLOW / 4 DEEP			1:00
2:00	6 SHALLOW / 2 DEEP	6 SHALLOW / 2 DEEP	6 SHALLOW / 2 DEEP	6 SHALLOW / 2 DEEP	6 SHALLOW / 2 DEEP			2:00
3:00	8 LANES SHALLOW					4 SHALLOW / 5 DEEP	4 SHALLOW / 5 DEEP	3:00
4:00								4:00
5:00								5:00
	2 LANES SHALLOW - ADULTS ONLY						ADULTS ONLY	
6:00	2 LANES SHALLOW - ADULTS ONLY / 1 LANE DEEP - ADULTS ONLY					4 SHALLOW / 5 DEEP		6:00
7:00	5 SHALLOW / 1 DEEP	2 SHALLOW / 1 DEEP	5 SHALLOW / 1 DEEP	2 SHALLOW / 1 DEEP	5 SHALLOW / 1 DEEP	ADULTS ONLY		7:00
								7:45
8:00	5 SHALLOW / 5 DEEP	4 SHALLOW / 1 DEEP	5 SHALLOW / 3 DEEP	4 SHALLOW / 1 DEEP	5 SHALLOW / 5 DEEP			8:00
8:20								8:20
9:00					5 SHALLOW			9:00
10:00 P.M.	8 SHALLOW / 4 DEEP		8 SHALLOW					10:00 P.M.

This Lap Lane schedule may be changed to accommodate special events or holiday activities. Check posted notices in the lobby.

Shaded areas indicate NO Lap Lanes Available

Test this lap-swimming schedule's usability. Could you swim laps now? How could you improve the schedule? *Designer: Aquatics— Montgomery County Recreation Department.*

- facial expressions and body language (for example, whether the participant uses a finger to scan the sheet)
- How much time it takes each participant to find the answer

6. If participants have trouble finding the answer, continue to just observe and probe for what's getting in their way; resist any temptation you might have to help them. (Ultimately you'll help at least their fellow humans by improving the design.)

7. Interview participants after the task about their experience. Get at any problems or delays they had. Ask open-ended questions such as "What did you think of it?" and "how was that for you?" Stay neutral in both your questions and facial expressions to avoid showing your hand or leading the participant. Test participants often try to "get it right" or please the interviewer, so keep your opinions ("Wasn't this a mess?") to yourself. For that reason, also make clear that any problems were with the design, not the participants' intelligence.

Analyze:
Solve participants' problems on paper
8. Take the test results to the drawing board and sketch versions that solve the participants' problems.* Also apply the information-design principles and guidelines in this book.

9. Choose the two sketches that seem clearest, and lay them out in digital format. Make them look as finished as you can for participants who find it tough to judge a rough sketch.

Test some more
10. Show the redesigns to the same participants, then six more. Divide your participants into two groups (even though you'll test them individually), with each group starting with a different version. After they finish the task, ask what they thought of the design. Then show the other version and ask what they think of that one. Use a neutral voice and facial expression, and use the same words to ask about each one to avoid showing any bias.
11. Make changes; test again.

Interview staff members
For any actual information design project, you'll get essential info by talking to staff members. For example, as at the swim center:

- the people who work the reception desk and phone could tell you about swimmers' problems and questions about the schedule. They could also give you a general sense of the type of people who use the schedule.
- the people who update the schedule could tell you how they produce, reproduce, and distribute it.
- the people who schedule teams and classes could tell you how much the schedule changes every season.

The schedule redesign in this book included interviews with fewer staff members than a commissioned project would need. They included a clerk (who greets patrons, collects fees, answers questions), three lifeguards, and a recreational supervisor. "I think (the schedule) works as well as it could work. . . . It reflects a very complicated schedule," said the supervisor, Peter Haack. And despite its complications, "the staff has it memorized." (But memorized with gaps, it turns out. When asked how long the lanes would stay open, one of three interviewed lifeguards didn't know; a second lifeguard was off by a half hour.)

As the designer or redesigner, you also might ask whether the schedule needs to be so complicated. But for our purposes, the complications add useful challenge to the exercise, so we'll work with it as is.

Staff interviews also would tell you that the center uses Excel to produce and easily update the schedule. So it makes sense to at least strongly consider using that program for the redesign. Possible reasons for *not* using Excel might also come out in the interviews. For example, maybe the center plans to move the updating to your studio, buy new software, or keep the new programming schedule permanently. Or maybe Excel just won't support a clearer schedule. That's not the case, but if it were, you could suggest new software or a permanent schedule. (Because this redesign is only an exercise, I used a page layout program just because I know it better.)

You'd also need to consult the staff on the internal feasibility of your ideas. For example, a design analysis—and turning the lanes into graphics in one redesign—revealed useful patterns: Tuesday's and Thursday's schedules match, and Monday's, Wednesday's, and Friday's schedules are identical to each other until 7:45 p.m. Those patterns aren't clear on the original, so later redesigns highlight

---

* Brainstorming toolbox: Experiment with both pencil and pen to find your preference. The look and sound of pencil on paper inspire some designers. Others prefer felt-tip pens for their speed in getting down ideas. If you use pencil, avoid erasing, which can plunge a brainstormer into idea-squelching perfectionist mode; just move on to the next sketch when you've finished exploring the previous one.

them, and test participants approved. But if the staff tells you that those day patterns change or even disappear from season to season, you're back to showing all seven days.

Tests also showed that the audience members didn't need the seal or other county references here. They already knew the center is a county facility. So because the project is just an exercise, the seal came out in later versions. If this were for real, the staff might tell you the seal must stay, for reasons ranging from identity to legal. Accept the answer if you can't fight it or shouldn't try to, and move on. (You might get permission to reduce its size, but avoid reducing it below legibility, as it might distract readers who think they have to decipher it.)

Interview the audience before you design
Whom to ask:
the "right" test participants
In the case of the schedule, even a nonswimmer or someone who's not familiar with the facility can shed light on a more functional design. Of course, also test those who represent the audience. In this case, the audience is a diverse public community, including all ages and a big share of people for whom English is a second or unknown language. That fact inspired design versions that relied on graphics, which, if they're clear, speak equally well to people of all native languages.

Whom not to ask . . . much: you
The first part of the previous exercise aside, you're not the audience, as you'll see throughout this chapter. At the very least, you're different because,

as the designer with an inside track to the organization, you know jargon and other things the audience doesn't know. Or you might represent only one segment of the audience, which could blind you to other segments.

What to ask and why
As you'll see throughout this book, every project should answer one big question for the audience. For the schedule, the big question—the one chosen for the test task—is "Can I swim now?" Other questions include "When can I swim?" and "How long can I swim?" But the clarity and value of your design also depend on knowing more about the audience members' diverse needs and preferences. So before you design an actual project, ask other questions to get at them.

Choose questions that seek to get to the heart of the audience members and their ideal experience, in relation to what you're designing. For example, if you were designing a swim center's schedule, you might ask audience members about:

their swimming times
- What times and days do you swim? (This will tell you high and lower traffic times; also ask staff members to keep track, if they don't already. It will also give you a sense of which audience members don't swim at regular times and so refer to the schedule more often than other users; these are the most valuable people to interview.)

the printed schedule
- Do you use the "lap lane availability" schedule?

- If you do, how does it help you?
- What has been your experience getting information about the swim center?
- Have you ever shown up at the swim center at the wrong time to swim?
- If not, how do you know when to show up?
- Do you use the Web site?

pool depths
- Will you swim in either of the two pools?
- What do you see as the difference between the pools?
- Do you have a preference?
- What do you prefer about it?
- With an equal number of swimmers in each lane, which pool would you prefer to swim in?

Why ask about depths?
Do swimmers care about the water depth? Won't they swim in either pool? Responses divided into three major categories:

- those who will swim in either pool but want to avoid heavy traffic. These swimmers want to know only the total number of open lanes.
- those who have a preference or will swim in only one of the pools. (Some people need deep water for doing underwater turns; others need shallow water they can stand up in.) They want to know the number of open lanes in their chosen pool.
- those who ignore the open-lane totals, the pools' depth, and the

printed schedule. Said one: "There's swimming every day till three-thirty. If I'm lucky, there aren't too many people in my lane." (That swimmer expressed relief she didn't depend on the printed schedule: She said that without her reading glasses, she found the (7-point) numbers too small. For her and others like her, the redesign made the numbers one size bigger than the words.)

If you're not sure what to ask for any given project, it might help to borrow the journalists' formula "5 *w*'s and an *h*": who (Who are the audience members?), what (What do they do there? What, if any, problems have they faced?), when (When do they swim?), where (In which pool do they swim?), why (Why do they swim there?), and how (How do they know when to swim? How do they get there?). Then try them out on audience members to see which questions work best.

At the end of the interview or test, ask a "what else" kind of question. In this case, that might be "What other information would you like this schedule to contain?" or, better and more neutral, "Is there anything you'd like to add?" The question might give you useful information you didn't think to ask about.

Collecting test results

Here's the process of a typical participant who was trying to answer the question, "Can you swim now?" while looking at the original schedule on page 43. After being briefly stalled by the clutter at the top of the page, he found the days of the week, then

Tuesday, his goal. But before he could find the hours, he got distracted and momentarily confused by the big *8*'s below it (showing the number of shallow and deep lanes). He wondered whether and how the big type might be different from the smaller type. (The big type does show that the schedule is the same for all five weekdays. But the absence of vertical lines to separate the days there is indication enough.)

Testing redesigns also showed a preference for putting the hours at the top of the schedule and the days down the side, instead of the opposite, as they are now. (When you test just one element, conduct a controlled experiment by creating versions that differ only in the element you're testing.)

Capture audience members' words to show you what terms they use and understand. Also test the audience's understanding of terms the staff uses. For example, you might explore how users understand the terms *shallow* (here it means 3 feet 10 inches to 5 feet) and *deep* (9 to 18 feet), and determine whether swimmers need to know how the staff are using them (yes, as it turned out).

Or let's say you found in your research that depths didn't matter to swimmers. So you might think of identifying the two pools as, say, "left" and "right," based on swimmers' perspective when they leave the locker room. You also would have to test the clarity of those terms with swimmers of all ages, native languages, and cultures. As another example, because there are adults-only swim times, how old is "adult"? Parents might wonder if their teenager can swim during those times.

If you can't change the terms to be clearer, define or explain them in a glossary placed where the audience members who need it can find it. (How do you know where the audience would look? Test, ask, observe.)

Analyze what's wrong

Testing swimmers showed that what confused people the most was the schedule's inconsistency:

1. Type is enlarged or shrunk to fit available space (different sizes of type usually mean different things, but that wasn't the case here).
2. The amount of space varies between lines of type that go together.
3. The amount of space varies for time periods of the same length (for example, the size of the 9:30–10 a.m. block is smaller than the size of the 10–10:30 block).*

The inconsistency starts at the top, in the page's competing titles. The eye easily can get lost in the elements, sizes, weights (bold with medium), and cases (some lines are in all caps, others in upper- and lowercase).

Analyze what works

Also look for any features worth saving, and test them with the audience to confirm it. Because the features are already in place, the audience might find them clear because they're familiar. And if they're compatible with any needed revisions, you'll also save yourself time. For example, on the original schedule:

- the shaded areas without type represent times when no lanes are available (this is clear even if you don't look at the key).

---

* An acceptable exception: See 7:45 and 8:20 among the otherwise half-hour increments. Those are the times when classes start or stop.

MONTGOMERY COUNTY DEPARTMENT OF RECREATION - AQUATIC SECTION

MONTGOMERY AQUATIC CENTER

AT NORTH BETHESDA

5900 Executive Boulevard, North Bethesda, MD 20852 • 301-468-4211

LAP LANE AVAILABILITY

Nov. 15, 2004 - Feb. 26, 2005

A.M.	MONDAY	TUESDAY	WEDNESDAY	THURSDAY	FRIDAY	SATURDAY	SUNDAY	A.M.
6:00								6:00
	8 LANES SHALLOW							
7:00	8 LANES SHALLOW							7:00
	8 LANES DEEP							
8:00						8 SHALLOW		8:00
						8 DEEP		
9:00	8 SHALLOW	3 SHALLOW	8 SHALLOW	3 SHALLOW	8 SHALLOW	8 SHALLOW		9:00
	2 DEEP	8 DEEP	2 DEEP	8 DEEP	2 DEEP			
10:00		8 SHALLOW		8 SHALLOW				10:00
		8 DEEP		8 DEEP				
	3 SHALLOW	8 SHALLOW	3 SHALLOW	8 SHALLOW	3 SHALLOW			
		3 DEEP		3 DEEP				
11:00		8 SHALLOW		8 SHALLOW				11:00
	8 DEEP	8 DEEP	8 DEEP	8 DEEP	8 DEEP			
12:00		3 SHALLOW		3 SHALLOW				12:00
NOON	4 SHALLOW		4 SHALLOW		4 SHALLOW			NOON
	8 DEEP	8 DEEP	8 DEEP	8 DEEP	8 DEEP			
1:00	4 SHALLOW	3 SHALLOW	4 SHALLOW	3 SHALLOW	4 SHALLOW			1:00
	4 DEEP	4 DEEP	4 DEEP	4 DEEP	4 DEEP			
	6 SHALLOW	6 SHALLOW	6 SHALLOW	6 SHALLOW	6 SHALLOW			
2:00	2 DEEP	2 DEEP	2 DEEP	2 DEEP	2 DEEP			2:00
3:00	8 LANES SHALLOW					4 SHALLOW	4 SHALLOW	3:00
						5 DEEP	5 DEEP	
4:00								4:00
5:00								5:00
	2 LANES SHALLOW - ADULTS ONLY					4 SHALLOW	ADULTS ONLY	
6:00	2 LANES SHALLOW - ADULTS ONLY					5 DEEP		6:00
	1 LANE DEEP - ADULTS ONLY							
7:00	5 SHALLOW	2 SHALLOW	5 SHALLOW	2 SHALLOW	5 SHALLOW	ADULTS ONLY		7:00
	1 DEEP	1 DEEP	1 DEEP	1 DEEP	1 DEEP			7:45
8:00	5 SHALLOW	4 SHALLOW	5 SHALLOW	4 SHALLOW	5 SHALLOW			8:00
	5 DEEP	1 DEEP	3 DEEP	1 DEEP	5 DEEP			8:20
8:20								
9:00					5 SHALLOW			9:00
10:00	8 SHALLOW		8 SHALLOW					10:00
P.M.	4 DEEP							P.M.

This Lap Lane schedule may be changed to accommodate special events or holiday activities. Check posted notices in the lobby.

Shaded areas indicate NO Lap Lanes Available

Look for and remove inconsistencies and clutter. *Designer: Aquatics—Montgomery County Recreation Department.*

- the columns for the days of the week are all the same width.

- times are listed on both sides of the schedule, so people don't have to scan across the page to find them.

- most of the labels are set in a consistent size and face.

- the title is appropriately bigger and bolder than anything else on the page.

- there are no 7:30 and 8:30 labels, because no swim period begins or ends then.

What's the least you can do to improve clarity?

Although it's worth doing everything you can to make things clear for the audience, it can be useful to first consider how you might limit changes to what's essential. The more elements you can keep from the original, the easier it will be for viewers to learn how to use the new schedule.

In this case, these changes were most needed:

- Make type sizes consistent for the same kind of information.

- Make leading (space between type within the boxes) consistent.

- Define terms (shallow, deep, adult, etc.).

- Separate the days more, using space or heavier rules.

- Match the amount of space given to equal time increments.

- Clarify the title section. The clutter of many squeezed elements makes it hard to find a place for the eye to land. The title is bigger than anything else, but it still tends to get lost in the crowd.

Guidelines to redesign by

Testing and analyzing this project inspired these guidelines for its redesign:

1. Use equal visual increments to represent equal quantities, unless your reason for unequal ones helps to clarify the information.

2. Use space to separate the title from the rest of the schedule, in this case the days of the week.

3. Every heading needs a clear focal point, and every information design needs an entry point for the audience.

4. Always ask how materials will be displayed or distributed, and design accordingly.

5. When you design seals or logos, simplify them enough that you can reduce and reproduce them on rough or textured surfaces without losing clarity.

6. Start with less detail, adding more only as needed (or logos and information design, in general). For example, that might mean just removing unavailable lanes, as in the redesign on page 50.

7. Question everything, including terminology. Always find out if audience members understand terms the organization takes for granted; if not, find out and substitute what the audience does understand.

8. Look at all of the materials the organization provides to its audience. See how the pieces relate to each other. See whether any of them need redesigning as part of a system to show how they interact and differ, or eliminating because they duplicate each other. If patrons don't find what they need on one sheet, how will they know whether it's on a companion sheet?

9. Connect all related materials clearly. For example, distribute them at the same place, give them similar design features, and, on each piece, refer to related pieces. Refer more specifically than saying just "Also see ["Public Use Times"] if the title doesn't describe what the audience will see there. One pool visitor admitted to searching the schedule for the hours of the center's third pool, which is not for lap swimming so the schedule doesn't include it.*

10. Choose words carefully, and test to determine whether headlines that describe what the information does for the audience (such as "When can I swim laps?" or "When you can swim laps") work better than label titles that tell only what the piece of information is (such as "Lap Lane Availability"). To either, you might add a subhead: "Hours when lap lanes are open to the public."

Improvements start at the top: focal point, hierarchy, chunking

The title needs space around it, without anything competing with it. In fact, the whole title section needs to be set off from the schedule itself. Here, typographic separation (serif titling compared with sans serif labels) isn't enough to do the job. Type can help, with a clear hierarchy of weights, sizes, and position to show the relative importance of various elements.

---

* By the way, that visitor felt stupid when he finally noticed the title of the schedule, because it referred only to lap lanes. But the schedule's clutter was really at fault. You'll commonly witness a similar emotion in test participants who can't figure out the materials they're testing. Always diplomatically remind the participants to blame the problem on the design, not on themselves.

LAP LANE AVAILABILITY
November 15, 2004 through February 26, 2005

Montgomery County Department of Recreation — Aquatic Section
MONTGOMERY AQUATIC CENTER
5900 Executive Boulevard, North Bethesda, Maryland
For more Information, phone (301) 468-4211

A redesigned title section features a stronger focal point, hierarchy, and chunking.

The section also cries out for "chunking" (grouping related elements and separating unrelated ones).

Always put the title at the top of any sheet (such as this one) that the audience picks up from a display stand in which only the title shows. And question what needs to be in the heading.

In the first redesign of the title section, "Lap Lane Availability" groups with the date, which is what most audience members (who already know how to get to the place) consider the second most important piece of information.

The phone number is bolder than the other contact info. But it's still below the address, close to the schedule that might raise questions (but, one hopes, fewer than before the whole schedule's redesign).

Another approach to the title section is similar to the original (and it works unless the display stand would cut off the title): Get the place info out of the way first, but play it down, with fewer caps and styles, and more space to separate it from the title.

Different takes: The final
Interviews, analysis, and design experiments resulted in more than nine versions of the schedule. More interviews would have limited the range of possibilities. (For example, the best versions turn the schedule on its side, which might not work with the center's display stands.) The final version is on the following page. Analyze it and see whether you can improve upon it. Major features include:

- a title section with the main info in the more prominent upper left corner, and contact info in the upper right. The county references came out (but only for this exercise).
- a landscape orientation, with days at the side and hours at the top, because it seemed more logical to the audience to swim across hours than days.
- grouped days that have the same or similar schedules.
- but separate Saturday and Sunday listings, because they differ too much to share space.
- only open lanes displayed, to keep closed lanes from distracting.
- shading that distinguishes shallow from deep lanes, adds contrast that helps the viewer track along the day.
- hours that are close to the lane blocks.
- plenty of space between the day groups.

(The redesigner considered breaking the timeline between lap periods because it would look cleaner [for example, between 3:30 and 5:00 during the week]. But she rejected it because it would make the floating evening periods look as close to other days' evening swims as to the rest of their own day.)

Intermediate versions
The sketches starting on page 51 represent the redesigner's thought process. Let's take a look and analyze them.

For the first few, the lanes turn into graphics. The first one relies too much on the key. As a general rule, use a key or legend only if you can design the diagram to explain itself without clutter and confusion.

And any key should be simple enough that the audience gets it in one glance—having to keep looking back and forth can hinder recall and add frustration. Avoid more than four or five key entries, and where possible, use intuitive codes (such as lighter screens for shallower lanes).

Also in the key, the two shallow lanes are stacked above the two deep ones instead of side by side, as they are in the main diagram, and the unshaded lines represent closed lanes (the opposite of the original, in which shaded areas are closed—a deliberate violation of the "what's familiar" guideline). Testing's needed for these elements.

LAP LANE AVAILABILITY
November 15, 2004 through February 26, 2005

MONTGOMERY AQUATIC CENTER
Executive Boulevard, North Bethesda, Maryland
For more information, phone (301) 468-4211

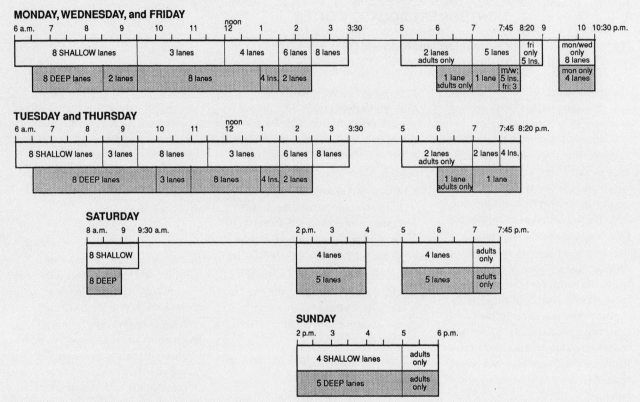

This final, total redesign gets closer to clearly answering the question "When can I swim?" Explain why, and how you'd improve it even more. *Series redesigner: Ronnie Lipton.*

LAP LANE AVAILABILITY
November 15, 2004 through February 26, 2005

Montgomery County Department of Recreation — Aquatic Section
MONTGOMERY AQUATIC CENTER
5900 Executive Boulevard, North Bethesda, Maryland
For more information, phone (301) 468-4211

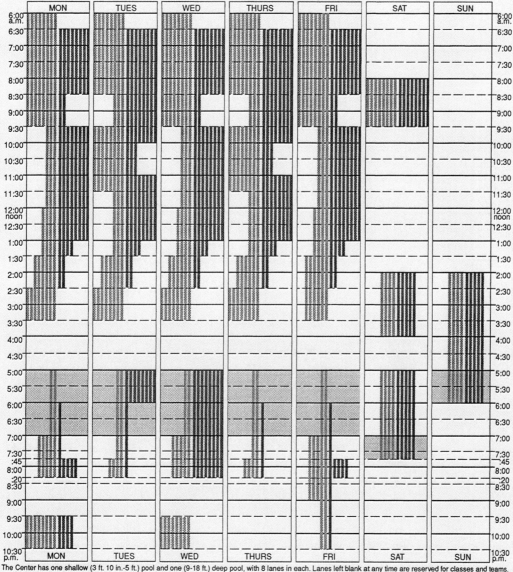

The Center has one shallow (3 ft. 10 in.-5 ft.) pool and one (9-18 ft.) deep pool, with 8 lanes in each. Lanes left blank at any time are reserved for classes and teams.

2 shallow lanes available — adult swimmers only (at least 18 years old)

2 deep lanes available — lanes not available

Schedule might change for holiday or other special events. You'll find changes posted in the lobby.

This project demonstrates the often evolutionary processes of design and redesign. The version that started the evolution keeps the vertical orientation, but replaces words with graphics. It also adds space between days and shading behind the adults-only swim periods.

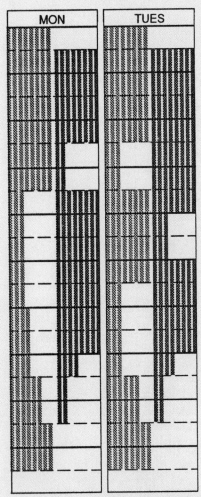

If shading won't survive the production process, change shallow lanes so they "read" open to closed from left to right. That way, the empty space between shallow and deep lanes reinforces their difference, as in this detail.

In the version on page 51, too, the half-hour scale increments get messy, especially at the "exception" times: 7:45 and 8:20.

That design and others assume viewers care about only the total available lanes, not their depths (before research proved the assumption wrong). At a glance, viewers can see the number of open lanes.

The final redesign and some of the other sketches (bottom of page 53, pages 54–56) assume staff approval for grouping. The overall drawback is messy variations on Monday, Wednesday, and Friday evenings.

Research dictated the return of depth distinctions, with shading (on the final and all sketches except page 53). Fortunately, the grouped days let lanes get taller, which helps them look more like lanes. But, on page 54, the closed lanes' high-contrast black, commands more attention than the open lanes do.

On page 55, along with too-strong verticals, notice two tries—one graphic, the other verbal—to show the meager weekend hours without taking up sixteen or thirty-two lanes' worth of diagram space. But using two different designs for the same type of information is confusing.

On page 56, the graphic weekend experiment in the previous sketch might also work for the weekdays, but not in this cluttered attempt. What other changes do you notice?

Information design student Ann Firth was inspired by the original to do her own version (on page 57). She didn't have the opportunity to do testing, so she focused on analysis. To make the schedule easy for the staff to update, she worked in Excel. She listed each day instead of grouping common ones, and put a single number in each time slot.

Firth added an adult lane to each day, but later thought that her shaded lanes and the letter A for "adult" were enough. Next, she says, she would add space between the days. (In fact, she says she kept the extra adult row to help separate them.) Her design also shows you at a glance which lanes are open, and it groups contact info at the bottom.

Firth agrees with putting days on the side. With the original, she says, "The inability to track lanes across one day bothered me the most. Jumping from time box to time box was very annoying, especially when some lanes remained the same." And, "It seemed more natural to visualize the day left to right, not up and down."

Building context into a series of materials

Few information design projects exist in a vacuum. When you take on a project, look at everything the organization provides to its audience. See whether the pieces relate to, supplement, or duplicate each other. If they supplement each other, how do they communicate that? If audience members don't find what they need on one sheet, does the sheet make clear where else to look?

Connect all related material clearly: Distribute them at the same place, give them similar design features, and, on each piece, refer specifically to related pieces. "Specifically" means more than "Also see [title]" if the title doesn't describe what the audience will see there.

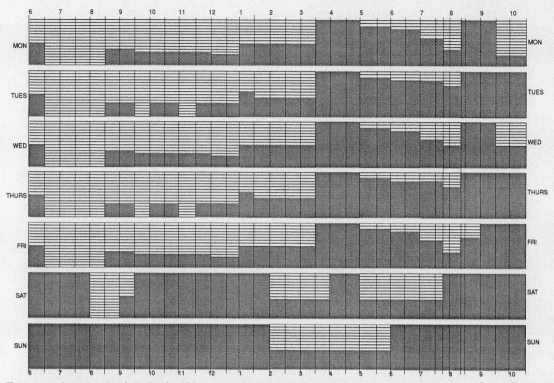

There went the swimming-lane depths. This version also rotated to horizontal.

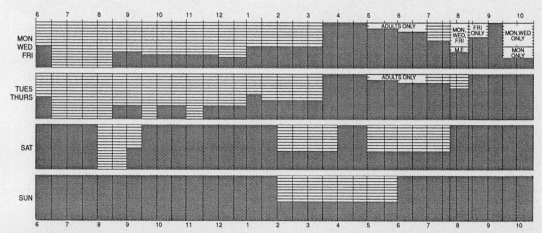

Patterns and their variations in daily schedules emerge.

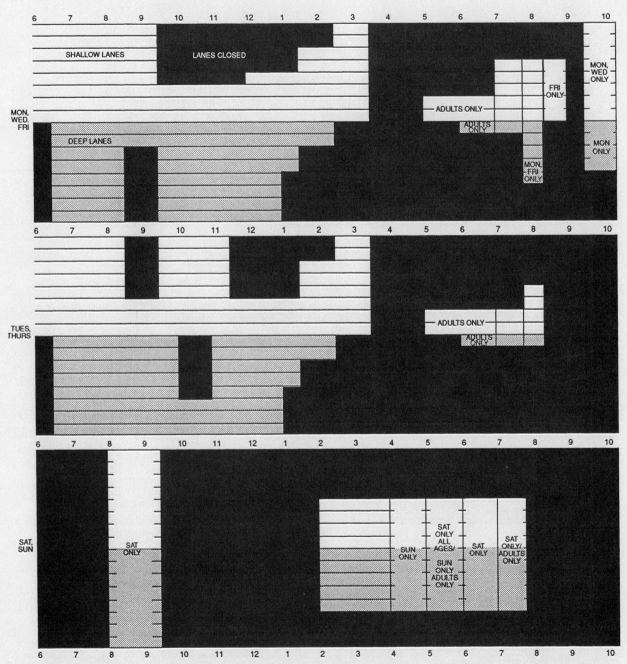

Depths return by popular demand. The version sees a virtue in only the essential vertical lines. But does that high-contrast black stay in the background?

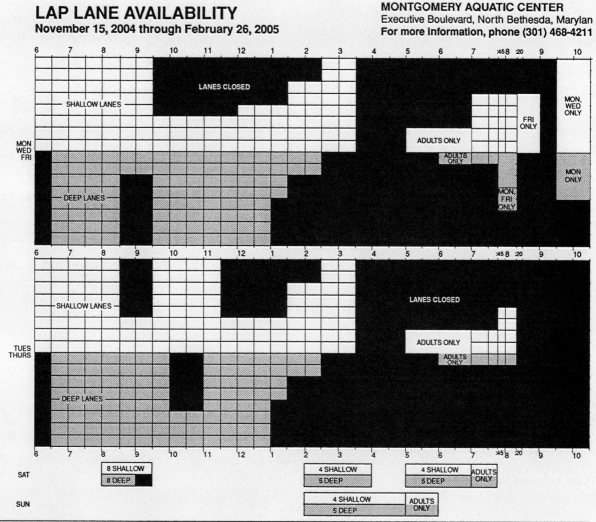

LAP LANE AVAILABILITY
November 15, 2004 through February 26, 2005

MONTGOMERY AQUATIC CENTER
Executive Boulevard, North Bethesda, Marylan
For more information, phone (301) 468-4211

Weekend Schedule
SATURDAY morning: 8-9 a.m. all lanes open; 9-9:30 a.m. 8 shallow lanes open.
　　　　afternoon: 2-4 p.m. and 5-7:45 p.m. 4 shallow lanes and 5 deep lanes open, 7-7:45 p.m. adults only
　SUNDAY afternoon only: 2-6 p.m. 4 shallow lanes and 5 deep lanes open, 5-6 p.m. adults only

Do more verticals help? If so, make them heavier than the lane lines for easier navigation, or the grid will distract from the info. At the bottom, you see two experiments in weekend schedule display.

LAP LANE AVAILABILITY
November 15, 2004 through February 26, 2005

MONTGOMERY AQUATIC CENTER
Executive Boulevard, North Bethesda, Maryland
For more information, phone (301) 468-4211

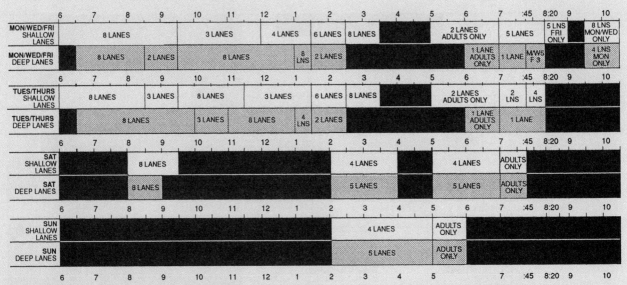

What happened here, and what you think of it?

Exercise: supplemental schedules

Now analyze both sides of a related information sheet from the same center on pages 58 and 59.

Context can take different forms

In the tests, most newcomers understood the terms *shallow* and *deep,* but not which pool was which without jumping in or asking someone. At this facility, the only clues are the depths painted in feet and inches along the upper walls of both pools (and the water color: In the deeper pool, it looks darker blue than in the shallower one). It's tough to see the labels across the large room.

So context in this case would mean posting a sign above each pool to identify it by name. In fact, any sheet label should correspond to big, clear, nonfogging pool signs that are visible and legible from a distance.

Also, displaying an enlarged copy of the schedule in the pool area would be helpful to tell people how much longer they can swim. Now the only poolside reference is the letter-sized sheet on a bulletin board. Because the schedule changes with the season, the sign would have to be changeable, too, maybe in electronic form.

More context:
"Visit us online"? Tell why

The back of the sheet (on page 58) offers an invitation to patrons: "Visit us online: www.montgomerycountymd .gov/rec." How will the audience know how this sheet relates to the Web site? Like so many organizations, this one needs to tell people *why* they should visit online. The schedule there (at this writing) is almost the same noninteractive table on one side of another sheet provided by the facility. That's a missed opportunity to exploit the Web's capabilities, which could've let patrons click on or type in a day and time for the current swimming schedule.

Montgomery Aquatic Center of North Bethesda
Montgomery County Department of Recreation - Aquatic Section

Lap Lane Availability
Current Dates: Nov 15, 2004 through Feb 26, 2005

Number of Lanes Available:

Day		6:00	7:00	8:00	9:00	10:00	11:00	12:00	1:00	2:00	3:00	4:00	5:00	6:00	7:00	7:45	8:00 8:20	9:00	10:00		Day
Mon	S	8				3		4		6	8		2 A		5				8	S	Mon
	D		8		2	8			4	2				1 A	1	5			4	D	
	A												A							A	
Tue	S	8			3	8		3		6	8		2 A		2	4				S	Tue
	D		8			8	3	8		4	2				1 A	1				D	
	A												A							A	
Wed	S	8				3		4		6	8		2 A		5				8	S	Wed
	D		8			2	8			4	2				1 A	1	3			D	
	A												A							A	
Thur	S	8			3	8		3		6	8		2 A		2	4				S	Thur
	D		8				3	8		4	2				1 A	1				D	
	A												A							A	
Fri	S	8			3			4		6	8		2 A		5		5 A			S	Fri
	D		8		2	8			4	2				1 A	1	5				D	
	A												A				A			A	
Sat	S			8						4			4		4 A					S	Sat
	D			8						5			5		5 A					D	
	A														A					A	
Sun	S									4			4 A							S	Sun
	D									5			5 A							D	
	A												A							A	

Type of Lanes
S = Shallow
D = Deep
A = Adult
░ = No Availability

Montgomery Aquatic Center of North Bethesda
5900 Executive Bld
North Bethesda, MD 20852
Phone: 301-468-4211

This Lap Lane schedule may change to accommodate special events or holiday activites.
Please check posted notices in the lobby.

Work with the staff's systems, as shown by this version done in Excel, the program the staff uses to make the schedules. *Redesigner: Ann Firth.*

Montgomery Aquatic Center AT NORTH BETHESDA

5900 Executive Boulevard, North Bethesda MD 20852 (301) 468-4211
Montgomery County Department of Recreation - Aquatics Section
2004-2005 POOL USE SCHEDULE: FALL, WINTER & SPRING: Sept. 7th, 2004 - June 12th, 2005

Visit us online at:
www.montgomerycountymd.gov/rec

Monday	Tuesday	Wednesday	Thursday	Friday		Saturday	Sunday
						8:00 - 9:30 A.M. • EARLY BIRD LAP SWIM	8:00 A.M.-2:00 P.M • MASTERS • SWIM & DIVE TEAM • WATER POLO • SWIM LESSONS • SAFETY TRAINING

4:45 - 6:30 A.M. MCRD SWIM TEAM PRACTICE

6:00 - 8:30 A.M. **EARLY BIRD LAP SWIM**
Deep water Running Available

8:30 - 11:30 A.M. **MID MORNING SWIM**
WATER EXERCISE CLASSES • MCRD SWIM LESSONS
Lap Lanes Available • Deep Water Running Available

8:00 - 9:30 A.M.
• EARLY BIRD LAP SWIM

9:00 A.M.-2:00 P.M.
• SWIM LESSONS
• HIGH SCHOOL SWIM MEETS

8:00 A.M.-2:00 P.M
• MASTERS
• SWIM & DIVE TEAM
• WATER POLO
• SWIM LESSONS
• SAFETY TRAINING

11:30 - 2:30 P.M.
NOON RECREATIONAL SWIM
Lap Lanes Avaiable (Diving Boards Open 1:00 - 2:30 P.M.)
Water Exercise Classes (Main Pool) • Deep Water Running Available

2:00 - 4:00 P.M.
Recreational Swim
• All Facilities Open (Ex. Diving Platforms)
• Lap Lanes Available
• Deep Water Running Available

2:00 - 5:00 P.M.
Recreational Swim
• All Facilities Open (Ex. Diving Platforms)
• Lap Lanes Available
• Deep Water Running Available

Limited Lap Lanes Available (See Lap Schedule) - Maintenance

3:30 - 5:30 P.M. **Slide & Dip** Leisure Pool & Slide Open	3:30 - 7:30 P.M. MCRD Swim Lessons	3:30 - 5:30 P.M. **Slide & Dip** Leisure Pool & Slide Open	3:30-7:30 P.M. MCRD Swim Lessons	3:30 - 5:30 P.M. **Slide & Dip** Leisure Pool & Slide Open

3:30 - 7:30 P.M. MCRD YOUTH SWIM & DIVE TRAINING
Limited Lap Lanes Available (5 - 7 p.m.) - Limited Deep Water Running Space Available (6 - 7:30 p.m.)

4:00-5:00 P.M.
Maintenance/Staff Training

7:00 - 8:20 P.M. **EVE. REC SWIM** ALL FAC. OPEN (EXCEPT DIV. PLAT.) • Limited Laps & DWR	7:00 - 8:20 P.M. **Slide & Dip** • Water Exercise • Limited Laps Avail.	7:00 - 8:20 P.M. **EVE. REC SWIM** ALL FAC. OPEN (EXCEPT DIV. PLAT.) • Limited Laps & DWR	7:00 - 8:20 P.M. **Slide & Dip** • Water Exercise • Limited Laps Avail.	7:00 - 9:00 P.M. **EVE. REC SWIM** ALL FAC. OPEN (EXCEPT DIV. PLAT. & DIVING BOARDS) • Limited Laps & DWR • Master's Swim • Safety Training

5:00 - 7:00 P.M.
Recreational Swim
• All Facilites Open (Ex. Diving Platforms)
• Lap Lanes Available
• Deep Water Run Available

5:00 P.M. - 6:00 P.M.
Adults Only

8:30-10:00 P.M. • Dive Training • Water Exercise • Adult Classes	8:30-10:00 P.M. • Master's Swim • Therapuetics • Adult Classes	8:30-10:00 P.M. • Dive Training • Water Exercise • Adult Classes	8:30-10:00 P.M. • Master's Swim • Dive Training • Therapuetics • Adult Classes	

7:00 - 7:45 P.M.
ADULTS ONLY

9:30-10:30 P.M. Late Laps		9:30-10:30 P.M. Late Laps		

6:00 - 8:00 P.M.
SWIM CLINIC

8:00 - 10:00 P.M.
Rentals & Special Uses

This pool use schedule may be changed to accommodate special events or holiday activities. Check posted notices in center lobby.

FAMILY REC SWIM   POOL CLOSED ON: Thanksgiving Day, Christmas Day, New Year's Day & Easter Day

Another sheet for swimmers kind of looks like a graph, but note the problems with the box heights, which represent the time periods in them just closely enough to be dangerous. And what do those terms mean? *Designer: Aquatics— Montgomery County Recreation Department.*

Montgomery Aquatic Center AT NORTH BETHESDA

5900 Executive Boulevard, North Bethesda MD 20852 (301) 468-4211
Montgomery County Department of Recreation - Aquatics Section
2004-2005 Pool Use Schedule: Fall, Winter & Spring: Sept. 7th, 2004 - June 17th, 2005

Vist us online at:
www.montgomerycountymd.gov/rec

Recreational Swim:

General swimming for all ages with the following facilities open: Lap Lanes, Diving Boards, Leisure Pool, Exercise Room, Hydrotherapy Spas, and Saunas. See Water Slide & 5-Meter Platform times below.

General Recreational Time

M - F:	11:30 a.m. - 2:30 p.m.
M, W, F:	7:00 p.m. - 8:20 p.m. (Fri 'til 9 p.m.)
Sat:	2:00 p.m. - 4:00 p.m.
	5:00 p.m. - 7:00 p.m.
	7:00 p.m. - 7:45 p.m. (adults only)
Sun:	2:00 p.m. - 5:00 p.m.
	5:00 p.m. - 6:00 p.m. (adults only)

Leisure Pool

M - F:	11:30 a.m. - 2:30 p.m.
M, W, F:	3:30 p.m. - 5:30 p.m.
M-Th:	7:00 p.m. - 8:20 p.m.
Fri:	7:00 p.m. - 9:00 p.m.
Sat:	2:00 p.m. - 4:00 p.m.
	5:00 p.m. - 7:00 p.m.
	7:00 p.m. - 7:45 p.m. (adults only)
Sun:	2:00 p.m. - 5:00 p.m.
	5:00 p.m. - 6:00 p.m. (adults only)

5-Meter Platform

Sat:	7:00 p.m. - 7:45 p.m. (adults only)
Sun:	5:00 p.m. - 6:00 p.m. (adults only)

Diving Boards

M-F:	1:00 p.m. - 2:30 p.m.
M & W:	7:00 p.m. - 8:20 p.m.
Sat:	2:00 p.m. - 4:00 p.m.
	5:00 p.m. - 7:00 p.m.
	7:00 p.m. - 7:45 p.m. (adults only)
Sun:	2:00 p.m. - 5:00 p.m.
	5:00 p.m. - 6:00 p.m. (adults only)

Note: On school holidays, the boards will open at 11:30 a.m. In addition, the boards will not open on some evenings. Please check lobby for details.

Public Use Times

Hydrotherapy Pools

Adults Only: 14-18 if accompanied by an adult.

Due to frequent cleaning and maintenance that these pools require, only one may be available for use during the following hours.

M & W:	6:00 a.m. - 10:30 p.m.
Tu & Th:	6:00 a.m. - 10:00 p.m.
Fri:	6:00 a.m. - 9:00 p.m.
Sat:	8:00 a.m. - 9:30 a.m.
	2:00 p.m. - 4:00 p.m.
	5:00 p.m. - 7:45 p.m.
Sun:	2:00 p.m. - 6:00 p.m.

Water Slide

(Recreational Swim)

M, W, F:	3:30 p.m. - 5:30 p.m.
M - F:	7:00 p.m. - 8:20 p.m. (Fri. until 9 p.m.)
Sat:	2:00 p.m. - 4:00 p.m.
	5:00 p.m. - 7:00 p.m.
Sun:	2:00 p.m. - 5:00 p.m.

ALL PATRONS WITHIN THE POOL AREA MUST BE ATTIRED IN SWIMMING APPAREL.

CHILDREN UNDER 10 YEARS OLD MUST BE ACCOMPANIED IN THE POOL AREA AND CARED FOR BY AN ADULT IN SWIMMING ATTIRE AT ALL TIMES.

Slide & Dip

A special after-school activity for all ages. The features available at this time will be Leisure Pool, the Spas, and a 230-foot water slide (must be 48 inches tall to use the water slide)

M, W, F: 3:30 p.m. - 5:30 p.m.

Weight & Exercise/Saunas

The Weight & Exercise Room and Saunas are available to patrons at any time the pool is open for public Recreational Swim.
Adults Only: 14-18 with permission slip.

M, W:	6:00 a.m. - 10:30 p.m.
T, Th:	6:00 a.m. - 10:00 p.m.
Fri:	6:00 a.m. - 9:00 p.m.
Sat:	8:00 a.m. - 7:45 p.m.
Sun:	10:00 a.m. - 6:00 p.m.

Lap Swim

Lap Lanes are roped off at either 25 yard or 25 meter competitive distance, or as 20 yard fitness lanes across the main pool. Some lanes are entirely in deep water. Patrons should "circle" swim from right to left and should swim in a lane with other lap swimmers of compatible speed and skills. In general lap lanes are available at all Recreational Swim periods.

M - F:	6:00 a.m. - 3:30 p.m.
M - Th:	5:00 p.m. - 8:20 p.m. (5 - 7 Adults Only)
Fri:	5:00 p.m. - 9:00 p.m. (5 - 7 Adults Only)
M & W:	9:30 p.m. - 10:30 p.m.
Sat:	8:00 a.m. - 9:30 a.m.
	2:00 p.m. - 4:00 p.m.
	5:00 p.m. - 7:00 p.m.
	7:00 p.m. - 7:45 p.m. (Adults Only)
Sun:	2:00 p.m. - 5:00 p.m.
	5:00 p.m. - 6:00 p.m. (Adults Only)

Note: On school holidays, lap lanes will be reduced between 11:30 a.m. - 1:00 p.m.

The management reserves the right to alter the pool schedule when it is deemed necessary.
Lockers are available - Bring a lock to secure your belongings - Proper Bathing suits required - NO CUTOFFS OR GYM SHORTS!

The terms are defined on the sheet's other side. With only words and numbers but no depths, see how compact the "Lap Swim" box in the lower right is. *Designer: Aquatics—Montgomery County Recreation Department.*

Shallow and deep pools (the deep one is closer in the photo) are divided by the white walkway in the middle.
Photographer: Ronnie Lipton.

Interviewing Guidelines: What to Ask and How

The typical survey question is a variation on "What content [articles, sections, answers] do you want?" Although you might get a few useful answers from such a direct question, don't be surprised if you don't get more. In fact, such a question at the start of a survey could suppress overall responses. That's because audiences often don't know what they want until they see it. They expect *you* to know what they want; if you don't provide it, expect them to look somewhere else.

Find out what the audience wants by reaching their heart: Ask psychographic, less-direct questions and observe the audience. The most valuable questions are oriented to emotional experience, such as "What frustrates you most?" or "What is your greatest challenge?" Compare that with the less effective wording of a similar question that engages the logical mind first, 'Tell me the five tasks you most would like to replace with a robot,'" says Nathan Shedroff, information designer and author of *Experience Design*.

For one subscription newsletter, responses to the challenge question painted a vivid picture of the audience that pervaded every design and editorial decision. Although subscribers were busy, they were so pleased to be asked that they responded in unprecedented numbers. They also responded from the heart and in depth, exceeding the provided space to write pages of their own stationery. Those letters translated into dozens of articles that targeted and solved subscribers' expressed problems.

Ask other questions to delve into audience members' motivations (see sidebar to the right), goals, and reward systems. But tailor the questions' choice and wording to the audience's tolerance level. Depending on the audience and the situation (as always), someone might be more likely to answer personal questions one on one than in a focus group or on the Web. Or not. Find out.

Find out what (else) audience members read, what Web sites they visit, where they shop, and how they spend spare time. But asking questions isn't the only way of getting at psychographic information. Shedroff likes to create a game and watch how people play it, so he can gauge "their problem-solving skills . . . or their emotional state through the process."

Observing the audience: What else to find out

Burkey Belser, partner of Greenfield Belser, Ltd., a design firm., combines university-based observational research with his firm's own

---

>> What's the Motivation?

Highly motivated readers are likely to tolerate less-than-ideal design (not that they should have to). But uncommitted readers decide to read or not based on their first impression of the content. To prove this to yourself, pay attention to how you decide to read something, and why you don't.

High motivation: You're probably highly motivated to read if you're alone at a bus stop in a strange city with only a sign to tell you when to expect your bus. At least you're highly motivated to get your bearings, which requires interacting with the sign. Motivation isn't the same as attraction; you might be highly motivated to fill out your tax form to avoid a penalty or get a refund, but you probably won't *like* it.

Medium motivation: Your mailbox gets crammed with mailings you'll never get to the bottom of. You might mean to read some of them, so you save them (in a pile that author Jan V. White calls the "mountain of good intentions"). But after a while, you toss them to make room for the next pile.

Low or no motivation: Comprehensible info design won't cause people to read what they don't want or have to. But it *will* help them tell the difference quickly. Design as if your audience's motivation to read your project is low or nonexistent. Save people time by helping them instantly identify what they want to keep and what they can toss or pass along.

research to find out how people interact with information. He looks at such essentials as:

- How does a consumer read a brochure?
- How does a consumer read an ad?
- How much time do you have before the reader loses interest?
- What part does the reader look at first?
- What can you learn from tracking eye movement?
- How do the human body and mind react to stimuli?
- How do psychographics and demographics influence consumer behavior?

How *does* a consumer read a brochure? From back to front is the typical pattern, Belser says. That means "if you anticipate telling your story in some strictly linear way," you might lose the readers before

 How does *your* audience "address the ball"?

When golf or tennis instructors show students how to "address the ball," they mean how to approach it. Similarly, think about how your audience will approach your design. First become aware of your own behavior when you approach, say, a magazine. Do you start with the front cover and read to the back? Or might you start with the back and thumb toward the front? Or does your path depend on your level of interest or the amount of time you have to spend?

If you ask a roomful of people, many will admit to back-to-front browsing—often sheepishly, as if it's perverse behavior. Actually, it's typical behavior. In fact, you're even more likely to start from the back if the publication came by mail and your name's on the back. You probably look at nothing else before your name on the address label. This fact should tell you something about any publication you design—consider that back panel valuable real estate. Start a good story there, or include a special offer, a formal table of contents, or just the big highlights. The lesson extends even beyond publications: Observe how the audience interacts with anything you design as a physical product, and see how your design can support that interaction.

Now notice this: As you continue from back to front of a magazine, one hand (probably the left) holds the spine while the other hand flips through. That should tell you to put the most attractive features in a publication—such as artwork and pull quotes—toward the trim side and away from what the clutching hand is holding closed.

you can engage them. He cites magazines such as the *New Yorker, Life,* and *Playboy* (" . . . the skin magazines are actually pioneers in many ways in information design") that engage readers with full-page pictures in the back. By contrast, most newsletters put "the best stuff in the front and the worst stuff in the back. You really need to create a rhythm and a movement for the reader throughout the piece." (See the sidebar on the facing page.)

How much time do you have before readers disappear? You have "maybe five seconds to capture readers and encourage them to . . . stop or slow down or do anything but go back to the scanning mode," Belser says. Every page must have a goal and "something for (the readers) to grab hold of." To help clients understand the concept, show them, he says: Hold up a page for five to ten seconds, then ask, "What was your take-away message?"

For example, the intended take-away message of the brochure to the right is that the advertiser can help law firms with an important goal: recruiting recent law school graduates. The brochure demonstrates research that found how students really choose their employers (nearby location and a salary high enough to let them repay student loans quickly), versus how law firms might think they do (impressive clients and a quick partner track).

Some researchers go even further than observing the audience, to try to see through the eyes of the audience. They give audience members disposable cameras to record their surroundings without directing their process.

➤➤ CASE STUDY:
Drug label design relied on research at the mall

Confusing information design can frustrate people. Confusing labels on drug packages risk much more. Such labels have to be clear to the broadest possible audience, including people who have low literacy levels and/or poor vision. So it's good that the design of the "Drug Facts" label came after that of "Nutrition Facts." For both Food and Drug Administration projects, research included "mall intercepts" (interviewing people at shopping malls about their reaction to presented designs). But the nutrition label test participants saw only a binder of big printed-out designs, Belser says. "An 8½-by-11-inch label in a binder that you stop me for is going to get a very different read than a tuna can that I'm running down the aisle for." So for the drug label research, he put actual-size labels on typical products such as

The cover of a design firm's brochure passes the five-second take-away message test. *Design firm: Greenfield/Belser Ltd. Designer: Siobhan Davis. Creative director/ Copywriter: Burkey Belser. Production artist/Illustrator: Brett Mannes. Photographers: John Burwell, Jason Hendricks.*

allergy medicine. The more realistic format made a huge difference in the quality of response, he says.

Adding to the project's challenge: Unlike nutrition labels, which need little more than calorie, fat, and vitamin counts, drug labels have to include "indications, contraindications, warnings, contents . . . probably three times as much to say in half the space," Belser says. So the type had to reduce accordingly. "The best we could do was 6-point," compared with 8-point for the nutrition labels. Even with 6-point type, he says, on some products the designers had to extend the available space with hang tags.

Although the research for the first labeling project informed that of the second one, the agency required a different look for the two projects, despite the success and familiarity of the first one. Half of the process "of getting people to understand labeling is when they see it again and again," Belser says. "That learning had already occurred in America [with nutrition labeling], so why not just copy it down to the last detail?" He believes the consumer "would benefit from a nation-wide labeling standard" on everything, including "mattress tags."

According to FDA's Office of Nonprescription Products, FDA developed and tested different labeling formats through industry and

Six-point type is enough to give you a headache on labels for U.S. drug packaging, but it's bigger and clearer than on earlier labels. Required legal and scientific language along with the contents limit the size. Bigger, bolder, and italicized headings provide contrast—the title's in 14-point type, subtitles are in 8-point. The 2^{1}/2-point dividing lines separate sections from each other and the label from the package, without stealing text space. *Design firm: Greenfield/Belser Ltd. Client: Food and Drug Administration. Creative director, Designer: Burkey Belser.*

Drug Facts

Active ingredients (in each tablet) — **Purpose**
Chlorpheniramine ....Antihistamine

Use temporarily relieves these symptoms due to hay fever or other respiratory allergies:
■ sneezing   ■ runny nose   ■ cough   ■ nasal congestion

Warnings
Ask a doctor before use if you have
■ glaucoma   ■ a breathing problem such as emphysema or chronic bronchitis
■ trouble urinating due to an enlarged prostate gland

Ask a doctor or pharmacist before use if you are taking tranquilizers or sedatives

When using this product
■ you may get drowsy   ■ avoid alcoholic drinks
■ alcohol, sedatives, and tranquilizers may increase drowsiness
■ be careful when driving a motor vehicle or operating machinery
■ excitability may occur, especially in children

If pregnant or breast-feeding, ask a health professional before use.
Keep out of reach of children. In case of overdose, get medical help or contact a Poison Control Center right away.

Directions

adults and children 12 years and over	take 1 tablet every 4 to 6 hours; not more than 6 tablets in 24 hours
children 6 years to under 12 years	take 1/2 tablet every 4 to 6 hours; not more than 3 tablets in 24 hours
children under 6 years	ask a doctor

consumer groups. To adhere to the requirement, Belser focused on the features of an informative label: strong typographical hierarchy, legibility, and contrast, which is especially important without color to help distinguish the information. He paired a 14-point black with a 6-point medium. Lines that separate sections also add contrast, but not too much: A thicker line would steal space from essential type. The lines around the drug info are essential to "prevent the [drug's] manufacturer from invading that territory" with marketing copy. The designers planned drug information labels to fit all possible package sizes and shapes.

EXERCISE: At the drugstore or in your medicine chest, look at six to ten products and notice what had to change in the "Drug Facts" section to accommodate the package size and shape, as well as what's common to all. This exercise should begin to give you a sense of the constraints of an information design project. Within those constraints, what, if anything, can you change to improve the label from a usability standpoint?

>> CASE STUDY:
Finding the tasks in a Web site

Web sites used by both an organization's insiders and an external audience tend to grow well beyond their value. That can happen because every department wants a prominent Web "presence."* Or a department wants to show everything it does. And maybe employees want to store everything there so they can easily find materials. So they add sections and pages without a structural plan to govern those additions.

The result is a site whose structure can't support all of its content and whose useful content hides from frustrated audience members. In fact, even a site of a reasonable size might contain "hundreds of different tasks people can do," says Sanjay Koyani, a senior usability engineer at the U.S. Department of Health and Human Services.

To find out which tasks and needs to emphasize in the redesign of his agency's Web site, Koyani's team created a process that involves users "through market research, interviews, and discussions, by looking at terms they enter into our search engines, through Web analysis" (what they click on during actual Web visits), and usability tests. The team strives for "a continued understanding of how these folks are interacting with the information, what's important to them," and whether the site continues to work for them.

---

* You might point out to these people what the word *presence* means: just being there, not doing anything for the audience.

The audience's searches and survey responses determined the order of the topic categories on this home page. The designers put what's most important to the audience on top. *United States Department of Health and Human Services. Design team leader: Sanjay Koyani.*

One of the specific insights that testing generated was the value of templates. So the team used pages that tested well as models for new pages. That way, users "don't have to relearn all the navigational stuff on each new page."

Nor did testing end with the design. Koyani advises developing a long-term plan for checking how people are doing with the site, and identifying new needs. To accommodate those new needs, his team designed a features section. "What you never want to do is just sit there and say, 'We've got a good site—people will find it if they want to.'" Instead, he says, make sure people are having a great experience.

» CASE STUDY:
Task-based focus groups help to redesign car manuals

A senior official at Ford couldn't figure out the clock-setting instructions in his car's owner's guide. He decided that if he couldn't understand them, at least part of the audience couldn't either. That led to testing, rewriting, and redesigning the manual and other customer materials at the former Document Design Center (DDC) in Washington, D.C.

Before and after the redesign, users were asked to use the manual to answer questions and do tasks. The tests pointed out problems that needed correcting in the redesign. The tests also showed that people aren't alike in how we look for information. Some begin with the index, some look at the table of contents, and others plunge right in, says Carolyn Boccella Bagin, who worked on the project at the DDC. The third group would appreciate tabs.

Other research-inspired improvements included:

- changing the format from horizontal (wider than tall) to vertical to make it easier to hold
- rewriting the information in plain language
- reorganizing it into digestible chunks
- adding categories to the table of contents based on users' needs
- adding white space
- indenting warnings and adding a vertical line to make them obvious

➤➤ CASE STUDY:
Surveys and recipe tests lead to a usable cookbook

"How do you cook? How do you choose a cookbook? What do you think of this recipe?" Before they designed a cookbook, Maria Giudice and Lynne Stile surveyed home cooks and asked them to test recipes. The answers, plus looking at outside research and other cookbooks and recipes, guided the designers to:

- list ingredients in the order of use
- group steps the way cooks would
- put ingredients in a different color than the steps
- group recipes by the amount of time they take
- put substitutions in the margins

Researching the audience "not only tests . . . or validates your assumptions, it allows you to come up with new things," Giudice says. For example, when the designers asked audience members to test recipes, feedback split regionally. The East Coast wanted "more butter, more cream," the West Coast wanted less of each, and the Midwest wanted more meat. Home cooks who live on the East Coast (where the cookbook author's restaurant was located) were the book's primary audience, so their preferences took priority. The substitutions listed in the margin were for everyone else. But the designers didn't label the substitutions by the region of the people who needed them. Instead of saying, "If you're from the West Coast, this is for you," they'd say "Instead of cream, you can use yogurt." That's a deliberate distinction, Giudice says. In information design, you shouldn't "tell people who they are" or make potentially insulting or inaccurate assumptions.

>> CASE STUDY:
Universal how-to graphics, minimum of type

A company needed clear, keepable, accessible instructions for operating its products—handheld or wearable scanning devices that ring up purchases, check prices, or take inventory. The goals for the instructions were to keep:

- users from injury, including back or repetitive-stress problems
- users' employers and the manufacturer from liability and added costs resulting from unsafe usage
- the products working properly

The main audience—the people who use the devices—vary widely in native language and in education, economic, and occupational levels. They range from inexperienced seasonal employees to "power users who . . . have figured out the shortcuts," says Sudhir Bhatia, senior manager of design research in the Industrial Design and Human Interface group at Symbol Technologies, Inc., which makes the devices.

The client's research looked at the "entire experience when someone gets a product." It found that a previous attempt to promote safety—instruction books that shipped with the devices—didn't work. The order departments often threw out the books with the box. Even books that survived failed to do their job, because they hid the essentials in too much information.

So the problem became, in Bhatia's words, "How can diverse and frequently changing populations of operators learn to use these devices effectively and safely?" Asking the question, the solution seemed obvious: "Use clear, accessible, and keepable instructions that work for every level of user." It also triggered another set of questions to address with research and design.

The company commissioned a poster for each device to display in a facility's break room. One side of each poster shows the best angles and body postures for safe scanning. On the other side, a "Quick Start Guide" answers another worthy question: "What does the user need to get off the ground?" It contains the most relevant content from the book, such as instructions for changing or charging a battery.

A pair of posters shipped with the device lets the recipient display both sides if they want to (see page 70). But it's the safety side that's most important (page 71). Most users sign scanners out from an IT (information technology) office each shift, so they don't have to deal with the set-up or maintenance, Sylvester says. And "the processes are simple and easy to remember—batteries only fit one way and are easily removed; scanners are set up once for their task and software type, not reprogrammed daily."

The value of nonverbal communication

The posters emphasize graphics over words, for at least three reasons. Graphics:

- project more clearly than words in break rooms with dim lighting or too much distance between chairs and walls.

- communicate across languages. In the posters, type is limited to the bare essentials to make instructions perform nonverbally as much as possible.

- can precisely describe objects. They *show* where to put the battery, while words can merely tell.

Depicting the products

The designer chose illustrations over photos for:

- *clarity.* Some of the emphasized details don't show up as well in a photo as they do in a black-and-white illustration, says art director/ designer Mark D. Sylvester, Interrobang Design Collaborative. In part, this is because the products tend to be "on the dark side . . . to keep them from showing dirt, scuffs and scratches."

- *emphasis.* Although you can emphasize a feature on a photo with an arrow or a circle, in an illustration you add even more emphasis by increasing the feature's size or by simplifying its surroundings. (With a program such as Photoshop you can do that in photos as well, but ethical issues come up, such as "Has the retoucher misled the viewer?" Users might wonder why their device looks different from the one in the photo.)

- *time.* "The product often is still being designed while we're getting these projects done," Sylvester says, so prototypes might not be available in time to incorporate photos of them.

A manufacturer found out that its instructions on how to quickly and safely use its portable scanners weren't getting to the scanner operators. So a series of instructional posters, designed to function across languages and to be displayed in work and break areas, replaced bulky instruction books. On one side of one product's poster, the "Quick Start Guide" shows how to insert and charge a battery and install accessories. (On these posters, the second color is actually red, not blue.) *Design firm: Interrobang Design Collaborative. Client: Symbol Technologies. Art director/Designer: Mark D. Sylvester. Illustrator: Richard L. LaRocco, Graymatter Illustration*

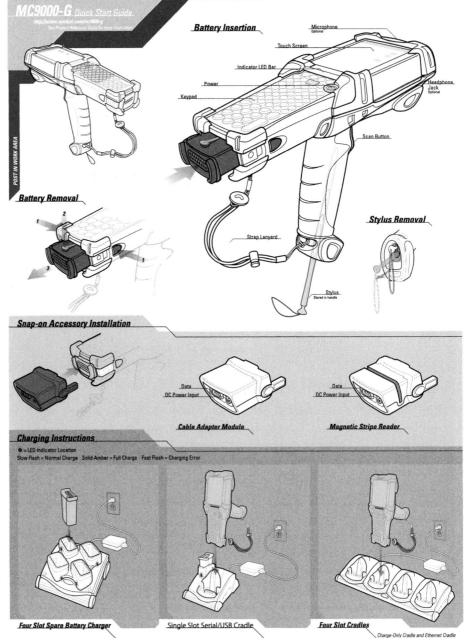

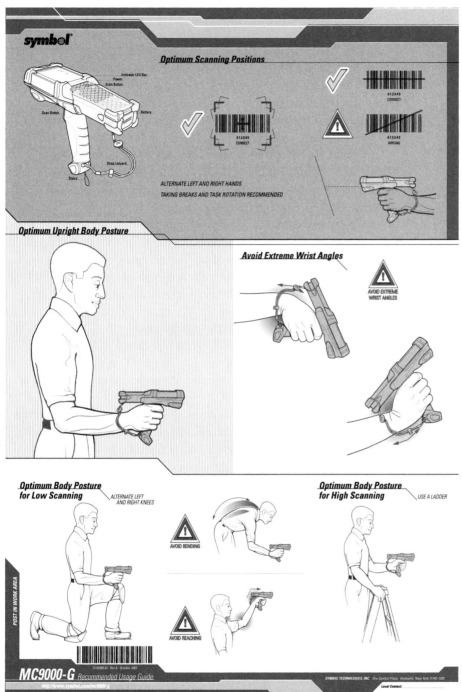

The other side, the "Recommended Usage Guide," demonstrates the body postures that will prevent repetitive-use injuries. *Design firm: Interrobang Design Collaborative. Client: Symbol Technologies. Art director/Designer: Mark D. Sylvester. Illustrator: Richard L. LaRocco, Graymatter Illustration.*

Depicting the user

When materials show a person using a product, what should the person look like? Art directors often struggle with decisions about the look, gender, race, and age of both live and illustrated models used to convey a message. This device's instructions use an illustrated man who looks racially ambiguous, which might help to avoid a racial stereotype about the products' users, and to connect with a range of users.

Of course, this might be true of only male users—the absence of a female demonstrator might suggest to some that the manufacturer thinks women aren't qualified to do the job. The designer could avoid that suggestion by using a woman in some illustrations. But that decision opens up more cans of worms: Which pictures? Who would demonstrate the do's versus the don'ts? And who would be shown bigger, who smaller? You also can argue that, like nonparallel construction, a different demonstrator might draw the user's attention away from the action (where you want it) to the person (where you don't).

Designing to enhance the user's experience

The poster arrives folded, and even when it's flattened for hanging, those fold marks remain to imply a grid, Sylvester says. He designed within that grid in case people refolded the paper "if they need to, and a lot of times they do."

Gray backgrounds help to separate different categories of information on the page. They also help to minimize contrast on secondary information. As a background, they create contrast from which black-outlined white objects "pop." That's another concession to the dimly lighted break rooms Bhatia and his colleagues saw in client visits. "Some of these back rooms . . . have one bare lightbulb hanging over the work area. It's not optimum lighting," Sylvester says they told him. So they're wisely "conservative about how dark a gray can be behind a field of copy. A 50-percent gray background with black 14-point text is not contrasty enough."

The designers didn't worry about matching the gray tones from product poster to product poster. "If somebody says, 'Gee, they went light to dark on this poster and dark to light on this one,'" Sylvester says, "it doesn't compromise the information." But red is a consistent element throughout the poster series as an emphasis and warning color, as well as a reinforcement of the brand identity. The backgrounds of bar codes also match on every poster. They have to be white for scanners, which demand higher contrast than even human eyes do.

Sylvester chose Univers type for its versatility. He underlined some headings, but no more than four words at a time because underlining poses a a legibility challenge. "The *g*'s do get closed off a little bit, but I think you tend to read through it."

What the people in the break room think

The lighting detail wasn't the only intelligence gleaned during research visits to the field. Answers to the industrial designers' questions informed the poster's content and design—"things like 'What kind of drop rate do you want when you're on the forklift and you're up on the third level of the storage area, restocking the bottom area?' 'What's working for you?' 'What's not working for you?' 'What would be more comfortable?'" Sylvester says.

Model numbers versus words

Why use letters and numbers instead of words to name products? It's tough to recall and distinguish model names such as LS/VS 3408 and MC9000-S. Indeed, Bhatia says, "we've gone back and forth on names," but the company standardized on numbers because "you can create a hierarchy" with them.

›› CASE STUDY:
Dealing with conflicting audiences' needs

You can't please everyone, you've seen in this chapter, so make sure you're pleasing your primary audience. But when audiences' needs conflict, sometimes those of a secondary audience take over. That's what happened in this case:

Tests by Discovery Channel TV showed viewers clicking away when programs' closing credits rolled, a company rep says. So the network tested removing the credits. That worked for the viewers, but not for another important constituency—the network's outside program producers. For them, the network proposed alternatives, such as a brief closing screen that directed any interested viewers to the Web site. There the network would post each program's credits for six months after the program's airing.

But producers and industry groups still complained, so on-air credits remain. The network continues to experiment with alternatives that work for everyone, including opening instead of closing credits.

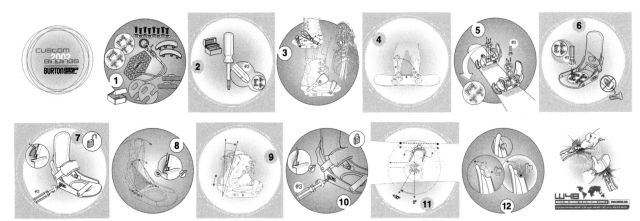

This project from the same design firm as the previous image relies even more on pictures and numbers to cross cultures without translation. In twelve steps, a folded manual shows how to adjust the snowboard bindings it comes attached to. Red (where the blue is here) stands out on the otherwise black-and-white piece to show action and direction, and to emphasize various steps and parts. *Design firm: Interrobang Design Collaborative. Client: Burton Snowboard Company. Art director/ Designer: Lisa Sylvester. Illustrator: Richard L. LaRocco, Graymatter Illustration.*

›› CASE STUDY:
Keeping the audience in touch

When recycled paper became popular in the 1990s, the editor of a newsletter for graphic designers knew from research that the audience needed to know the paper's pros and cons. So the editor not only wrote about the paper but also let the audience test it. She printed five consecutive issues of the publication on a different variety of recycled paper each time. (See the images on the following two pages.)

Getting inside your audience through personas

Use your psychographic research to group audience members into categories. Then you might find it useful to create what usability people call "personas" to represent your primary and secondary audiences. A persona is an imaginary person, with a name and a life story, whose traits represent a typical audience. It's used to help everyone on a design or development team speak to the audience's needs.

Build personas from individuals' words, attitudes, even appearances to give audience members a real voice in the project and its development. Use them to form a picture of your audience members that's so accurate and convincing you think and speak of them as one person. You refer not to "them" but to "he" or "she," or, better, by the name you've given him or her. When you talk *to* them, you use "you." You might even find a picture (maybe from a newspaper or magazine) of the person who represents your primary audience. Display it where you work, and distribute copies to your colleagues.

PAPER

Taking stock of the stocks

*I*f you've been reading *In House Graphics* for a while, you know we've experimented with five recycled papers since we switched from virgin stock in October. In case you've had trouble convincing your management about the quality of recycled paper, we thought it would help to show them five printed samples that look like the 70-lb. Hammermill Cream virgin stock we used to print on.

So we asked our printer to collect five recycled papers that look like the other stuff, but contain at least 50% recycled fiber, including at least 10% post-consumer waste (paper that would've gone to a landfill). We asked for relative costs and ordering turnarounds. Follow along with your back issues as we look at some of the characteristics of the various sheets.

66 *I*f your boss claims recycled paper means low quality, compare our five recycled-paper issues to those on virgin paper, and ask 'Which is which'? 99

The flock of stocks
Some of the papers may now contain even more post-consumer waste than when we printed on them, as paper mills busily try to respond to customer demand. Also, note that because regions, paper reps, printers and projects vary like mad, the costs, turnarounds and minimums you get may also vary. We offer our experience only as a case study.

In the chart on this page, you'll see what papers we used, in the order of their appearance.

How they look
With 20%, Proterra led in post-consumer-waste content — twice as much as the other stocks.

"Expect more pliability from recycled than from virgin stocks," we'd heard, but the samples didn't necessarily back up that claim. Only Medallion and Sycamore felt more pliable than Hammermill Cream — the other three felt stiffer.

We were surprised to see more show-through in the 80-lb. Proterra than in the 70-lb. Hammermill. Taking into account the difference in ink coverage and density among the issues, we thought the other stocks showed through the same as Hammermill.

The recycled stocks		% of recycled fiber	% of post-consumer waste	weight/color/finish	costs*	turnaround
make	manufacturer					
Proterra	Hopper Paper Co.	50%	20%	80-lb. Ivory Vellum	37% more**	3-4 days
Medallion	Cross Pointe Paper Corp.	50%	10%	70-lb. Ivory Text	16% more	1 day
Graphika	James River Corp.	50%	10%	70-lb. Cream Vellum	8% more	3-4 days
Sycamore	Cross Pointe Paper Corp.	50%	10%	70-lb. Ivory Text	25% less (!)	10 days
Crestline	George Whiting Paper Co.	90%	10%	70-lb. Ivory Vellum	23% more***	7 days

*compared to Hammermill Cream per monthly issue of *In House Graphics*
**here we're comparing apples to oranges: 80-lb. paper to 70-lb. (It doesn't come in 70-lb.)
***minimum order: 4,800 sheets

12 • IN HOUSE GRAPHICS

PAPER

The guinea pigs in our recycled-paper experiment. *Use this matching guide and your back issues to follow along with the chart on p. 12.*

October printed on Proterra. November, on Medallion. December, on Graphika. January, on Sycamore. February, on Crestline.

Proterra and Graphika demonstrated the cleanest folding and hole-punching.

For our future newsletters, we ruled out Medallion as too textural and absorbent — halftones muddied up. We'd choose it instead for letterhead or brochures with line art, but without photos. We also ruled out Crestline because it's yellower than what we're used to (and it requires a minimum order). We prefer Sycamore's and Graphika's Ivory to the yellower stocks.

We also prefer Sycamore's cost, but not its flexibility, and turnaround for our area. We'll continue to experiment when we hear of worthy recycled papers with more post-consumer-waste content. But in the meantime, you'll probably be seeing Graphika (we'll have to convince our beancounters of the benefits of paying more for a sheet that stays firm in your hands).

Useful "green" resource costs little green
Responsive to criticism that it's a villain to the environmental movement, the direct marketing industry got busy. At the end of 1989, The Direct Marketing Association (DMA) formed a Task Force on Environmental Issues. And you can benefit from at least one of the results of that task force's work: *The DMA Environmental Resource for Direct Marketers* provides comfort, help and action plans for organizations that want to do the right thing.

The 68-page handbook tells you how to set ecological goals for your workplace and your products (including recycled-paper use), enlist support within your organization, clean lists to cut down on wasted mailings and train your suppliers to package responsibly. You'll get strategies

Can you afford recycled paper?
Although most people expect to pay at least 10% more for recycled than for virgin paper, and most of the samples we tried cost even more than that, one actually cost 25% less.

So if you're interested in a specific look, ask your printer or paper rep to give you a choice of stocks and samples. Ask your printer to fill out a chart like the one on the facing page with vital statistics about papers that may work for you.

Back to the question: "Can you afford it?" From a bottom-line point of view, 94% of respondents to an *Advertising Age* survey conducted by Gallup said they prefer to buy from companies that demonstrate environmental concern. From an environmental point of view, we counter the first question with another: "Can we afford not to?"

for in-house recycling programs, tips on educating your consumers and implementing the 3 Rs and a P of environmental responsibility (Recycle, Replant, Reduce and Publicize).

It's a well-designed resource filled with resources, like the American Paper Institute's Paper Matching Program that'll tell you the nearest paper mill, recycling center, or waste paper dealer that can accept your paper waste: (800) 878-8878. Or get a free copy of the booklet, *Keeping Your Company Green*, by contacting Rodale Press, 33 East Minor St., Emmaus, PA 18098, (215) 967-5171.

Get *The DMA Environmental Resource for Direct Marketers* (on recycled paper, of course) for $7.15 (including s&h) from DMA, 6 E. 43rd St., New York, NY 10017, (212) 768-7277, ext. 194.

The DMA Environmental Resource for Direct Marketers: It's packed with ways to help companies care for the earth... plus it's a visual treat.

IN HOUSE GRAPHICS • 13

The process of identifying and building personas, shared by everyone in the project team, can:

- add dimension, reality, and familiarity to major audience types; add recognizable human face and characters
- solidify the shift in focus from the client's needs to the audience's needs
- redirect the source of design and content decisions to the audience

If you use personas, go beyond the surface, information designer and author Nathan Shedroff advises. Personas are no more valuable than the research that goes into them. He cites typical—and useless—personas in Web site development as "'Mark is twenty-eight years old and he's a software programmer. He's young and energetic and curious. He loves computers and he plays a video game.' We create this whole

Buyers of printing paper got to sample five makes of paper in as many issues of a trade publication. In the issue following the experiment, an article, including a pictorial guide and a table helped readers compare the five. (See details on the following page.)

PAPER

The guinea pigs in our recycled-paper experiment. *Use this matching guide and your back issues to follow along with the chart on p. 12.*

October printed on Proterra.   *November, on Medallion.*   *December, on Graphika.*   *January, on Sycamore.*   *February, on Crestline.*

Here's a closer look at the pictorial guide.

And here's a closer look at the table. How would you improve the table? (*Hint:* Eliminate unneeded repetition.) *Publisher: United Communications Group. Newsletter:* In House Graphics. *Designer: Ronnie Lipton.*

fictional story about him, and move on to Heather, 'thirty-six and a writer who works out of her house.'"

The problem is, Shedroff says, although the demographics might shift in the stories created, the psychographics don't. "They all end up being the same person," the minority who are in love with technology, "curious, not afraid of the computer, and who love their job and their work." What's lacking in these cases are realistic, insightful profiles, such as people who are mean or who just don't understand. For them, realistic scenarios will "take people through the help system,

The recycled stocks		% of recycled fiber	% of post-consumer waste	weight/color/finish	costs*	turnaround
make	**manufacturer**					
Proterra	Hopper Paper Co.	50%	20%	80-lb. Ivory Vellum	37% more**	3-4 days
Medallion	Cross Pointe Paper Corp.	50%	10%	70-lb. Ivory Text	16% more	1 day
Graphika	James River Corp.	50%	10%	70-lb. Cream Vellum	8% more	3-4 days
Sycamore	Cross Pointe Paper Corp.	50%	10%	70-lb. Ivory Text	25% less (!)	10 days
Crestline	George Whiting Paper Co.	90%	10%	70-lb. Ivory Vellum	23% more***	7 days

*compared to Hammermill Cream per monthly issue of *In House Graphics*   ***minimum order: 4,800 sheets
**here we're comparing apples to oranges: 80-lb. paper to 70-lb. (it doesn't come in 70-lb.)

or have people call up customer service" because they can't figure something out.

And although even made-up personas help a development team talk about Web site navigation, Shedroff says, authentic ones "highlight potential problems" and go beyond "Where do I click?" to "Would I do it this way?" The personas you develop "should be the synthesis of similar people and their problems and attributes . . . that come from real interviews that included psychographic questions."

You begin to see audience members you might not have considered before, Shedroff says, such as those who have trouble using computers. "They don't hunt around the screen, and when they can't find the next thing to do, they go into panic mode . . . or they turn off the computer." When you understand how they approach a problem, you can create a meaningful test scenario, he says.

Personas personified: an example

Let's take a look at how personas work. Meet Frances, a single twenty-two-year-old woman about to buy her first new car. You're doing a Web site for a car dealership that finds her typical of the audience it wants to pursue. So you'll want to find out as much as you can about Frances. And you'll want to see how she's like and different from others who seem to be in the same audience.

To create the persona, you'll interview and observe Frances and other audience members, and interview management and staff members. But before you begin your research, notice and eliminate any assumptions you might have about Frances, so you'll be open to hearing the real story. For example, maybe you assumed she wants a car that's:

- cute. (Uh-uh. When asked, she describes a homely and reliable car that won't attract carjackers in the city or police attention on the highway.)

- compact. (No again. Her car should be big enough to take along three friends, but small enough to save on gas. Here she starts getting passionate about the world's energy problems and briefly considers getting a bike instead. Now you're getting at attitude; this might be the time to probe gently for any contradictions. Maybe being *seen* as environmentally conscious is more important to her than actually *being* that way if it means giving up what she wants more.)

• affordable. (Most people want that, but what's considered affordable varies from low-range to expensive. And not only will she haggle, but she also enjoys haggling.)

• low-maintenance. (Reasonably; she'll do oil changes.)

Other questions and observations will help you get deeper inside Frances's head and heart:

• What else does she like?

• What does she value?

• What are her goals?

• What does she read?

• How does she dress?

• Where does she live?

• What are her image and expectations of the car-buying process?

• What does a car represent to her?

• What's her history/experience with cars, and car shopping and buying?

• What have been her biggest challenges with cars, and car shopping and buying?

• How often and when will she use the car, and to go where and how far?

• What are her information-seeking habits and skills?

More: Does Frances have a specific car make and model in mind? If so, find out where she first noticed it and what she likes about it. And how does she shop? If she says she does at least part of her shopping on the Web, how does she search? And what questions does she want answered, in what order?

Part of avoiding assumptions is favoring open-ended questions over multiple-choice ones. For example, ask, "How do you shop?" not "When you shop, do you drive to dealerships, talk to friends, look in the newspaper, go on the Web, use more than one method?" That's because multiple-choice questions limit the range of possible responses; the real answer might be something you never thought of. Also, hearing respondents' own words will give you greater insight into their thought patterns.

And observe, rather than just interview. Observing Frances's and others' search process will tell you even more than asking about it.

That's because we're not always aware enough of our behavior to describe it accurately. Both methods will help you develop a clear picture of your typical audience members that will help you design well for them.

≫ CASE STUDY:

More about how to use personas

To create a health and nutrition book that would attract and serve its audiences, its information designers developed three personas. In any project, there might be as many as five, because most products, including publications, have more than one audience. After you identify those audiences, also identify—and focus on—the primary audience.

"I think people make a real mistake trying to be all things for all people, because you're going to be half-assed for everybody," says Maria Giudice, principal of HotStudio, the design firm that worked on the nutrition book. "If you satisfy this person who represents the majority of the audience 100 percent of the time, the others might be satisfied 50 percent of the time. You have to allow them to be successful as well, but you're not dividing it up equally."

Typically and optimally, those personas would come from direct qualitative audience research (interviews with the audience, one-on-one or in small groups).* This sort of research defines values and opinions and helps with identifying personas. For Web sites in particular, "we'll interview six to ten people the client identifies, we collect information from these interviews, and we turn them into personas," Giudice says.

This project's budget didn't permit such research. So the designers could only interview the two authors (who are doctors) and marketing staff to identify the audience, product attributes, and business needs. They looked at competitive health books, magazines, and weight-loss programs. And they had to fall back on their own health and diet experience, and personal identification with the audience. That's better than no audience focus at all, but it risks false assumptions.

Testing the book with the audience would come only toward the end of the project, another budgetary effect Giudice would rather avoid: "When you test later, you don't get to make that many changes, so you better feel confident that your assumptions [were] right."

Internal research guided development of the three personas:

1. Shelley, age thirty-four, married to Bert, two young children, lives in Minnesota. "She's fifteen pounds overweight . . . doesn't know why.

---

* Quantitative research, on the other hand, refers to info collected en masse, as in online or written surveys.

She thinks she's got a slow metabolism. And it's hard for her to follow a diet because she's got kids. Shelley's husband, Bert, "is thirty-five and overweight, too, but doesn't seem to care about it." (That's useful because the content can address the challenges and solutions when her family members don't share her concern.) Her activities: Tupperware parties, children's play groups (she might discuss the book with other Shelleys), Sunday school, reading (*Family Circle* and *Parenting* magazines), and TV (*Trading Spaces* and *This Old House*).

2. Connie, a twenty-four-year-old single teacher, wants to lose five or ten pounds to wear a bikini without embarrassment. "Usually when people are a little overweight, there's a goal to weight loss: 'I want to look better in a bikini or I have a wedding I have to go to.'" She drinks Coke and coffee for energy, but she feels too tired to exercise, which she feels guilty about.

3. Michael, a fifty-year-old book sales rep, will sell this book. He's well connected, overweight, and quietly concerned about his health. He's interested in the book, but he wants sound bites instead of having to read it. He wants to sell the book, but he also wants to know whether the book can help him.

Each persona has three or four quotes identified with it. Ideally, these would come from the words of interviewed potential audience members. But in this case, the designers had to make up the quotes (see the sidebar on this page).

For Shelley:
- "I've tried all kinds of diets and I can't lose weight."
- "I exercise, but my metabolism is so slow."
- "I want to see results."

For Connie:
- "Why am I so tired?"
- "Is there something wrong with me?"
- "I'm hungry—what should I eat to bring my energy up?"
- "I'm stressed out."

Michael has dual motivations:
- "I know which pills to take, but I'm not sure why I'm taking them."
- "My joints always hurt."
- "I want a source of information that speaks my language."

>> Incorporate actual audience quotes gathered from research in your projects. For example, a capabilities brochure for Allfirst Investment Advisors used the very words of investment clients. The quotes, which came from phone interviews conducted by the brochure's creator, Carla Hall Design Group, suggest the company understands what its clients want and don't want.

- "The book helps me sell."
- "Now I know what I'm talking about."
- "Who wouldn't want to do this?"

Shelley's and Connie's needs proved so different from Michael's that the designers kept him out of the book. Instead they designed a separate sales and info piece for him.

Clear personas help the team evaluate content ideas through the eyes of the audience. They "help everybody focus," Giudice says. Here, the team only had to ask, "What would Shelley want?" when proposed content went off track. For example, the designers knew she wouldn't care about such things as "glutamine . . . so there was a constant back-and-forth between what the users want versus what the doctors think the users want." But that dialogue is useful for everyone. The designers listened carefully, because the clients "are the content experts, we're not."

What also helped to keep the team on track was a diagram designers drew and taped to the studio wall. It read: "I feel tired, overweight, stressed out. Help me lose weight, gain energy, and relax. I'll need to pay attention to how I eat, exercise, sleep, breathe and relax. But . . . I'm busy, so I want something that's easy to understand, that's easy to follow, that (shows me) results. . . . So give me choices or a specific plan to follow."

The two main personas inspired a list of questions whose answers turned into content for the book. Every spread had to answer one big question, such as "What is [the topic of the spread]?" or "How is it important?" The questions and conversations with the authors guided the content. For example, Giudice would say: "'We're going to design a spread on 'Why am I tired?' . . . Well, why *am* I tired? What's happening in my body?" The authors' answers "became part of the book."

What stayed out of the book were questions the personas would never ask. "It's more important to take out than to include," Giudice says. "People tend to put so much stuff in that readers can't digest it." (See Color Plates 7, 8, and 9.)

Burkey Belser uses research to avoid putting in too much stuff. When he finds out how much the audience already knows, he can see what to leave out. For example, in the law firm brochure, he avoided repeating info students will get from law firms' Web sites. The printed materials only have to "communicate the spirit, the charm, and the working style of the firm."

Keeping the audience in mind . . . literally

Some designers strive to put themselves in the audiences' shoes even if or when they don't do research. Mental modeling and audience intuition are valuable skills to develop as supplements to, rather than substitutes for, actual audience research. For example:

- Joel Katz is guided by "modeling myself as different people, and different kinds of people." He tries to "think of all the people who will see it and what their life experience has been."

- Richard Saul Wurman tests clarity against two internalized audience models: his mother, "who wasn't really interested in everything," and a "literate twelve-year-old boy" with a short attention span. Wurman also uses himself as the audience model because his projects come out of his interests. For example, he wanted to do a book about raising a dog because he couldn't find what he needed to raise his. "All the information was given out absolutely without the person— the owner of the dog—in mind . . . and nothing made any sense to me. Wow . . . what an interesting problem to solve: how to do a book on raising a puppy for the various me's in the world." So his questions and their answers formed the content.

- Carolyn Bagin says she always begins by putting herself "in the place of a user, which I usually am." Then she adds research, such as interviews, focus groups, and cognitive testing.

- Nathan Shedroff says a designer should have a "somewhat universal appreciation for people," which isn't the same as liking all people or hanging out with average people. But he advises you to cultivate "at least a general understanding of what 'average' is in the culture you're designing for." Designers are trained to do this in a visual way, Shedroff says. "They scan text and say, 'This would make a great photograph or this would be a great cover.' But they're sort of trained *against* saying 'That doesn't make any sense' or 'This could be much clearer if I just did a diagram here.'" Understanding the audience often inspires going those extra steps.

- John Grimwade of *Condé Nast Traveler* magazine illustrates "for myself in many ways . . . it's not as if I know our readers personally. I'm doing what I think people want. It's hard otherwise to know where to begin." But he also pays close attention to research, observing focus group participants' reactions to magazine pages. He reads letters from readers who've used his guides to cities and museums. He also looks at how his audience members are different from him.

Caution: The audience *is different, and you're not it*

Avoid stopping at your own assumptions, especially the idea that you represent the audience. That's because as soon as you start to work on a project or for an organization, you start to know more about it and its language than its audience does. It's also because audiences are complicated: You might be similar in some ways, but never alike enough. And keeping the focus on yourself prevents you from looking at and responding to changes in the audiences and their needs.

Sanjay Koyani describes the risk when content and technology people make decisions that "match their internal perspective" instead of the audience's. These people tend to assume that if a design is intuitive to them, it'll be intuitive to the audience, he says. They also tend to assume that the audience has more skill and better equipment than it has. But if you test by bringing in "outside folks who have none of this institutional knowledge . . . they don't know what the devil we did."

So for every information-design project, aspire to the Buddhist goal of "beginner's mind," working to erase preconceived notions so you can experience a situation as if for the first time. Do so by talking to first-timers and current audience members, and being open to what you hear. That doesn't mean you need to ignore your instincts or any experience you might have as an adjunct audience member. They can be valuable at least as a starting point, but avoid letting them replace listening to the "unaffiliated" audience.

Expect resistance to change . . . inside and out

Often, listening to the audience in any form suggests the need for a redesign. Go ahead, but present the redesign only *after* you let the audience in on what you're doing and why. *Here's* why. (It'll be easier to understand if this has happened to you.)

As a subscriber, you feel possessive of your favorite magazine, so you're not happy when it shows up with a new look. "They say 'new and improved' on the cover and then you find everything you liked is gone," says art director Ellie Barber about redesigned magazines she has subscribed to. Think of it as another usability issue: The magazine is no longer familiar, so you can't get around by habit anymore. It's as if someone redecorated your bedroom while you slept, so you trip over a chair on the way to the bathroom. Oh, you'll get used to it eventually, but only after the bruise goes away. It's also a perception issue—kind of insult added to injury—because readers often assume the change is not for their benefit (for example, that it's for cost savings that won't get passed on to them).

So avoid redesigning just because *you're* bored. When you work on a periodical, you see it every day, so it's no wonder you tire of it. But your readers probably see it much less often, and (again) find comfort and convenience in its sameness. Redesign *only* if the current design fails in some way:

• It bores or hinders your readers.
• It interferes with the content.
• It looks old-fashioned, suggesting out-of-date content.
• Its content category has changed.

You'll limit or even eliminate readers' resistance to the change if you prepare them for it. If you can, even involve them in the change.

›› CASE STUDIES:
Three ways to prepare the audience for a redesign

Build a bridge

Talk about change: A publication changed size, color, paper, frequency, editorial features, and even title in one issue. The journal of the Association of Governing Boards of Universities and Colleges went from 6 by 11 inches to 8½ by 11, from black-and-white uncoated cover stock to four-color coated stock, and from the title *AGB Reports* to *Trusteeship,* among other things. And it did all that without ticking off the readers. "Nary a soul complained about the switch," says editor Dan Levin. (See Color Plates 10 and 11.)

The editor wrapped the new publication in a full-sized replica of the old one. Because of the old one's narrower width, it became a bound flap to show off one of the few common features of the old and new: the illustration. Under the flap, a letter from the president introduces and explains the new publication, its new editorial features, and its relationship to the previous, familiar publication. It's a verbal follow-up to an expressive nonverbal presentation.

Prepare the audience at every step

Here are other ways to introduce readers to a stranger in the mailbox. On the first redesigned issue, you might prominently show a picture of the old cover with a letter that details and explains the changes. Say that the publication changed to respond to readers' requests, maybe to give them more of what they want in less time. You might back up your statements with results from your readership research.

Or put a notice on the cover of the new issue, as did *Hemispheres*, a magazine published for United Airlines passengers. (See Color Plate 12.) A circle in the lower left that color-coordinates with the cover art announces, "New Look! More Substance! More Style!" The president's letter inside gives details.

A still better way to link the old with the new: If you finish the new cover layout far enough in advance, show it with explanatory text in the final issue before the change.

Involve the audience at every step

The Bureau of Business Practice (BBP) took on the redesign of its thirty-three business-to-business newsletters in one year. The move was overdue; some of the designs hadn't changed in decades, and it showed. Before the redesign, each editor mailed a survey to each newsletter's readers. Beyond typical content questions, the survey asked readers what they thought of the newsletter's design and what they'd like to see.

You might not expect nondesigners to be able to answer such questions. But readers came through with useful results. Readers said they wanted:

* updated designs

* more charts and graphs to explain and break up text

* articles that are continuous rather than jumping multiple pages

* hole punching*

* less clutter

* shorter articles

Each newsletter's editor and designer incorporated the survey results into the redesign. And they prepared the audience for the change by sending two announcements with the redesigned issues: a "Welcome to [newsletter's name]'s New Look!" box on the front page and a letter.

---

* When your readers ask for hole punching (known to offset printers as "drilling") for a print publication, assume you're doing something right. The request says readers value your publication enough to save it in three-ring binders. By the same token, if you take it upon yourself to hole-punch your publication before you distribute it, the holes might send a subtle message that the publication's worth saving. (And send a free binder with the publication's name on it to store them.) On the other hand, you'll waste the touch and send a mixed message by punching holes in a publication whose info goes out of date the day after it arrives.

The letter explains changes that sometimes involved a new name and focus, not just a new look, Barber says. It also gives this reassurance: "The information you've come to rely on is all here—but in a more attractive, easy-to-read format," along with a list of features and their locations.

Survey 'em again

After you go to the effort of a massive redesign, you might be tempted to take a break. But it's time to check reactions, as BBP did. After readers got the redesigned newsletter, they also got a postcard with these questions, most about design:

1. What do you think of the redesign of our publication?
2. What do you like the most about our new appearance?
3. What do you like the least about our new appearance?
4. What additional information would you like to see in upcoming issues?

Responses to the first questions ranged from "eye-catching" to "you went too far," with the majority mostly pleased with the redesigns. But complaints about distracting "fancy" effects caused the design team to scale back. They yanked screened photo backgrounds behind text, and anything that got in the way of finding story beginnings. Nor did the editors stop there in their efforts to show concern for the readers: after a few months, they checked in again.

More advice: For faster and easier-to-tabulate responses, do online surveys if you communicate with your audience on the Web. And make sure the survey device you send includes a photo of the new look.

The case against "art" versus content

You might wonder why the designers in the BBP example above needed to hear the scale-back message. When the previously restrained designers got a mandate to update designs, they sometimes tried out all their Photoshop tricks in one publication. That's easy to understand—but not to condone, as the audience reminded them.

Information design is graphic design combined with usability. It's the victory of:

• substance over sizzle

• function *combined* with form, not sacrificed to it

• how well information connects with the audience and delivers the content, over just how it looks

• building the layout from the content up, over just pouring in type

• respect for content *and* white space, over contempt for the first

• meaningful elements, over gratuitous decoration.

So work for the audience members on every project. Learn all you can about them, become an advocate for them, and encourage your clients or supervisor to do the same. Also read what you design. (Well, if it's a seven-hundred-page book on an unfamiliar technical topic, at least ask for a summary of the content and the audience.)

Color Plate 1. High-contrast colors and type weights deliver an organization's message in a subway car. *Creative firm: Fixation Marketing. Client: Bread for the City; Dan Hoffman. Creative director: Bruce E. Morgan. Designer/illustrator: Elizabeth Ellen. Copywriter: Kathryn Tidyman.* (See page 21.)

Color Plate 2. Red and blue shown side by side in equally strong intensities seem to produce a shimmering effect on the eye, not conducive to comfortable reading. Graph Design for the Eye and Mind *by Stephen M. Kosslyn.* (See page 32.)

Color Plate 3. Caffeine-starved color-blind patients have to rely on legible type for direction to an eye hospital's coffee shop because they can't see the cup in the graphic on Paul Mijksenaar's signs. It's one sign in a series that spoofs a colorblindness test. *Design firm: Bureau Mijksenaar bv. Client: Oogziekenhuis [Eye Hospital] Rotterdam.* (See page 32.)

Color Plate 4. A poster to promote Iraq's interim-government election in January 2005 uses symbols that mean something to the audience. Even audience members who don't read Arabic only had to recognize the flag as Iraqi and the slot as a ballot box to get most of the point. Also note the poster's strong direction: The wrist, hand, and thumb lead the eye into the focal point, the flag "ballot." The highest-contrast white stripe of the flag, bordered by red, reinforces the eye's destination. The flag's off-center placement adds interest to the poster's otherwise symmetrical balance and more contrast and attention to the flag. (See page 35.)

Color Plate 5. Symbols—and styles—clutter a poster created for the northern Iraqi city of Erbil, a Kurdish stronghold. Symbols compare and contrast the city's five-thousand-year history (represented by the city's founders in the hilltop citadel and other ancient people on the right) with the present and future (on the left, a boy wearing Kurdish-flag colors and holding a Kurdistan Democratic Party campaign poster, a modern hotel, and a dove, a symbol of peace among many cultures, with the poster in its beak). Like the Arabic language, the symbols also "read" from right to left, where the future lies. To tell a similar story to Western people, of course you'd put the past on the left. (See page 35.)

Color Plate 6. On this poster, symbols reinforce two of the words in the name of a festival. Filmstrips form the cross that's common to all Nordic flags; the cross is on a popcorn bucket. People who might've missed the flag-cross connection can see it at the bottom of the poster. The bucket colors come closest to the colors of the Finnish flag, which the designer could justify because that country's film is the first in the series. *Design firm: Design Army. Client: Nordic Film Festival. Creative director/Designer: Pum Lefebure. Illustrator/Account manager: Jake Lefebure.* (See page 35.)

If you want to improve your health, you really are asking to take control of three things: your energy, your weight and your stress level. And you can. But first you need to clearly see what has thrown one, two or all three of these elements out of balance.

Change Begins with Asking Why

To get started, let's look at where you are right now. What choices are you making that contribute to feeling stressed, fatigued or overweight? How are these three factors affecting your overall health? Once you understand what is going on, we will show you what you can do: make choices that boost your health and your energy. It's not as hard as you might think. This section will show you what to change and, in the rest of the book, we'll tell you how.

WHY AM I TIRED?

WHY AM I OVERWEIGHT?

WHY AM I STRESSED?

FATIGUED
OVERWEIGHT
STRESSED

Do you wake up tired or feeling like you need more sleep? Do you run out of energy every afternoon? Do you need to nap when you come home from work? In this section, you will learn what factors make you feel tired, how this fatigue affects your overall health and what you can do about it to boost your energy.

Have you been struggling to lose those extra 10 pounds for the past six months? Are you constantly jumping on and off different diets with little or no success? Take a look at how the things you eat, do and feel influence your body. You'll see how making good choices can give you back control of your weight.

Do you feel panicky, unfocused or overwhelmed? Do you get depressed, frustrated or lose your temper easily? Stress has a huge impact on every aspect of your health. In this section you'll come to understand the stressors in your life and how to manage them to feel less stressed.

Color Plate 7. A book about energy and nutrition begins by introducing three typical audience members whose likely questions form the content. They're the result of internal work on personas. *Design, Content development: Hot Studio, Inc. Creative director: Maria Giudice. Art director/Designer: Piper Murakami. Information architect/Designer: Renee Anderson. Producer: Hazel Sharpe. 848 Folsom Street, Suite 201, San Francisco, CA 94107, 415.284.7250, info@hotstudio.com.* (See page 81.)

6

WHY

Why Am I Tired?

You aren't "just tired." It's more than that. Feeling a lack of energy is the most basic way your body tells you that something is out of balance. Your energy level is related to every system in your body and to everything you eat and do. Even small and simple changes can give you an immediate boost. Look at all the factors that drain your vitality so you can make energy-enhancing choices.

FATIGUE AND YOUR BODY

Blood
Poor blood oxygenation from not enough exercise reduces energy.

Lungs
Lack of exercise reduces oxygen intake and makes you feel worn out.

Heart
Being overweight makes the heart work less efficiently, making you tired.

Liver
Toxins from food and the environment overwhelm the liver's ability to purify the blood.

Adrenal glands
Too much stress weakens the adrenal glands.

Digestion
Food allergies and imbalance in stomach acid (caused by stress or genetic factors) prevent efficient conversion of food into energy.

Immune system
Food allergies cause overload, making your system work harder.

Hormones
Stress hormones lower the levels of energy hormones like thyroid, DHEA and testosterone.

7

FATIGUED

What is "chronic fatigue"?
Extreme tiredness, along with other symptoms like pain, loss of mental focus and frequent illness, could be the condition called chronic fatigue syndrome. It is a result of multiple system failure.

Ask your doctor to check for:
Anemia (not enough healthy red blood cells)
Thyroid levels
Low cortisol
Food allergies
Heavy metal toxicity (mercury, lead)
Chronic viral infection

WHAT YOU EAT

Nutrient deficient diet
Foods that are high in sugar and refined flour, most snacks, sweets and fast food, fill you up without giving your body what it needs for energy. These foods throw off the body's ability to regulate blood sugar. The resulting low blood sugar is called hypoglycemia and causes sluggishness and irritability.

Food allergies
For many people, certain foods like wheat and dairy products can cause allergic symptoms like fatigue, headaches, joint pain and frequent colds. The body's energy is drained by constantly going through an allergic reaction.

Dehydration
Not drinking enough water thickens the blood, which is mostly water. Thicker blood circulates more slowly and carries nutrients to your cells less effectively.

WHAT YOU DO

Lack of exercise and toxicity
The act of moving your body and using your muscles helps eliminate toxins—chemicals in our body that can't be used and can interfere with cell function. Exercise helps to circulate and remove waste products from your cells. In a body that doesn't move enough, the toxins linger and accumulate.

Lack of exercise and mood
Exercise stimulates the production of endorphins in the brain. These are "feel-good chemicals" which give a natural sense of well-being and energy. Without them, you feel tired and depressed.

Lack of exercise and metabolism
Lack of exercise lowers your metabolic rate, the speed at which your body operates and produces energy. The lower the rate, the less efficiently your body will convert the food you eat into energy for your cells, organs and brain.

WHAT YOU FEEL

Stress
Stress makes you feel tired and overwhelmed because it releases the stress hormone cortisol. This chemical puts the body in a state of emergency which, when sustained over time, causes exhaustion.

Poor sleep
Without sufficient sleep, the nervous system cannot regenerate itself, replenish lost energy reserves in brain cells and restore chemical balance.

Negative emotions
Negative emotions cause the brain to produce adrenaline, the emergency "fight or flight" hormone. This depletes available blood sugar and leads to a "sugar crash," a sudden lack of energy.

THINGS YOU CAN DO TO IMPROVE YOUR ENERGY LEVEL

Eliminate food allergens
Get tested for allergies or avoid common allergy-causing foods (such as dairy) for a while to see if it changes your energy level.

Supplement your food intake
Nutritional supplements and energy drinks stimulate cellular function to increase energy production.

Regulate stress hormones
You can control your hormone levels by controlling your stress levels. Taking time to relax each day reduces the exhaustion that comes from stress.

Get more sleep
Give yourself at least 8 hours of restful sleep each night to rejuvenate your mind and body. Short-changing yourself on sleep leads to exhaustion.

Color Plate 8. The following spreads of the nutrition book reveal solutions gained from looking into each persona's problems. *Content development, information architecture and design: Hot Studio, Inc. Creative director: Maria Giudice. Art director/D designer: Piper Murakami. Information architect/Designer: Renee Anderson. Producer: Hazel Sharpe. Hot Studio, Inc., 848 Folsom Street, Suite 201, San Francisco, CA 94107, 415.284.7250, info@hotstudio.com.* (See page 81.)

20

THE THREE KEYS

The Energized Plate

You can eat delicious, diverse meals and still lose weight. The key is eating the right amount of each type of food. Use your hand as a portion guide and leave the table full of energy, instead of just full.

You can measure healthy food portions with the parts of your hand. Use a fist for grains, a palm for meats, and thumbs for cheeses and oils.

Fish, poultry, lean red meat
1 palm = 6-oz serving

Hard cheeses (cheddar, parmesan) or feta
2 thumbs = 1-oz serving

Olive, flax seed and plant oils
1 thumb = 1 tablespoon

Vegetables (and fruit)
Make sure your meals contain many servings of fruit and vegetables.

Whole grains, legumes, yogurt
1 fist = 1 cup

Nuts and seeds
1 handful = 1-oz serving

21

Size matters
American portion sizes have increased drastically over the past 25 years. Today's restaurant servings, "super-size" meals and giant soft drinks contain much more fuel than your body can use.

Less is more
Eating is a very visual experience. You will think you're eating larger portions if you serve your meals on a smaller plate...

...versus the same serving portion placed on a larger dinner plate.

EATING

Color Plate 9. The book also contains general nutritional advice, including the answer to another question—"How much can I eat?"—that could have come directly from audience members if they'd been interviewed. (And "How can I measure it?" Use your hands, suggests the diagram-like illustrations.) *Content development, information architecture and design: Hot Studio, Inc. Creative director: Maria Giudice. Art director/Designer: Piper Murakami. Information architect/Designer: Renee Anderson. Producer: Hazel Sharpe. Hot Studio, Inc., 848 Folsom Street, Suite 201, San Francisco, CA 94107, 415.284.7250, info@hotstudio.com. (See page 81.)*

Color Plate 10. A wise editor prepared his audience for his publication's major reposition and redesign by flapping the old cover over the new one (with the car pointing and the wind blowing from old to new). *Cover image: "Windy Day in Atchison," by John Falter, © 1952 SEPS: Licensed by Curtis Publishing, Indianapolis, IN. All rights reserved. www.curtis-publishing.com. Sheldon Memorial Art Gallery; University of Nebraska. Journal: Trusteeship. Publisher: Association of Governing Boards of Universities and Colleges. Editor: Daniel J. Levin.* (See page 84.)

Color Plate 11. Beneath the black-and-white replica of the old, the president's letter details the changes on the left, and reveals the whole new look on the right. *Image on cover, "Windy Day in Atchison," by John Falter, © 1952 SEPS: Licensed by Curtis Publishing, Indianapolis, IN. All rights reserved. www.curtispublishing.com. Sheldon Memorial Art Gallery; University of Nebraska. Journal: Trusteeship. Publisher: Association of Governing Boards of Universities and Colleges. Editor: Daniel J. Levin.* (See page 84.)

THE ASSOCIATION OF GOVERNING BOARDS OF UNIVERSITIES AND COLLEGES   JANUARY/FEBRUARY 1993

──TRUSTEESHIP──

Dear AGB Colleague:

Welcome to the pages of *Trusteeship*, AGB's new magazine, which you now will receive bi-monthly in lieu of *AGB Reports* and *AGB Notes*.

Trusteeship combines the best features of *Reports* and *Notes* — practical articles about important issues in higher education, thoughtful discussions of board policies and practices, and succinct, timely information about current events.

New features include columns by an experienced public university president, a private college board chair, and a professional board secretary, whose views reflect key perspectives in institutional leadership. For 1993, these columnists are Michael Schwartz, president emeritus of Kent State University; Robert E. Tranquada, board chair of Pomona College; and John B. Hicks, secretary to the board of trustees of the University of Alabama.

Another new feature is "Board Adviser," a concise discussion of some of the common and more challenging dilemmas faced by trustees. "Perspectives on the News" offers an overview of important developments affecting higher education in the preceding two months. "Presidential Search" continues to provide advice on the board's all-important task of presidential selection, and "First Order of Business" draws on the expertise of AGB's Programs and Research staff to help keep trustees and presidents up to date.

Please let us know what you think of *Trusteeship*, as well as your suggestions for how this, AGB's flagship publication, can best serve you and your board. Happy reading!

Sincerely,
Richard T. Ingram
President, AGB

Color Plate 12. Found under an iguana and a beach rock: an announcement that a magazine for an airline's passengers has not just changed but improved. Inside, the CEO's letter, titled "Reinventing Ourselves," gets a little more specific, mentioning that the revamped magazine is "easier to navigate." *Illustration by Dieter Braun, larkworthy.com. From* Hemispheres, The Magazine of United Airlines; *Pace Communication.* (See page 85.)

Color Plate 13. The headline links artwork through color (and through kerning—too-tight letter spacing subtly reflects the cloth's close-knit weave). © *Element Media, LLC, 2000. Element magazine. Photographer: Jill Wachter, www.jillwachter.com. Art director: Daniel Chen.* (See page 154.)

Color Plate 14. A photographer groups her portfolio by one-word descriptions established on her home page: "swank," "jolt," "groove," "grit," "exquisite," "attract," "amuse," "origin," or "wonderland," as well as the dominant color of the photos in each group. *Web site: www.jillwachter.com. Web designer: Deb Unger Design, www.debunger. com.* (See page 154.)

Color Plate 15. For example, here's a photo in the photographer's red-keyed "jolt" group. *Web site: www.jillwachter.com. Web designer: Deb Unger Design, www.debunger.com.* (See page 155.)

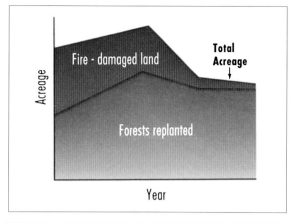

Color Plate 16. Green is for growth; red is for fire damage . . . (See page 157.)

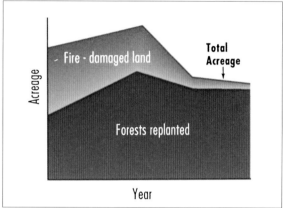

Color Plate 17. . . . mix them up and you risk doing the same to your audience. *Graph Design for the Eye and Mind by Stephen M. Kosslyn.* (See page 157.)

In Korea red is an unlucky colour.

At HSBC we never underestimate the importance of local knowledge. Because what's right for one person can often be completely wrong for someone else. That's why we have local banks, staffed by local people, in more countries than anyone else. So you always talk to people who see things the same way as you do.

HSBC
The world's local bank

Issued by HSBC Holdings plc

Color Plate 18. A global bank changes its logo color to show it understands its local audience, but red's unlucky there only in certain cases. (See page 158.)

Color Plate 19. The front of a poster looks like a map. © *The Regents of the University of California. Design firm: Gregory Thomas Associates. Creative director/Principal: Gregory Thomas. Designer/ Illustrator: Julie Chan. Additional design: David La Cava.* (See page 160.)

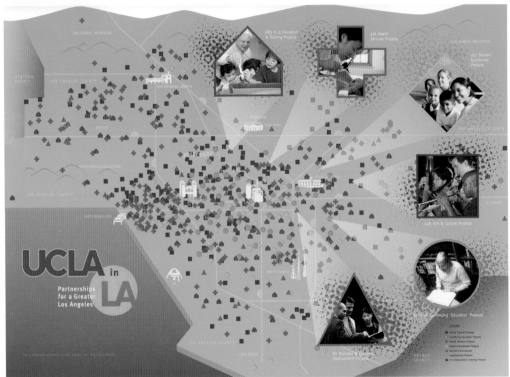

Color Plate 20. Unfolded, the map analogy continues to show the density of sponsored programs. A series of symbols, shapes, and colors identifies the various program categories. © *The Regents of the University of California. Design firm: Gregory Thomas Associates. Creative director/Principal: Gregory Thomas. Designer/Illustrator: Julie Chan. Additional design: David La Cava.*
(See page 160.)

Color Plate 21. Portland signs use a code of different hues (blue, green, etc.), but the same chroma (brightness). That gives the colors equal prominence, and the backgrounds equal contrast against the white type. *Design firm: Joel Katz Design Associates. Client: Portland Development Commission.* (See page 163.)

Color Plate 22. A color code distinguishes airport terminals . . . but not with equal power. The letters on higher-contrast blue and red, even green, "speak" across a greater distance than the one on lower-contrast gold. *Photographer: Ronnie Lipton.* (See page 163.)

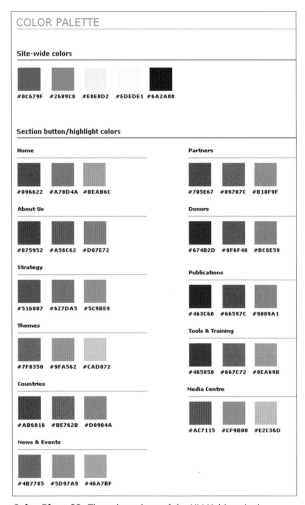

COLOR PALETTE

Site-wide colors

#0C679F #2689C8 #E8E8D2 #EDEDE1 #6A2A00

Section button/highlight colors

Home

#896622 #A78D4A #BEAB6C

About Us

#875952 #A56C62 #D07E72

Strategy

#516887 #627DA5 #5C9BE9

Themes

#7F8350 #9FA562 #CAD072

Countries

#AB6016 #BE762B #D0904A

News & Events

#4B7785 #5D97A9 #46A7BF

Partners

#705E67 #89707C #B18F9F

Donors

#674B2D #8F6F48 #BC8E59

Publications

#463C60 #66597C #9089A1

Tools & Training

#465850 #667C72 #8EA69B

Media Centre

#AC7115 #CF9B00 #E2C36D

Color Plate 23. The color palette of the UN Habitat site is a design system within a design system, ensuring consistency that aids navigation throughout the site *Design firm: Hot Studio, Inc. Project manager: Clancy Nolan. Information architect: Renee Anderson. Lead visual designer: Laura Haertling. Creative director: Henrik Olsen.* (See page 164.)

Color Plate 24. Here are the color mixes in use and in comparison. *Design firm: Hot Studio, Inc. Project manager: Clancy Nolan. Information architect: Renee Anderson. Lead visual designer: Laura Haertling. Creative director: Henrik Olsen.* (See page 164.)

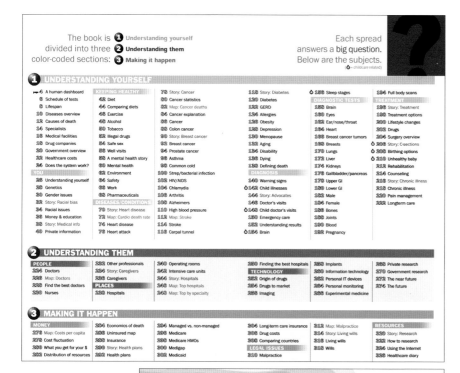

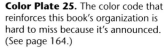

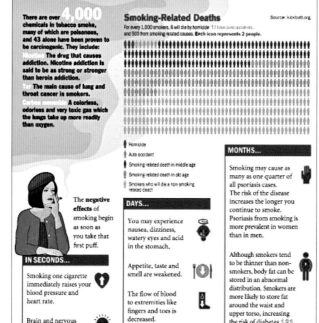

Color Plate 25. The color code that reinforces this book's organization is hard to miss because it's announced. (See page 164.)

Color Plate 26. Color also distinguishes and identifies categories in graphs. In "Smoking-Related Deaths," five colors might be too many to recall if the key weren't so close and the red so appropriate for "Homicide." But the categories— "Homicide," "Auto accident," "Smokers who will die a non-smoking-related death," "Smoking-related death in middle age," and "Smoking-related death in old age"—don't fit the title or the book spread's apparent goal to discourage smoking. *Exercise:* Analyze the graph to explain why, and how you can improve it. *Designer: John Sotirakis, Agnew Moyer Smith, Inc. Art director: Richard Saul Wurman. Production designer: Loren Barnett Appel.* (See page 164.)

Color Plate 27. Four-color printing and labels remove challenges to naming the fruit types. *Photography: The Food Group for the Florida Department of Citrus.* (See page 166.)

Color Plate 28. The background's as interesting as the foreground in this photo. So you'd keep it if it means something, such as setting the tone or telling the story of a carousel. *Photographer: Ronnie Lipton.* (See page 173.)

Color Plate 29. But use a silhouette to direct the viewer to one animal, maybe to show the results of its restoration (or how manes hang only on the audience side, as you saw in the Introduction). (See page 173.)

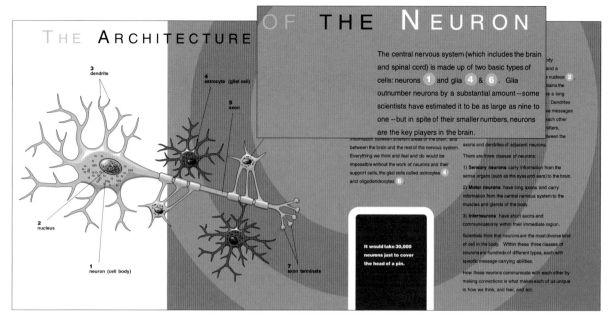

Color Plate 30. Numbered diagram labels correspond to numbers in the text, but not as clearly as they would if the numbers looked the same in both places. Those numbers interrupt the text, run distractingly out of sequence, and meaninglessly share a color with part of the diagram. *Courtesy of the National Institute of Neurological Disorders and Stroke (NINDS), National Institutes of Health.* (See page 176.)

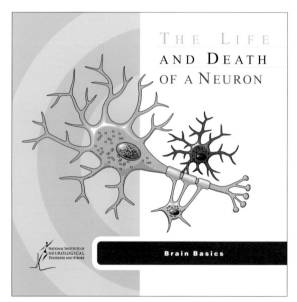

Color Plate 31. The brochure's cover title also violates the laws of consistency and meaning: The color of the words "The Life" matches the neuron, "of a Neuron" matches a secondary cell, and "and Death" matches only the illustration's outline. *Courtesy of the National Institute of Neurological Disorders and Stroke (NINDS), National Institutes of Health.* (See page 176.)

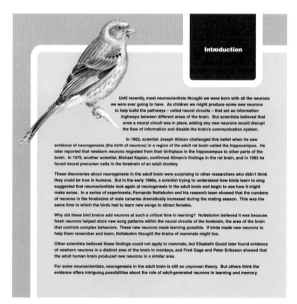

Color Plate 32. Readers don't find out what a bird's got to do with neurons until the third paragraph, not soon enough to keep the image from looking out of place. But nonscientific readers in particular might appreciate the natural touch. Also note the bird's direction—toward the text to help lead readers' eyes that way. *Courtesy of the National Institute of Neurological Disorders and Stroke (NINDS), National Institutes of Health.* (See page 176.)

Color Plate 33. The train faces off the page, and so could send readers the same way. But the strong leftward arrow at the photo's base and the graphs' contrast and colors (wisely picked up from the photo) counteract the photo's inherent direction. *Project: National Mediation Board annual report. Design Firm: Design Army. Creative director/Designer: Pum Lefebure. Account manager: Jake Lefebure.* (See page 177.)

Color Plate 34. Call it a pie graph even if it serves other dishes. Here, a photographic background depicts each slice's category. *Design, Content development: Hot Studio, Inc. Creative director: Maria Giudice. Art director/Designer: Piper Murakami. Information architect/Designer: Renee Anderson. Producer: Hazel Sharpe. 848 Folsom Street, Suite 201, San Francisco, CA 94107, 415.284.7250, info@hotstudio.com.* (See page 181.)

FY 2003   Arbitration Services   **31**

FY 2003 ACTUAL   FY 2004 ESTIMATED   FY 2005 ESTIMATED
6,002   5,136   4,795
CASES PENDING START

4,295   4,643   4,643
CASES DOCKETED

5,161   4,984   4,984
CASES CLOSED

5,136   4,795   4,454
CASES PENDING END

◄ **ARBITRATION FORECAST** | F

14   **THE THREE KEYS**

Eat for Energy

Every meal is an opportunity to boost your health and energy. But what makes a healthy meal? It's simple. All you have to do is shift your thinking from "eat to get full" to eat to "feel good." A few simple guidelines will steer you towards the foods and the quantities that energize you and keep your weight under control. Your choice of what to eat is one of your most powerful tools for feeling your best.

What is soluble fiber?
Soluble fiber is found in vegetables, fruit and legumes. It removes toxins from the digestive system and slows down the absorption of carbohydrates (sugar) into the blood. This prevents the sugar highs and lows that can lead to diabetes, obesity and cardiovascular disease.

15

Fruits
Whole fruits contain soluble fiber and bioflavonoids, nutrients that help prevent and cure disease.

Dairy
Low-fat fermented dairy products like yogurt and skim milk cheeses provide calcium, protein and beneficial bacteria for digestion. Soy, rice and almond milk are good substitutes for cow's milk because they are easier to digest.

Fish, poultry, lean red meat and eggs
High quality protein from lean animal sources provides minerals and protein to prevent fatigue.

Whole grains
Whole grains contain carbohydrates that fuel your body with energy.

Legumes
Legumes contain antioxidants to boost immunity and fiber to balance blood sugar and prevent diabetes.

Vegetables
Vegetables contain minerals, vitamins and fuel for energy. They help reduce the risk of cancer and regulate body weight.

Beneficial oils
Olive oil is rich in antioxidants, which promote cell health and prevent inflammation and heart disease. Flax seed oil and other plant oils build and regenerate cell walls. Fish oil can prevent and treat many diseases of the heart, immune system, hormones and nervous system.

Nuts and seeds
Raw nuts and seeds are good sources of protein for energy and contain oils that benefit the brain and skin.

EATING

5% Dairy
40% Fruits and vegetables
20% Fish, eggs, and poultry
30% Whole grains and legumes
5% Nuts and seeds

Color Plate 35. Numbers next to the bars are as prominent as they need to be because they quantify what's represented (mediation cases) more accurately than the bars do. There is also a blown-up detail of the "cases docketed" section on the spread. The graph is titled "Representation Cases." *Project: National Mediation Board annual report. Design Firm: Design Army. Creative director/ Designer: Pum Lefebure. Account manager: Jake Lefebure.* (See page 192.)

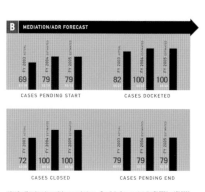

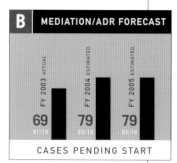

Color Plate 36. White numbers below the red ones look insignificant enough to miss, raising questions about whether the information itself is, too. (See page 192.)

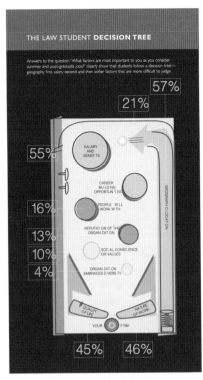

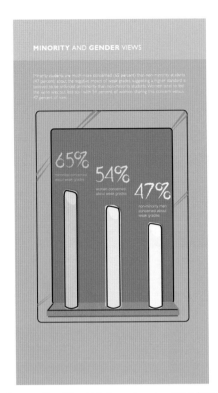

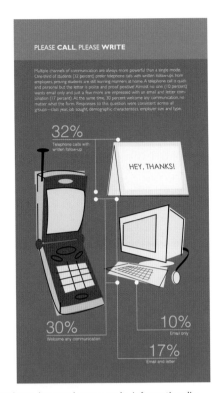

Color Plates 37, 38, and 39. A design firm's self-promotional booklet shows how to recruit law students, but not how to make informative diagrams. Its creators meant the icon-filled tables, maps, and bar (chalk) graphs only to demonstrate the design firm's creativity and knowledge of its audience's audience . . . typically college-age students. (The chalk bars in the middle, "Minority and Gender Views," graph the degree of concern of "minorities," "women," and "non-minority men" about weak grades. The diagram on the right shows students' preferred contact methods.) *Design firm: Greenfield/Belser Ltd. Designer: Siobhan Davis. Creative director/Copywriter: Burkey Belser.. Production artist/Illustrator: Brett Mannes. Photographers: John Burwell, Jason Hendricks.* (See page 192.)

Color Plate 40. One screen on a design firm's Web site answers this question for potential clients "For whom have you designed what and how many projects?" Then they can click on the dots to answer the likely follow-up question: "What do the projects look like?" *Design firm: Carla Hall Design Group. Art director: Carla Hall.* (See page 194.)

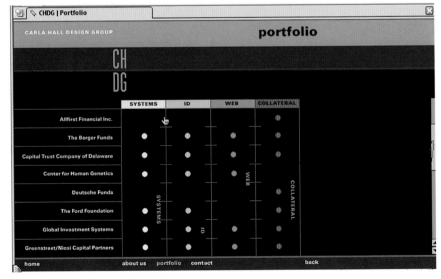

Color Plate 41. The cover of a sailing association's magazine introduces the theme of emotional connection with the sport. *Design firm: Magma [Büro für Gestaltung]. Art direction: Lars Harmsen.* (See page 199.)

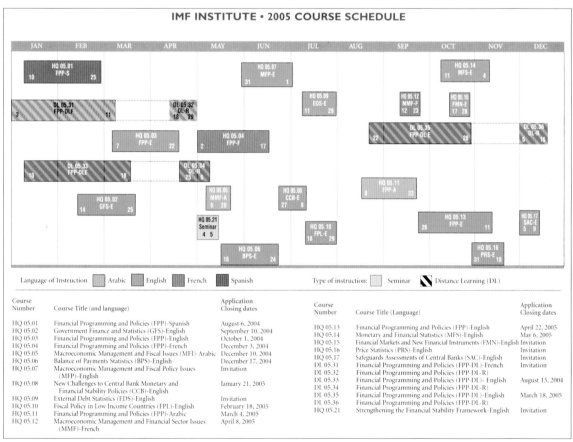

Color Plate 42. Here's the at-a-glance full page of a course schedule that runs horizontally (landscape) to fit everything in at the end of a vertical (portrait) booklet. See a detail on the next page. *Reprinted by permission of the International Monetary Fund. 2005 IMF Institute Program booklet.* (See page 202.)

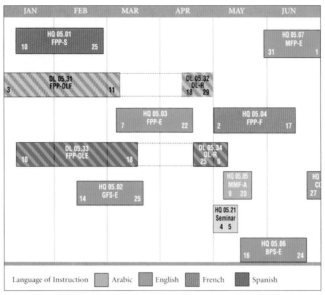

Color Plate 43. And here's a detail from the course schedule. *Reprinted by permission of the International Monetary Fund. 2005 IMF Institute Program booklet.* (See page 202.)

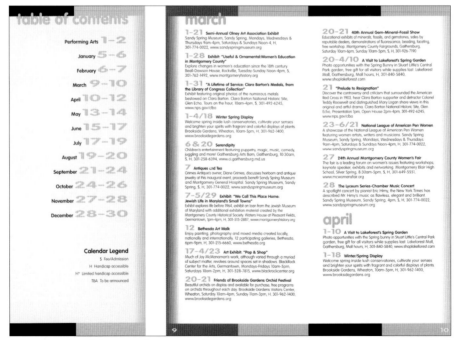

Color Plate 44. All the categories are set in the same typographic style. Does that suit their meanings? *2004 Calendar of Events, Conference and Visitors Bureau of Montgomery County, MD., Inc.* (See page 202.)
Color Plate 45. Gold type that was used for page numbers in the table of contents becomes dates in the calendar's body. Instead, the same style should convey the same meaning consistently throughout an information-design project. (See page 205.)

Color Plate 46. A tour map to London's Victoria and Albert Museum is designed to help visitors hit the highlights in an hour and see how floors correlate. This is the first spread of a booklet that inserted in a travel magazine. *Design director: Robert Best. Graphics by: John Grimwade. Condé Nast Traveler ©️ Condé Nast Publications, Inc.* (See page 218.)

Color Plate 47. Other spreads in the booklet give previews of the featured floor's attractions. *Design director: Robert Best. Graphics by: John Grimwade. Condé Nast Traveler ©️ Condé Nast Publications, Inc.* (See page 218.)

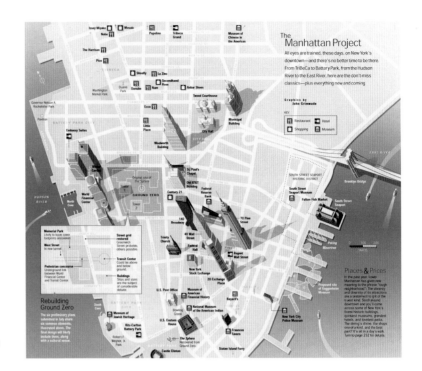

Color Plate 48. This spread's illustrator drew the buildings three-dimensional to aid identification, shadowed to connect them to the map, and tilted to avoid the magazine's binding. *Design director: Robert Best. Illustrator: John Grimwade. Condé Nast Traveler © Condé Nast Publications, Inc. (See page 219.)*

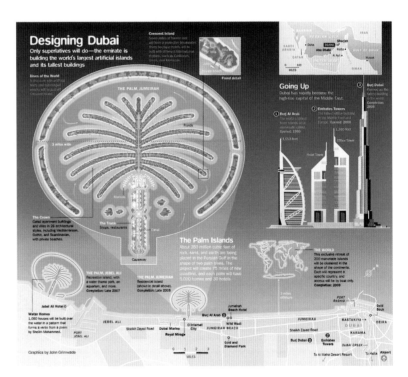

Color Plate 49. A legible sans-serif typeface works best against a busy or dark background. *Design director: Robert Best. Graphics by: John Grimwade. Condé Nast Traveler © Condé Nast Publications, Inc. (See page 220.)*

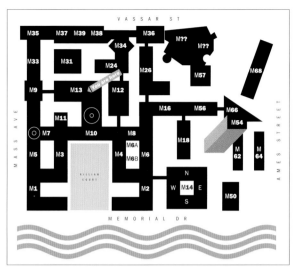

Color Plate 50. Heads up! The maps are designed and placed based on where the viewer is standing. For example, if you're on the main campus and looking at this map, the river's behind you and the map reflects it. The "you are here" banner (which prints in gold) does even more to nail down your viewing position: in Building M13 with Building M10 behind you. Design firm: Joel Katz Design Associates. *Client: Massachusetts Institute of Technology.* (See page 223.)

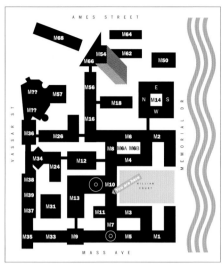

Color Plate 51. If you're on campus looking at this map (if the system's adopted), you also know where you stand: The river's to your right, and you're in Building M10 between Buildings M8 and M7, both accessible by corridor. *Design firm: Joel Katz Design Associates. Client: Massachusetts Institute of Technology.* (See page 223.)

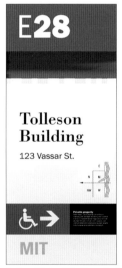

Color Plate 52. On a building sign, words and symbols combine clearly, and every element informs. The heads-up map's simplified almost into an icon. *Design firm: Joel Katz Design Associates. Client: Massachusetts Institute of Technology.* (See page 223.)

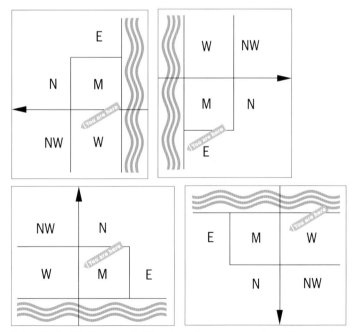

Color Plate 53. As always in this system, the maps come in north-up, east-up, west-up, and south-up to suit the viewer's standpoint. The golden banner reads "You are here."*Design firm: Joel Katz Design Associates. Client: Massachusetts Institute of Technology.* (See page 225.)

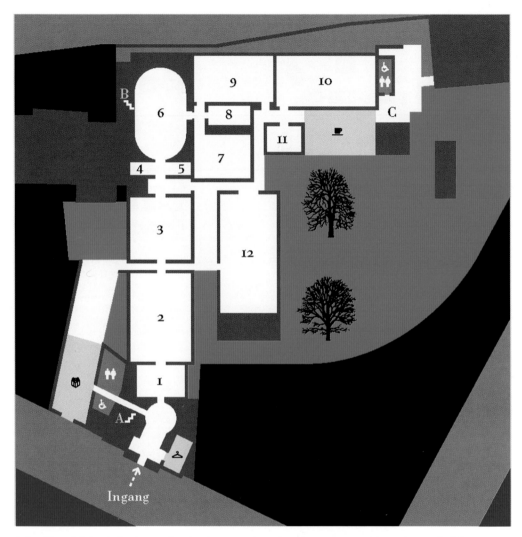

Color Plate 54. Symbols take up a fraction the space of words to show museum visitors where to find the coat room, the gift shop, and more. If only they were big enough to see on the brochure. There, the map measures 3¹/16 inches square. It's enlarged here to clarify the symbols. *Design firm: Bureau Mijksenaar bv. Client: Teylers museum.* (See page 226.)

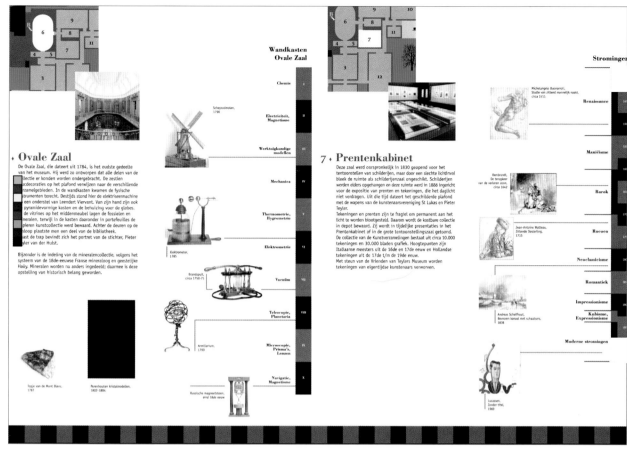

Color Plate 55. "Down-to-earth" features of this museum guide, such as photos, beat typical aerial-view floorplans alone for giving wayseekers signals that they've arrived. *Design firm: Bureau Mijksenaar bv. Client: Teylers museum.* (See page 228.)

Color Plate 56. This sign helps passengers at Schiphol Airport who want to know not just where their gate is but how long it will take to get there. Walking times are in white inside the big black gate letters. *Design firm: Bureau Mijksenaar bv. Client: Schiphol Airport.* (See page 228.)

Color Plates 57 and 58. These handheld devices are in the works to direct passengers through an airport. What's more, links to databases can provide info such as gate changes and answers to passengers' questions. *Design firm: Bureau Mijksenaar bv.* (See page 229.)

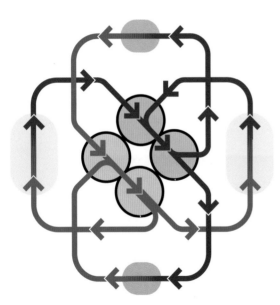

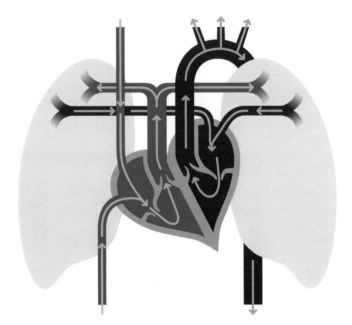

Color Plate 59. Katz re-created this sketch to show his first idea for explaining how the heart works. Inspired by Harry Beck's London Underground map, the subway analogy "made it so much easier to understand the pathways." But what made it too radical to use, the illustrator decided, was "the stuff coming out of the bottom." *Design firm: Joel Katz Design Associates. Client: The Ovations Press.* (See page 230.)

Color Plate 60. Blood that's lost its way through the body might do well to consult this "map," drawn to explain how the heart works. This final version shows conventional pathways around a valentine-shaped heart. *Designer: Joel Katz Design Associates. Client: The Ovations Press.* (See page 230.)

Color Plate 61. Art penetrates normally secure boundaries to illustrate an article about security surveillance. *Illustrator: Mirko Ilić Corp. Client: National Geographic magazine. Illustrator: Mirko Ilić. (See page 231.)*

Color Plate 62. The light square text area on the face of this parking machine got a much-needed makeover. *Design firm: Bureau Mijksenaar bv. Client: Amsterdam Stadstoezicht. (See page 231.)*

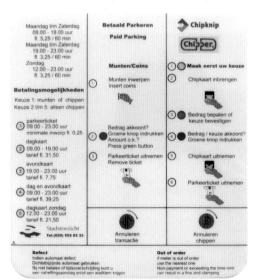

Color Plate 63. The old text area suffered from lack of hierarchy, contrast, and clarity. *Design firm: Bureau Mijksenaar bv. Client: Amsterdam Stadstoezicht. (See page 231.)*

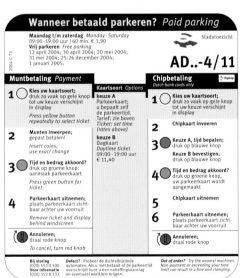

Color Plate 64. On the redesigned text area on the parking-fee machine, drivers navigate the left or right column depending on their method of payment; the time options in the center apply to each, say the common color and the "downdent," the top indention of the column. *Design firm: Bureau Mijksenaar bv. Client: Amsterdam Stadstoezicht. (See page 231.)*

7D Maxey Andress 28, 78
2D Samuel Antupit 26, 64, 78
3H Dana Arnett 28, 44, 78
2A Stuart Bailey 65, 78
9A Jonathan Barnbrook 48, 64, 78
8B Burkey Belser 44, 79
1H Michael Bierut 26, 44, 79
9F Peter Bil'ak 65, 80
1G Tina Blaine 66, 80
9C Andrew Blauvelt 42, 80
4C Nicholas Blechman 66, 80
0I Steve Brodner 66, 80
0E Class Action 43, 45, 81
9E Sue Coe 38, 81
3F Robbie Conal 45, 81
1C Siân Cook 43, 81
7B David Crowley 65, 84
6H Gideon D'Arcangelo 84
4D Chris Dixon 44, 84
2G William Drenttel 84
1I Dave Eggers 70, 84
0G Experimental Jetset 85
9D Mario Garcia 66, 85
8H Ken Garland 36, 85
2E Joanne Leigh George 85
3G Carin Goldberg 27, 85
8C Fernando Gutiérrez 44, 86
6D Allan Haley 86
3B Peter Hall 66, 86
3I Sylvia Harris 37, 42, 86

7I Luke Hayman 44, 86
2B Jaime Hayon 64, 87
6C Steven Heller 26, 42, 87
5B John Hockenberry 36, 87
5C Terry Irwin 44, 87
3A David Isay 38, 87
8A Alfredo Jaar 48, 90
3D Natalie Jeremijenko 42, 59, 90
6G Judy Kirpich 42, 90
6B Naomi Klein 61, 90
5D Kalle Lasn 60, 90
6F Brenda Laurel 37, 91
8G Golan Levin 49, 66, 91
1F George Lewis 66, 91
7F Loser's Lounge 26, 91
5F Luba Lukova 45, 92
7G John Maeda 28, 91, 92
2H Saki Mafundikwa 58, 92
8F Roger Mandle 58, 92
1A Bruce Mau 70, 92
1B Geoff McFetridge 42, 93
7H Andrea Moed 42, 93
4E Clement Mok 17, 93
9H Jennifer Morla 28, 93
9I James Nachtwey 39, 93
2I Dan Nakamura 66, 70, 96
4B Kali Nikitas 44, 96, 118
5A Emily Oberman 29, 96
1D Plazm 67, 96
3C Chris Pullman 26, 97
3E ®™ark 66, 97
2C Mark Randall 65, 67, 97
6A Susan Roth 42

5I Ben Rubin 64, 66, 98
0H Stefan Sagmeister 48, 98
2F Louise Sandhaus 64, 66, 98
4H Paula Scher 26, 98
4G Sam Shelton 26, 98
7A Mike Simons 60, 99
7C Brian Smith 66, 99
5G Loretta Staples 67, 99
0F Stiletto 44, 100
5H Bill Stumpf 58, 102
4A Ward Sutton 66, 102
4F Terry Swack 44, 102
5E Seth Tobocman 66, 102
6E Cheryl Towler Weese 64, 103
1E Teal Triggs 43, 103
6E Bruce Turkel 42, 103
9B Masamichi Udagawa 42, 104
4I Jop van Bennekom 42, 104
6I Julia Whitney 44, 104
8D Lorraine Wild 67, 104
9G Shawn Wolfe 60, 105
7E Margaret Youngblood 28, 105
8I Bob Zeni 42, 105

Lectures and biographies of the
speakers can be referenced by
the page numbers in blue.

Color Plate 65. A conference brochure's designer borrowed map coordinates to help identify speakers. *"AIGA Voice"* brochure. © Cahan & Associates. *Creative director/Art director: Bill Cahan. Art directors/Designers: Michael Braley, Bob Dinetz, Kevin Roberson, Sharrie Brooks. Designer: Gary Williams. (See page 232.)*

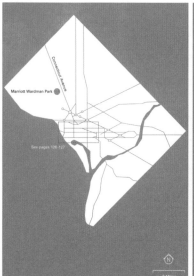

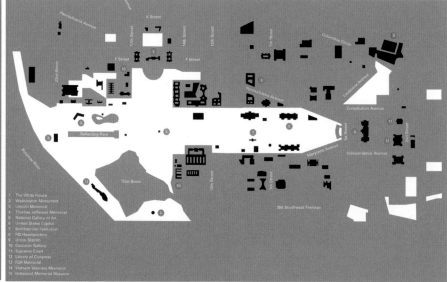

Color Plate 66. In the same brochure, a drawing of a simplified map gives conference goers a general sense of how the hotel's location relates to nearby tourist areas (represented by the rectangle). *"AIGA Voice"* brochure. © Cahan & Associates. *Creative director /Art director: Bill Cahan. Art directors/Designers: Michael Braley, Bob Dinetz, Kevin Roberson, Sharrie Brooks. Designer: Gary Williams. (See page 233.)*
Color Plate 67. On the next page, the rectangle's blown up. *"AIGA Voice"* brochure © Cahan & Associates. *Creative director/Art director: Bill Cahan. Art directors/Designers: Michael Braley, Bob Dinetz, Kevin Roberson, Sharrie Brooks. Designer: Gary Williams. (See page 233.)*

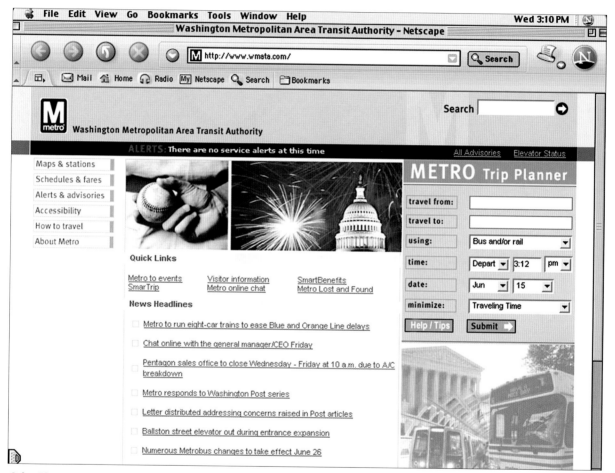

Color Plate 68. On the subway system's Web site you can plot your trip. *Washington Metropolitan Area Transit Authority (WMATA). www.wmata.com.* (See page 234.)

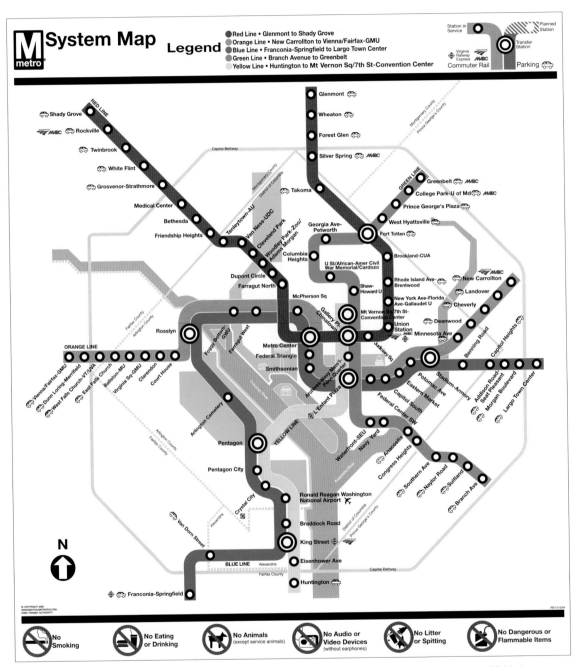

Color Plate 69. Here's the subway's map. *Washington Metropolitan Area Transit Authority (WMATA).* (See page 234.)

Color Plate 70. This Web site's redesigned to put the news front and center, with a plan for frequent updates. *Design firm: Hot Studio, Inc. Client: UN Habitat. Project manager: Clancy Nolan. Information architect: Renee Anderson. Lead visual designer: Laura Haertling. Creative director: Henrik Olsen.* (See page 234.)

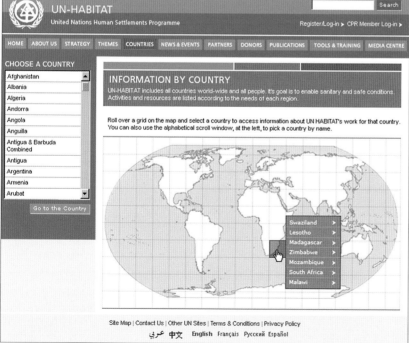

Color Plate 71. Internal site links follow this style. *Design firm: Hot Studio, Inc. Client: UN Habitat. Project manager: Clancy Nolan. Information architect: Renee Anderson. Lead visual designer: Laura Haertling. Creative director: Henrik Olsen.* (See page 234.)

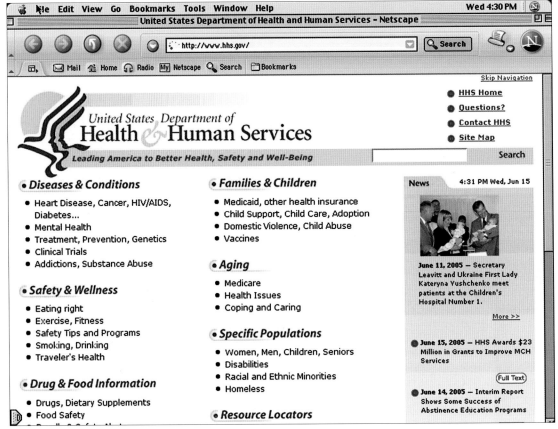

Color Plate 72. The category links you see "above the fold" on this government department's Web site are, as they should be, the ones the audience searches for the most. *United States Department of Health and Human Services. Design team leader: Sanjay Koyani.* (See page 239.)

Section II: word design

How to Design Understandably

«

CHAPTER 3

How to work with type and layout

It's not enough to focus only on how people perceive information. Having perceived, your audience members must *understand*. As Miles Tinker wrote in his 1963 book *Legibility of Print,* "reading without comprehension is not reading."

To help your audience members understand, and to reflect and serve their needs, preferences, and abilities:

- develop useful content
  - present just what your readers need, not everything you've got
- write clearly
  - be consistent, precise, and concise
  - use language and reading level that are appropriate for your audience
  - present content in the order the readers need it
- design clearly: stick to an effective design style sheet for consistency and clarity
  - set easy-to-read type
  - create an easy-to-navigate layout that shows where to begin reading, in what order to read the text that follows, and where to end
  - plan space between and around elements consistently
  - use color as an information-design tool, not as decoration
  - choose, crop, place, and caption photos to tell a story
  - design, label, and caption diagrams clearly
- consider your audience's perspective, setting, context, needs, and abilities in your decisions (as you saw in the previous chapter), and test your project with your audience

Hey you with the sinus problem—

Now there's a new sinus medicine that clears the pain and pressure which also clears the fog.

The clear your head sinus med.

This ad uses fuzzy type to make its point clearly, meaningfully, and memorably. But don't try it at home, or on any information-design materials for which unclear type fights both perception and understanding. That applies to most materials.
© *The Procter & Gamble Company. Used by permission.*

"What's in it for me?" reader asks; answer quickly, the clock's ticking

What encourages viewers to read (right away or at all) is perceiving that they'll benefit from the material. Expect them to take mere seconds to decide. In those seconds, they'll register a first impression based largely on how long the material takes to announce its content. They'll decide whether they need it or care about it, and if they do, how much, compared with everything else they've got to read and do. They'll decide to either read it, defer the decision (tossing it on the reading stack for "later," another way of saying "throw out in thirty days"), pass the buck, or trash it.

Comprehensible design supports rather than interferes with the content. It supports reading in at least three ways:

- It quickly delivers a preview of the contents to help viewers decide whether or not to read on (if it's voluntary).

- It helps readers get through the content with minimal time and effort and no confusion.

- It *looks* clear, as if it won't take much effort or time to read, so it encourages the decision to read.

That last one was confirmed by surveying readers of a sixteen-page monthly newsletter. "I read the newsletter cover to cover right away," wrote many of the respondents. Big deal, you might say; it's only sixteen pages. But to these readers, who regularly reported being overworked, it *was* a big deal. They were amazed to be taking time to read *anything* during a workday, let alone sixteen pages of it. They read it all right away because the content addressed their needs, and the design and writing delivered it clearly. If instead the design or writing had interfered, the reader might have relegated the piece to the "later" stack.

Readers got right into and through the newsletter because it looked as if it wouldn't take up a lot of their time. And *that's* because it avoided common design and writing crimes against reading motivation, such as:

- unclear or inconsistent type

- disorderly layout

- lack of alignment

- lack of grouping

- too many elements

- too many styles of elements (rule weights or colors, for example)
- random amounts of space between elements
- poor contrast, including backgrounds that interfere with the foreground
- poor writing or useless content, which even the best typography and layout won't make up for

Clear design and clear writing, then, are the controllable comprehension factors you'll explore in this section. We'll start with the first.*

Use a design style sheet: Why and how

The design style sheet—a blueprint for your design and the elements within it—is your essential tool for consistency, whether you're working on just one item or a whole series. It sets the tone, establishes a system of codes, and gives clues to the content. It speeds readers through the information. Regular readers find the design familiar from previous encounters. New readers quickly get familiar with the design because it reinforces itself by being consistent. Most important, the style sheet keeps readers from being distracted by random changes.

In addition to creating familiarity, a thorough style sheet considers the needs and flow of the entire project. (It also saves time for the designer, who doesn't have to lay out each page from scratch.)

When you follow a style sheet, readers quickly get the idea. By the second page of, say, a Web site that uses a clear style sheet, readers know what kind of information they're looking at *before they even read a word.* They don't have to figure it out on every page; they know their way around.

The style sheet includes all the type elements that recur (headings, text, captions, callouts, and more), the kinds and sizes of artwork, and the grid (placement, size, and amount of columns and empty space). Elements that are the same should look the same everywhere they appear. That means you don't want to begin the text in one size and shrink it on another page because, as you saw in the chapter on perception, people expect changes in design to signal a change in meaning. If they notice the change, they'll wonder what it means. And what they might assume is that smaller text is less important than what came before, because people connect size to importance—they assume what's bigger is more important.

If the change in size doesn't translate to a change in meaning, you'll confuse readers, maybe even lose them. For example, even if

---

* In actual information projects, content selection and writing often come first. But in the most effective projects, the designer gets involved from the earliest stages of planning. The early interaction between writing and design increases the likelihood of developing design that supports and clearly conveys the content.

readers aren't consciously aware that the text got smaller when they turned the page, suddenly reading probably started to feel like work. That's where a reader who isn't highly motivated will put the reading aside (if only to make an appointment with the eye doc).

Usually all a size change really means is that the designer had to fit more on the page. Running out of space or cramming in type with a shoehorn isn't the sort of meaning you want to convey, so choose a size that'll work across the project.

A consistent style sheet also imparts a sense of familiarity. Beyond the logo, the look of the grid, the layout, and the type help viewers recognize a Web site or publication when they come back to it. That sense of familiarity can even lead people to feel possessive about "their" publication.

Make things easy to find

The value of consistency extends to object placement. Regular readers look for the same items in the same place each time. Sometimes moved objects are merely annoying, such as when a newsletter's masthead turns up on a different page in every issue. But inconsistent placement also can lead to mistakes. For example, in at least one version of America Online e-mail windows, important buttons switch places. In the "Incoming/Saved Mail" and "Old Mail" windows, the delete-message button's on the right. But in the window where users can permanently delete mail, the delete button's on the left, and the read button's on the right. So customers used to deleting on the right and not paying close attention easily could open a letter they never meant to.

Sensible styles

More than being consistent, styles also have to make sense. Readers will get your style code more quickly, lastingly, and meaningfully if it matches readers' expectations of how things should look:

Japan Airlines' *JAL Newsletter* distributed only a print version until its 2002 switch to e-mail. As you can see, it adheres to a strong design style sheet in most cases (see the sidebar on pages 96 and 97). The headlines, initial cap, and text are consistent from story to story, so after the first story, the reader can tell the kind of info by its style.

Now notice the 18-point italic type blocks in the wide margin. The blocks look the same and run near articles. Without reading them (even if they reproduced big enough to read), what kind of info would you guess they are?

Doesn't the type look like pull quotes?* But readers who agree will look in vain for the margin type's appearance in text. The type chunks often are freestanding stories, unrelated to the text. The style confuses because it doesn't match readers' expectation. There's another principle: Type styles must be consistent *and* give clues to the nature of the type based on what's familiar to readers.

More about type

The design of words usually has the strongest impact on a project's ability to look clear and easy to navigate. Although you can design work that informs without words, most information designs rely on them. So how you present those words becomes all-important. The presentation of words depends on—*is*—typography, the graphical display of words and one of the most important parts of any design style sheet.

Type can't be understood if it can't be read. That's not as obvious as it sounds. The quest for style, creativity, and peer awards often drives designers away from clarity, even when they know how to achieve it.

For your intended readers' sakes, you'll make type clear, easy to read, and appropriate for the audience, message, and medium by carefully considering:

- size
- typeface
- line length (actually the *width* of the type line or column)
- style
- alignment
- spacing
- placement
- color

As you'll see, each of those variables affects the others, and your knowledge of your readers and your purpose should affect them all. For example, 9-point type, the recommended minimum for sustained reading, looks too big on most business cards. On the other hand, plenty of designers go to the small extreme with the type on their own business cards, putting even phone numbers and e-mail addresses in 6-point gray or debossed type.

---

* Also known as "blown-up quotes," pull quotes are excerpts from the text that are blown up and run near the text to draw attention to it.

3

Hong Kong report

Airport '98

The construction of Hong Kong's new airport is proceeding apace, and Chek Lap Kok is expected to be operational in just over a year. The airport, along with its supporting infrastructure, will be the second most costly public works project in the world (US$20 billion) and includes a high-speed rail link to downtown, a six-lane highway, two suspension bridges (one longer than Golden Gate), a third under-harbor tunnel, and an entirely new town that will be home to as many as 20,000 people.

"Kung hei fat choy"

Your noisemakers are long gone, but the Chinese New Year is just around the corner: February 7. If you should find yourself in Hong Kong for this holiday — the most important of the year — be sure to watch the afternoon parade along the Tsim Sha Tsui waterfront, and later, a spectacular display of fireworks over the harbor. Welcome in the Year of the Ox in Hong Kong style, a year that will see historic changes to this territory.

More than 'good vibes'

Feng shui translates from the Chinese as "wind, water," but it means a lot more. It is the practice of aligning objects or living spaces with natural geographic features and energy fields to ensure good fortune and harmony. It's a very, very important element in determining how and where an edifice is erected and how its internal components are arranged, including decoration and color. Among the Chinese peoples, no sane architect or engineer would consider the construction of a building — from an apartment to a massive skyscraper — without employing the skills of a geomancer — feng shui master. Ideally, your home should face the right direction — usually south — and should look out over calm water. Doors must not open directly to the outside world (evil will get in, good luck will escape). The right kind of indoor plants will help you become rich, especially if placed in a lucky corner. If you live in an apartment with no sea view, bring the water indoors with an (auspiciously placed) aquarium — with the right kind of fish.

The basis of feng shui has roots in Chinese folk culture; ancient scholars systematized classical writings on the subject, establishing meticulous mathematical formulae and principles through which the laws of life forces might be divined. A geomancer must study for many years before competently interpreting the geomantic compass. Astrology and numerology come into play too, and colors are vital. Certain hues are auspicious for some, toxic for others; workers in certain professions should wear certain colored clothing (writers and editors should wear green, red, all black or multicolored clothes), and office interiors and exteriors must be decorated in the appropriate colors, determined by the type of business transacted there.

Even many westerners are looking into feng shui; in areas with a large concentration of Asians, architects, builders and real estate people are very attuned to the importance of feng shui to many of their customers. The eminently practical Donald Trump has used it in some of his projects, so perhaps there *is* something to it.

At a late-December car license plate auction in Hong Kong, "HK9797" sold for a modest US$27,100, but the number "99," which in Cantonese sounds like "longevity and endless luck," went for $350,000. The record, however, still belongs to "9," for which someone paid $1.7 million!

Look at the italic type in the margin. Without reading it, guess what kind of info it is. (Here at least, the type *is* related to the story next to it, but in most issues, the same type that looks like a pull quote is really a freestanding story.) See the newletter's style sheet to the right. JAL Newsletter. *Publisher: Japan Airlines International Co. Ltd.*

» As you create your design style sheets, it might help to look at a simple one, such as that of *JAL Newsletter*.

You can see a page from that newsletter on the left.

Format: 8½ by 11 inches, 4 pages (one 11-by-17-inch sheet folded in half), 60 lb. uncoated cream-colored paper

Self-mailing panel: upper third of the last page, includes return address (name in 14-point bold, address in 9/11 regular), mailing indicia (7/10 Book Antiqua centered caps in a half-point-ruled box), and reduced (36-point) version of the logo in the nameplate

Margins: 1-inch top and bottom on first three pages; side margins tend to shift from ¾ to 1 inch to accommodate more or less type. (They shouldn't; make margins consistent throughout a publication to help to unify the pages.)

Columns: one 5-inch main text column, one 2-inch column for other information, artwork, boxes

Nameplate: half-point-ruled box around it; letters *JAL* set without punctuation (throughout) in 110-point bold with ⅛ inch of space between letters (the *A* gets a hint of a crossbar from the spot-color rectangle it overlaps, and the *L*

overlaps a gray rectangle formed by a 30 percent dot pattern of black); hairline-ruled box within the box, containing the word *Newsletter* set in 24-point extra-bold expanded caps; type below in 10-point regular Helvetica

Main stories: a 3-point, 3-inch horizontal rule placed 3 points (not precisely) above each headline

Headlines: 24-point type set downstyle (initial cap just for first word and proper nouns, acronyms; one-line maximum); flush-left alignment

Amount of space between stories: varies, but should always be the same; in this case, it could be 23 points, double the leading (space between lines) of the text

Drop cap lead-in: 20-point, same typeface as the headline face, except for some characters (e.g., *T* is in Book Antiqua); drops into two lines of type

Text: 10-point Book Antiqua on 11.5-point leading (also known as 1.5 points of leading); flush-left, ragged-right alignment, except where margin type is set on the right of it and it's justified aligned on the right, often on page 3; text sets wider than the nameplate box (but they should align)

Text bullets: hanging; in text size and face

Margin type: gray (black-screened) hairline vertical rule the length of the type; gray (black-screened) 14-point Book Antiqua Italic type on 17-point leading (3 points of leading)

Margin bullets: dropped-shadow outline squares, same size as margin type

Headers/footers: black hairline grid-width rule at the bottom of every page, and at the top of pages 2 and 3 aligned with the 14-point page number

Story end marks: 9-point drop-shadow outline squares

"Continued from" lines: truncated title portion with ellipses in the headline face in 14-point and "Continued from page __" in 9-point black italics, with a 3-inch hairline between it and the jumped story

Occasional special-info boxes: same size and leading as text, often over a 30-percent screen inside a hairline-ruled box, and set into the text

Artwork: clip art in a similar style from the same provider, set into the text column or in the margin

Masthead: 8/9 Book Antiqua, two lines centered below hairline at the bottom of the last page.

How to set clear text type

Let's focus first on text type, also known as body type, which is a quantity of words meant for sustained reading. It's the meat of the article or the chapter—what isn't titles, enlarged quotations, captions, or other forms of display type. It's also the part that tends to carry the message, but that people are less inclined to read.

One way to encourage reading text is to make it—and make it *look*—easy to read. To make text look easy to read, make good decisions about the various factors that affect its appearance. The factors interact, so read all the guidelines before you use any to design type.

SIZE

A common, general guideline about text size for print and the Web is no smaller than 9-point and no bigger than 12-point. But that's a big range, so you usually can start by lopping off the bottom end.

In fact, you might start with 10-point and go up from there, depending on those just-mentioned variables that affect clarity. Also consider the medium (paper, computer screen, plastic, steel, glass, etc.), method of production, and quality.

For example, look at how you might change point size to serve the audience. Choose from the bigger end of the range or even beyond if the average age or the eyesight of the audience demands it. By age fifty, visual acuity begins to decline, according to the American Federation of the Blind (the Federation's Web site lets viewers customize its size and background colors).

Nonetheless, member publications from the American Association of Retired Persons (AARP) don't exaggerate text size, which is no more than $10^1/_2$ point. But, says AARP art director Eric Seidman, the typefaces are highly legible. He uses Mercury for the main magazine and Pointer for the newsletter but plans a design overhaul that would include a custom-made typeface. As a newcomer to the organization,

This size guide (like one you can easily make on a computer to compare any type sizes and typefaces) shows the relative heights and lengths of consecutive sizes in the same typeface.

The text you're reading now is 10 pt.

The text you're reading now is 11 pt.

The text you're reading now is 12 pt.

he says, he was reluctant to change typefaces because readers were familiar with them. Besides, he says, he doesn't need to boost text size because readers tend to correct for imperfect vision with eyeglasses.

But bigger text makes sense for any audience of any age with more severe vision impairment. For such audiences, argues Lighthouse International's Aries Arditi in "Making Text Legible: Designing for People with Partial Sight," use type as big as 16- to 18-point, which would be too big for most projects targeting audiences with at least average vision.

Also consider bigger-than-average type (and sans serif) with low-resolution printing, rubber stamping, or other legibility challenges, such as:

- reversed type (light on a dark background, also known as "dropped out" or "knocked out")
- printing on (or reversing out of) a photo
- patterned, rough-textured, glossy, or highly absorbent printing surfaces
- slides, Web sites, and other media with backgrounds formed by light
- posters and other media designed to be read from farther away
- anything that could be faxed or photocopied

THE PROBLEM WITH STRONG BACKGROUNDS

Try to keep backgrounds a similar tone, advises John Grimwade, graphics art director at *Condé Nast Traveler* magazine. It's hard to read type over changing backgrounds. For example, monotonal type of any color will fade in and out of the changing contrast in the background. Varying the type color to keep up with the background doesn't work either because it looks contrived, choppy, and still hard to read.

Another way designers try to compensate for busy backgrounds is to put a solid panel between the photo and the type. But that won't work when what's outside the panels is more interesting than what's in them, Grimwade says. Another problem is that "you end up with

reversed   reversed

Reversed type is less legible for reading sections of body copy because the background can dominate and dilute the type. Even in these samples with only one word, you can see the type's shrinking potential. That's especially true in the serif version on the right because of its fine and varied-weight strokes.

If you stare at the photo, you might see a hint of these lines printed five times:
"Type that prints on—or reverses out of—
a photo gets stronger or weaker
according to the contrast of the photo."
Your readers should never have to work that hard to read, so avoid putting type—especially body type—on a photo.

a sort of patchwork-quilt look." Even putting labels outside of the graphic can pose a problem if viewers have to search for them.

HOW TO CHOOSE A TYPEFACE FOR TEXT

Designers who love typefaces and appreciate their subtle differences, or "personalities," tend to spend a lot of effort on choosing typefaces. And there's no question that typeface choice goes a long way in setting a tone, creating an image, and establishing a brand, especially for a logo, a food package, or an album cover.

But (at the risk of being accused of blasphemy), to audience members who depend on the words for essential information, the typeface's

How to measure type

You don't need to know how points relate to inches in order to size type. You just click on the chosen size in the type menu of the software program you're using. But knowing the relationship of points to inches will help you estimate the size in a finished document.

Because 72 points equal one inch, you might conclude that 72-point type measures an inch in height, 36-point type a half inch, 18-point type a quarter inch, and so on. It's not exact, but it's a fairly close approximation if you allow for the fact that type is measured from the top of the longest ascenders (the parts of certain lowercase letters that extend above the other lowercase letters, as in *b, d, f, h, k, l*) to the bottom of the longest descenders (the parts of certain lowercase letters that extend below the other lowercase letters, as in *g, j, p, q,* and *y*), and that distance can vary from typeface to typeface. So, for example, a 36-point Arial capital *T* measures $^3/_8$ inch (rather than $^1/_2$ inch) because it has no descender.

$$ \text{T T T } \boxed{\text{T}} \rbrack{}^{3"}_{8} \qquad \text{closer to } {}^{1"}_{2} \lbrack \textbf{Type} $$

You can relate point size to inches in measuring type if you measure from the top of the tallest character, such as a "d," to the bottom of the lowest-extending character, such as a "p." This 36-pt. "Type" measures just less than an half-inch because the cap is a little shorter than a "d" in the same typeface would be.

"personality" is less important than its clarity and use. What's more, "picking a typeface is actually not as important as manipulating the spacing attributes of the typeface," says typographer and designer Alex W. White. "Typography is 90 percent space management and only 10 percent letterform management."

Typeface selection also might be less critical to comprehension (within reason) than other design elements. That's the finding of a 1972 study Paul Mijksenaar cites (Dirken, 1972). The participants of the study, by J. M. Dirken at Delft University, ranked eight design elements in this order of importance (from most important to least):

1. Order (in space)

2. Place (on a page)

3. Type size

4. Contrast (bold versus light)

5. Direction (roman versus italic)

6. Column width

7. Vertical spacing

8. Typeface

But Mijksenaar says he's noticed for years that "graphic designers work this list from the bottom up! They spend most of their time discussing typefaces, and never come to the top of the list."

So (it might comfort you to know) you don't have to become an expert on typefaces and their nuances to set clear type. (See sidebar on the following page.) Nor do you have to know your way around tens of thousands of typefaces, and their subtle personality or historical differences. They're certainly fascinating topics for study, and exquisitely set typography is an art form. But for the kind of practical designs we're talking about, you probably don't need to be familiar with more than a handful of legible typefaces.*

If you do want to become a type expert, you might start by absorbing these books: *Thinking in Type* by Alex W. White, *Elements of Typographic Style* by Robert Bringhurst, and *Stop Stealing Sheep and Find Out How Type Works* by Erik Spiekermann and E. M. Ginger. (Embrace the Spiekermann book's teachings but not always its design, especially the sidebars of challenging red tiny type on almost every spread. You might also find yourself questioning type decisions in the exquisite Bringhurst book, along with design decisions made in this book. You're supposed to. Type and graphic designers, and information-design-book designers and authors live in glass houses.)

You *do* need to know what factors contribute to clarity enough to be able to recognize a clear typeface when you see one. For example, you should be able to distinguish among the major categories of typefaces as they contribute to clarity. You need to know about spacing, both within and between words, and between lines and paragraphs. And become aware of the overall tone of type to make sure your type

---

* You might choose to emulate Nigel Holmes, a noted information designer and illustrator, who says, "If there were only Gill Sans in the world, I'd be happy." Holmes says he likes the look of it, and it comes in so many weights, "you'd never need anything else." (At least not in the sans serif category. Accepting the argument that serifs make a lot of text easier to read, he turns to serifs, including Hoeffler, by Jonathan Hoeffler, in those cases.) Holmes cites the even greater loyalty of Austrian sociologist, philosopher, and designer Otto Neurath to a version of Futura: "He just always used the same typeface." But you can make a strong case that Neurath, whose work inspired the development of an international symbol system, preferred images to words. In more recent times, Burkey Belser, of Greenfield/Belser Ltd., includes Gill Sans and Futura on his short list of legible typefaces for brochures and books; the list also includes Garamond, Bembo, Frutiger, and Franklin Gothic.

The least you need to know about type

As in everything else in information design, you'll find opinion differences here, too. Alex W. White addresses the question of the minimum amount of typographic knowledge needed to design effectively: "You might as well ask, 'What's the least a non-physician needs to know about the human body to effectively heal it?' The answer is obvious: If no one *who is qualified* is available, then as much as possible. Having said that, typography is an art and a craft driven by common sense at least as much as by artistic vision." White predicts more success for the nondesigner who applies common sense to the design problem than for the one who just follows his or her own tastes.

More support for the familiar

In information design—where materials are meant to inform, not entertain—White agrees with the need to stick with the familiar, because "a reader's familiarity and comfort with 'normal' lettershapes will make them more open to using the designed material." But, he adds, that doesn't mean you're stuck with Helvetica—just choose typefaces that "fit within the range of 'normal' and 'familiar.'"

Nor does type for information design mean ignoring aesthetics; rather, it involves thinking about them differently. Aesthetics plays a different role in informative materials than in reading meant just for pleasure.

Unlike aesthetics' role in voluntary reading, where readers have to be drawn into the copy, White says, readers of manuals and tax forms "are there to get information as quickly and painlessly as possible. They *have* to be there, so help them get in and out with alacrity."

But does appeal also improve a reader's attitude about task-oriented reading? For example, is a typeface capable of improving a taxpayer's attitude about a tax form?

White's answer is yes, especially if it obviously improves upon a poor choice such as ". . . an Extra Condensed anything.' Don't ever give the reader/user an excuse to go do something, anything, else. They're looking for it and they'll take it. Reader's preferences are based on familiarity. . . . So find out what your audience prefers." He adds, "Remember that a designer's job is to make the reader unaware of the act of reading. [Your job is] not to draw attention to the designer's great taste."

choice not only *doesn't contradict* the message you want it to deliver but also *reinforces* it.

White's list for effective headline/text combinations includes those that share shape and width characteristics. For example, an oval shape in serif rounded lowercase letters (*b, d, o, p, q*) needs pairing with a similarly oval shape in a sans serif typeface. (See examples on page 105.)

Sans Serif Typefaces

Akzidenz Grotesk	mockingbird's autobiography
Avenir	mockingbird's autobiography
Franklin Gothic	mockingbird's autobiography
Frutiger	mockingbird's autobiography
Futura	**mockingbird's autobiography**
Gill Sans	mockingbird's autobiography
Meta Plus	mockingbird's autobiography
Monotype Grotesque	mockingbird's autobiography
News Gothic	mockingbird's autobiography
Officina Sans	mockingbird's autobiography
Rotis 55	mockingbird's autobiography
Syntax	mockingbird's autobiography
The Sans	mockingbird's autobiography
Trade Gothic	mockingbird's autobiography
Univers 55	mockingbird's autobiography

Serif Typefaces

Baskerville	mockingbird's autobiography
Berling	mockingbird's autobiography
Bodoni	mockingbird's autobiography
Boton	mockingbird's autobiography
Californian	mockingbird's autobiography
Caslon	mockingbird's autobiography
Centennial	mockingbird's autobiography
Century Expanded	mockingbird's autobiography
Clarendon	**mockingbird's autobiography**
Galliard	mockingbird's autobiography
Garamond	mockingbird's autobiography
Goudy	mockingbird's autobiography
Jenson	mockingbird's autobiography
Memphis	**mockingbird's autobiography**
Modern No.20	mockingbird's autobiography

Various typographers have named one or more of these typefaces among their recommended, versatile favorites, grouped by category (sans serif or serif). Exercise: Comparing each typeface with the others, list all the differences you find. *Typographer: Alex W. White.*

Mockingbird's Autobiography a Must-Read

Giving fresh meaning to the phrase "bird's eye view," this new book has just one flaw: The author speaks with too many voices.

Good head/text combinations share shape and width (such as this Meta Plus Black above Century Expanded) . . .

Mockingbird's Autobiography a Must-Read

Giving fresh meaning to the phrase "bird's eye view," this new book has just one flaw: The author speaks with too many voices.

. . . or x-height (such as this Frutiger 75 above Californian) . . .

Mockingbird's Autobiography a Must-Read

Giving fresh meaning to the phrase "bird's eye view," this new book has just one flaw: The author speaks with too many voices.

. . . or just something right (Griffith Gothic Bold above Concorde).

Or match x-heights (the height of the lowercase *x* compared with the typeface's uppercase characters). X-height varies with the typeface and affects text legibility. Look at the x-height of any text face you consider, and consider it at least as important as point size. (As you'll see later in the chapter, x-height also affects the number of characters you can fit on a line.)

An x-height on the bigger side tends to add clarity, because of its open counters (the enclosed spaces in certain type characters, such as the lowercase *e*, *a*, and *o*, or the uppercase *B*, *P*, and *R*). Make sure they're open enough to keep them from filling in at the smallest sizes you'll need.

But x-heights can get too big, as Avant Garde demonstrates. Full circles make up most of its lowercase characters, so they take up as much width as height on a line. To get anywhere near an ideal number of characters on an average line, the text would need to drop more than a full point size.

The enormous interior space of Avant Garde's lowercase characters at any point size attracts the eye away from a more useful destination, the characters' shapes. And the typeface's tiny strokes and extenders

Too much x-height for its own good.

The typeface Avant Garde combines a huge x-height with full circles, which hinders the legibility of text and headlines. Eyes tend to get lost in its characters' interiors . . .

and a naugahyde blimp   ad nh bp dq

. . . and sometimes even confuse characters.

make it easy for readers to confuse characters. That's especially true of character pairs that need the extender to tell them apart, such as *ad*, *nh*, even *bp* and *dq*.

X-height also affects the density on the page; as you'd expect, a big x-height usually looks denser. So consider adding one or more points of leading to avoid a page that looks cramped and daunting.

SERIF VERSUS SANS SERIF

For text, choose whichever category and face is clear and familiar to your audience and works for your purpose. (I usually use a legible serif for text on paper, and always a legible sans serif for the Web or slides.) Consider:

• *direction.* Serifs—the horizontal bars at the ends of the strokes of some typefaces—form a subtle yet sure reinforcement to the baseline, the imaginary horizontal line on which type sits. So they might help to lead the reader's eye in a horizontal direction instead of down and off the page.

• *enforced letter space.* Serifs come with a little extra space between characters to keep them from overlapping. They're more forgiving than sans serif, which needs more space—both between letters and between lines—"to help the eye traverse the horizontal line with equivalent smoothness," White says. The extra space between lines keeps the eye from losing its place. And "with default settings (unthinkingly favored by nondesigners), serif types are a much safer bet for text."

• *usability* (discussed in the previous chapter) in terms of audience familiarity and preference . . .

. . . *by geography:* We tend to find it easier to read what we prefer than what we don't. And often we prefer what we find most familiar. For example, serif type is more familiar than sans serif in the United States, because it's usually what children learn to read here. But when in Rome (or Geneva), set type as the Europeans do—European audiences prefer sans serif, for the same reason.

. . . *by industry, age, attitude:* Regardless of where your audience members learned to read, their professions might affect their preferences. For example, scientists, doctors, engineers, accountants, or Web programmers often prefer sans serif. Designers and audience members who prefer sans serif often point to its uncluttered and contemporary look compared to most serif faces. Sans serif typefaces tend to look newer than serif typefaces, because they are. They came along much later than serifs did.

. . . *by kind of info:* Preferences change with the kind of material, not just with the person, according to *Dynamics of Document Design* by Karen Schriver. The author asked a group of sixty-seven people whether they preferred the serif or sans serif (or neither) version of an instruction manual, a business letter, a tax form, and a short story. More audience members favored sans serif type overall, particularly for the letter and the manual. But serifs captured the most votes for the story, and twice as many for the form. The letter and form serif victories lose some punch when you consider that as many people chose neither as either. So use the study to remind you to test your own choice.

• *stroke weight and uniformity.* What matters more to legibility than a letter's ending are the qualities of the strokes that make up the letter's body. Notice whether the curves and strokes (the spines of the letters) are a uniform weight throughout the letters, or whether they vary. Most serif text faces have those stroke variations (known as "thicks and thins"), which reinforce the identity of each character and its distinction from others. Those variations support legibility when conditions retain their subtleties, as with good-quality printing on high-quality paper.

• *legibility challenges.* Use sans serifs for their uniform weight when you have less-than-optimal reading conditions. Those might include small type sizes, diagrams, reversed type, poor printing, low-resolution or pixelated type, textured or dark paper, an inconsistent background such as a screen or photo, or a light-projecting background such as a slide or Web site. Delicate, curved serifs with strong variations between their thick and thin strokes can lose their power and seem to fade, while showing up just enough to clutter. If you want to use serifs in these cases, favor square-serif fonts that have more uniform strokes such as Boton, Clarendon, or Memphis, which hold their own in such conditions, unlike, say, Bodoni or Modern No. 20. But they're generally too strong for text, and those blocky serifs tend to call too much attention to themselves and the space between the letters. (See the sidebar on the following page.)

HOW TO DETERMINE LINE LENGTH

Your text should set a comfortable reading pace that supports comprehension because it fights fatigue. Too-wide columns of sustained text

>> The best research plays no stroke-end favorites

The horizontal bars at the end of letters on some typefaces have no real effect on legibility, according to most researchers who've studied it, and plenty have. In text sizes, "there are no differences in legibility depending on presence or absence of serifs alone," Aries Arditi, senior fellow in vision science, Lighthouse International, writes. But, as he pointed out, those two categories usually differ in many other ways that can affect legibility. That's why Arditi designed typefaces for his experiments that differed only in the absence or presence of serifs.

The "only situation in which one would find legibility differences" between sans serifs and serifs is when the point size "is so small as to be only barely decipherable—only a few points in size at typical reading distance,"

Arditi notes. But even then, "serifs appear to have mixed effects." Although they "enforce a little extra space between the letters," Arditi also found evidence that their presence diminished the extra-space advantage. So enhance legibility by adding a little extra space between letters in both serif and sans serif text, but not so much that letters cease to read as word units.

The bottom line: The difference between serifs and sans serifs is negligible, especially for motivated readers. For most applications, a clear, open face in either category will serve readers if it's well set. Let your preference (or your boss's or client's) lead you. That is, use what you like as long as it's clear for the medium, the audience, and the method, and you use it consistently.

force the reader to work too hard to follow the path. They don't build in enough momentary reading pauses, and make it tough to stay on track and find the start of the next line. "A long line length absolutely defeats the reader, period," says Burkey Belser of Greenfield Belser Ltd., a design firm in Washington, DC.

The opposite extreme is almost as bad. Long sections of narrow lines containing too few characters make the eye jump too quickly for comfort.

With a comfortable reading pace, readers are more likely to focus on content, not on what they could be doing besides reading. And you'll help to set that pace by counting characters in a line. What

Reading too-wide columns of sustained text is kind of like watching a tennis match. Eyes have to swoop back and forth, requiring too much effort without a built-in opportunity to pause. Too many too-wide lines also make it tough for readers to find the beginning of the next line.

determines the number of characters in a line are type size, typeface, style, and column width (often called "line length").

So what's a comfortable count? As with almost every other question that comes up in information design, the answer again is that it depends. In this case, what it depends *on*—in addition to the usual variables of audience, purpose, and medium—might be whose research you follow. Miles Tinker's early but seminal study caused him to recommend an average of 50 to 70 characters (including word spaces and punctuation points) per line. That's a workable guideline for books and manuals, although the top of the range is too many characters for some eyes and tastes.

For other projects, such as newsletters with more than one column on a page, an easier-to-read range (and easier-to-recall guideline) is an alphabet and a half to two alphabets (39 to 52 characters, including word spaces and punctuation). Some designers, such as Paul Mijksenaar, get to the same range by counting words instead of characters. He works toward an average of six to eight words a line (40 to 53 characters in Dutch words, which average 6.6 characters).

White adds this advice: "Never set anything the full width of a page" regardless of page size or medium (paper or electronic). "The problem with [full-width type] is that it looks as if it would run wider if the page were wider." Type should relate to other material on the page, never to the perimeter of the page, he says.

A single column that leaves a wide margin (also called a "scholar's margin"), such as this page's layout, can work fine. On the Web, a single column offers the important benefit of preventing a viewer from having to scroll up while reading. (You know this irritation if you've ever tried to read a multicolumn print-to-PDF document on the screen instead of printing it out.)

WHAT ELSE AFFECTS CHARACTERS PER LINE COUNT . . .
. . . x-height: Bigger often means wider
Given the same typeface, words, and line length, you know you'll fit more words on a line if they're set in a smaller point size than a bigger

Long sections of narrow lines containing too few characters make the eye jump too quickly for comfort.

EXERCISE: Count an average line of characters, punctuation, and spaces on this page. Then type the same line in a software program that counts words and see how the number of words per line changes as you change the line's type size and face.

Same typeface, different size: 12 pt.

Same typeface, different size: 18 pt.

Of course the same typeface in a bigger point size takes up more space than it does in a smaller typeface.

Same typeface, different size: 24 pt.

Less intuitive: These two sentences have the same point size. Only the typeface and x-height (and width) change, so the amount of space the sentences take up changes, too. Because Garamond has a smaller x-height than Bookman (and almost anything except some script faces), it looks and sets smaller.

This is set in 18-pt. type.   Garamond, small x-height

This is set in 18-pt. type. Bookman, big x-height

This is set in 9-pt. type.   Garamond

This is set in 9-pt. type.   Bookman

This is set in 13-pt. type.   Garamond

A tiny x-height without a compensating increase in point size can do more harm to legibility in text than it can in display type.

This is set in 10-pt. type.   **Bookman**

In these display sizes, Garamond needs to grow by four or five point sizes to look as big as Bookman. So if you use a typeface with a small x-height, use a bigger point size than you would for one with an average x-height.

This is set in 23-pt. type.   Garamond

This is set in 18-pt. type.   Bookman

one (see the top series of samples on the facing page). But what you might not have known is that different typefaces in the same point size often set to different widths (see the second series of samples). That's because the x-height varies among typefaces. The cap size stays more consistent, truer to point size.

Although the two type samples have the same point size (and the same characters), the typeface with the bigger x-height looks bigger and takes up more horizontal space than the one with a smaller x-height. So if you choose a typeface with a small x-height such as Garamond, you'll probably need to punch up the point size (see the other samples on the facing page).

. . . compression: Avoid it

As you've just seen, often x-height differences are reflected in character width (the name *x-size* might have been more accurate). But generous x-heights don't equate to generous widths in typefaces that are condensed—stretched vertically, compressed horizontally. Some typefaces are naturally condensed (such as Franklin Gothic), some are a condensed form of an uncondensed typeface (usually identified by the word *condensed* in their name, such as Univers Condensed or Univers Extra Condensed), and some typefaces get condensed when designers deliberately distort them.

Extra Condensed

And typefaces that are expanded—stretched horizontally, compressed vertically—take up extra space on a line. These often can be identified by the words *Expanded* or *Extended* in their name. For optimal text legibility, limit both horizontal and vertical compression. Avoid typefaces whose names identify them as compressed, and never compress by distorting. Typefaces often overstretch—in either direction—at the expense of legibility.

Expanded

(To keep from inflicting the effects of compressed type on your audience, you might be able to get them out of your system at the food market. Broccoli growers often print their names in condensed type on the thick rubber bands that bind the stalks. Stretch the band and you expand the type.)

. . . text wraps: Avoid skinny ones

Good artwork can interest readers in the text by connecting with and expanding on the text. Text really flaunts its connection with the artwork when it wraps around it. But use restraint. Leave enough words—more than a couple—in the wrapping text to keep from throwing off the reading pace. And put artwork on the right side of the text column to keep the left edge intact and encourage readers to stay on track.

. . . point size: Bigger should mean longer, and vice versa

Achieving a comfortable reading pace means increasing point size for longer lines (within reason). The inverse also is true: If you must set text bigger than average (because your client or organizational standards demand it, for example), plan a longer line to accommodate it.

Longer lines also need more space between lines (leading). After traveling so far to the end of a long line, eyes tend to fall on their way back to the source of the next line. Extra leading helps them find their way.

STYLE

Watch your posture: Roman versus italics

Roman type, which stands straight up (you're reading it now), works best for large quantities of type. Reliable tests show italic type to be less legible than Roman, especially for sustained reading. And that's using italics that were designed to be italics—legibility really goes out the window when a word-processing program merely tilts letters to create pseudo italics. Use only real italics—typefaces with *italic* in the name—and use them sparingly in print as:

- a brief key sentence, word, or phrase
- short questions, to distinguish them from their longer Roman answers in a question-and-answer section
- book titles
- photo captions (also known as cutlines)
- foreign words and phrases
- words that are defined in a nearby glossary

Don't ask readers to read italics on a computer screen at all, according to *Stop Stealing Sheep* by Spiekermann and Ginger. On a screen, italics are "simply stupid" because "the pixel grid is square" and can't accommodate the curves of italics.

Watch your weight

Bold type is an effective way of showing contrast and emphasis. Readers identify it as a code for more important information. So in text it works to highlight people or company names that will attract readers. (In fact, you've probably heard celebrities referred to as "bold-faced names," given their usual typographical treatment in magazine and newspaper gossip columns.)

Bold styles emphasize more powerfully than italics do, because of their increased contrast. Although italics contrast with regular type, some italic styles have finer strokes, so they have limited emphasis power. Bold not only contrasts with regular type but also stands out more from the background.

But boldface doesn't always stand up under pressure as you might expect. Here's another legibility challenge: In small sizes in particular, and especially in typefaces with small x-heights, ink tends to fill in small counters (the enclosures in the letters). Begin with a typeface that has a bigger x-height if you intend to use the bold at all; then test it in the smallest size you'll use.

Like italics, but even more, a little boldface goes a long way.

The case against all caps

All-uppercase text and headlines are foes to legibility. They persist from days of the typewriter, which offered limited ways to emphasize something. Today you have no excuse for all-caps text. We read lowercase text about 5–10 percent faster than we do all-caps, according to some studies. So just don't set it. In fact, according to *Guidelines for Document Designers,* limit all-caps type to four words.

The main problem with caps, many say, is that caps in any typeface have the same height, and plenty have the same width. So text in all caps presents no visually graspable shape to help us distinguish one word from any other that's the same length. As readers, we look for these clues. Squint at the word TYPOGRAPHY, for example. It's a ten-

Words that have the same number of characters, such as these two, have few distinguishing qualities when they're in all caps.

UNDERSTAND

TYPOGRAPHY

understand

typography

But in lower case, the same words have more to set them visually apart.

The case against the word-shape theory

Kevin Larson, a psychologist at Microsoft, contests the word shape theory of word recognition. Caps slow reading not because they lack a "graspable" shape, he contends, but because we're not as accustomed to reading them. As further proof, Larson cites studies that find shorter words to be recognized more quickly than longer ones. For word shape to count, he writes, the opposite should be true because longer words contain more visual clues than shorter ones do.

Instead, Larson advances the idea that "we use the letters within a word to recognize a word" by citing eye flow research. While reading, our eyes land in the middle of a word as they jump along the line. There we read the word and its immediate environment, then plan our next landing, usually to the right.

Those are compelling arguments, yet I contend—citing only my well-honed intuition—that Larson is missing something with his if-this-then-it-can't-be-that thinking. Surely it would take too long to decipher words by their guts alone. His theory also discounts the value of reading experience. As he says, we *are* best at reading what's most familiar. So wouldn't we learn to recognize by shape the words we encounter often? And might we encounter shorter words more frequently than longer ones? Or might shorter word shapes just be more memorable?

It might be interesting to test Larson's theory with people who were trained with word shape exercises. If you learned to recognize word shapes when you learned to read and write, wouldn't you keep that word shape awareness?

Draw your own conclusion. Read Larson's paper—"The Science of Word Recognition, or How I Learned to Stop Worrying and Love the Bouma" (a bouma is a word shape)—at http://www.microsoft.com/typography/ctfonts/WordRecognition.aspx.

character word with a shape that's hard to distinguish from most other ten-character words, despite distinctive-shaped characters on either end. Now look at UNDERSTAND. (See the sidebar above.)

But with lowercase's dots, ascenders, descenders, and greater differences among letters come easily recognizable word shapes that readers can perceive more quickly than they can caps. Readers more easily see the words as the sums of their parts.

In any given size and face, caps also take up about 30 percent more space than lowercase, which is reason enough to avoid them in almost any medium. In print, text in caps means paying for extra pages to convey the same amount of information; in a Web site, such text asks the reader to scroll further for the same information. In an e-mail, add the potential for insult, given the widely held perception that all-cap messages "shout."

But setting type in all-caps does work sometimes. In signage, unlike more stationary forms of reading, all-caps setting text is no less legible than mixed-case characters, according to *The Signage Sourcebook*. We tend to recognize characters in all caps more easily, which can come in handy when viewing signs from a distance. The problem with using caps in close-up and sustained reading is that we also tend to read them as individual characters more than as part of a word. Lowercase characters, more easily read in words and phrases, have the edge there. (See the sidebars below and on the next page.)

More styles you can use in text, but should you?
Underlined type is a throwback to the days of manual typewriters. Besides all-caps (and centering), it was the only other way to show emphasis. But underlining chops off those valuable descenders and violates the leading, so use italics instead when you can.

⟫ Stacked case against stacked type

Before the last U.S. presidential election, Stefan Bucher wore the T-shirt shown in the photo (designed by Isaac Mizrahi for declareyourself.com) to a party attended by graphic artists . . . visual people all. The shirt stacks the letters of the word *vote*, but the *v* is formed by the shirt's contrasting V-neck. "All night, people asked me, "Hey, so who's 'OTE'?" Because the V-neck is a convention, stacked type isn't legible, and the *V* is bigger and bolder than the other letters, party-goers missed the fact that the collar doubled as the first letter of the word.

The example also doubled as art, not just information; it has the all-important hip factor that was a big part of the get-out-the-vote marketing for that election. And the message was all the more memorable when people heard the real meaning. So the design worked for those who were interested enough to ask about it, but it could have communicated more powerfully as a walking billboard to less curious and outspoken passersby.

Confusion about meaning should trigger looking into the need for change in anything designed to inform. Those "OTE" people almost certainly felt stupid when they learned what they'd missed, and if Bucher had not pointed it out so tactfully, they might not have felt warmly about him.

"Who's 'OTE'?" Most people who see this T-shirt miss the neckline's initial cap. *Shirt designer: Isaac Mizrahi. Client: declareyourself.com Model: Petra Algerova.*

>> SMALL CAPS HAVE THEIR PLACE, BUT THIS ISN'T IT

Within text and without small caps, acronyms (IBM, NASA), abbreviations (P.M., B.C.), and numbers can overpower a paragraph. "Lowercase" numbers are called old-style or nonlining numbers. (Make them with small caps, unless the typeface comes with old-style figures, as the example, Meta Plus Book, does.)

Book and periodical designers often use small caps for the first few words (the lead-in) of a chapter or an article. Although a small-cap lead-in can look elegant there, it's not a good idea. Small caps have most of the legibility disadvantages of big caps, so they interfere with legibility in a most important spot: at the start of reading.

They ordered 1,200 planes on Monday; 3,000 more on Tuesday.
Regular lining numbers can overwhelm a sentence.

They ordered 1,200 planes on Monday; 3,000 more on Tuesday.
Old-style numbers make a more subtle statement.

Shadow
OUTLINE
Avoid shadow type because it has muddied edges and outline type because it's made from only edges.

Avoid reversing quantities of text in print or on the Web. Also avoid putting a shadow on type or turning it into an outline, with limited exceptions. Shadows can help type stand out from a dark background on a Web screen or a slide, but they often get the job of rescuing display type from a busy Web or print background. They're not strong enough, and their attempts result in weakened type edges and word shapes; better to lose the busy background.

Then there's outline type. Neither here nor there, it lends only the hint of the shape, but without conviction enough to fill itself in. So type appears to fade into the surface, giving more power to the background glimpsed through the outline than to the type itself. In text type in particular, consider outlines the worst violation of the principle that mandates separating foreground (figure) and background (ground). Outline type is even less legible than reversed type.

ALIGNMENT IN TEXT TYPE
The easiest-to-read type columns align to the left margin, and let the right margin go ragged (flush left, ragged right) such as this book. That style puts equal spaces between each word in each line, so it supports a consistent reading pace.

speaking   slowly   on   one   line,   few   characters,

then speeding up on the next line because so much more fits on it,

then   really   dragging   on   the   next…

annoying, isn't it?

Reading justified text is like hearing a speech in which every line varies in tempo (based only on the number of characters in the line, not the line's meaning). Instead, set a uniform reading pace by setting text flush left, ragged right.

By contrast, type columns that justify (align left and right) leave word spaces of varied lengths. Word space size varies because the number of characters and words in each line varies. Especially when those numbers vary a lot, reading becomes as awkward and annoying as listening to someone slow down and speed up from line to line.

So ragged-right text wins the text-reading contest. Its other advantage over justified text, say ragged-right fans (including me), is its look: approachable, accessible, even friendly. Justified-text fans call that a disadvantage, preferring the traditional symmetry of formal, precise, conservative columns. Certainly they have a point for some projects and audiences.

Traditionally, you'll find more books using justified columns. Also, engineers, doctors, and military and other government officials tend to prefer more formal-looking documents. Another reason justifiers die hard: You generally can fit more justified than ragged-right text in the same amount of space. But consider whether the loss of reading ease is worth it. And justification works only on wider-than-average columns because those have plenty of word spaces to divide up.

But even ragged-right text columns need help. They need hyphens where appropriate to avoid distracting gaps between the widest and narrowest lines. Then edit to avoid more than two hyphens in a row, which also distracts. (Some editors forbid more than one, while others permit as many as three.)

What about other alignments—ragged left, centered? "We read best what we read most," according to *Stop Stealing Sheep,* the type book by Spiekermann and Ginger. And we prefer what's familiar. And flush-left type is what readers of Western languages read and know best. Our eyes are accustomed to starting to read on the left and returning to the left to continue. But with both ragged-left and centered text, the eye has to float for a bit—even if it's only a second—to find its place. In both ragged-left and centered edges, only the number of characters and word spaces, not content, determines placement.

Fortunately, ragged-left and centered edges don't turn up much in text, and they shouldn't in yours.

SPACING AND PLACEMENT: WHAT'S GRID GOT TO DO WITH IT?

The grid might be the most important part of a style sheet. It's a physical plan—a framework or structure—for consistently placing the elements within an information design. It's to information designers what a blueprint is to architects. The plan includes the number of columns, the size of the margins, the space between columns and paragraphs, and the size, number, and position of artwork. A well-designed one does all that while still remaining flexible enough to be interesting. "Grids should not be straitjackets," according to *Editing by Design* by Jan V. White.

To make a grid, the designer creates a series of lines on the page that guide space use on that and every other page (or project part— grids work for any project with multiple parts, such as a series of signs). Those lines don't show in the final design (except on the facing page, in blue, as an example), only the organization imposed by them does.

A grid serves readers by organizing the info and establishing continuity within a design. When a grid's in place, readers' experience with one page tells them what to expect and where to find things on subsequent pages. The grid imparts layout structure, consistency, and alignment—elements are anchored rather than seeming to "float," because everything lines up with something on the grid. That helps readers flow from one element to the next.

Readers also might appreciate the balance and proportion a well-designed grid brings to a design. For example, the grid helps to balance more prominent elements against less prominent ones, to avoid top- or bottom-heavy pages. It also balances the amount of empty space in proportion to filled space.

The two most important elements of the grid are margins and columns.

Margins frame a page

Top, bottom, and side margins contain the content within a design. Notice the ones on this page, then look at those on a few other books and magazines. Are the margins the same size all around the page, or is there more space in one of the margins? And do margins match from page to page?

Hey you with the sinus problem—

Now there's a new sinus medicine that clears the pain and pressure which also clears the fog.

The clear your head sinus med.

This ad uses fuzzy type to make its point clearly, meaningfully, and memorably. But don't try it at home, or on any information-design materials for which unclear type fights both perception and understanding. That applies to most materials.
© The Procter & Gamble Company. Used by permission.

"What's in it for me?" reader asks; answer quickly, the clock's ticking

What encourages viewers to read (right away or at all) is perceiving that they'll benefit from the material. Expect them to take mere seconds to decide. In those seconds, they'll register a first impression based largely on how long the material takes to announce its content. They'll decide whether they need it or care about it, and if they do, how much, compared with everything else they've got to read and do. They'll decide to either read it, defer the decision (tossing it on the reading stack for "later," another way of saying "throw out in thirty days"), pass the buck, or trash it.

Comprehensible design supports rather than interferes with the content. It supports reading in at least three ways:

- It quickly delivers a preview of the contents to help viewers decide whether or not to read on (if it's voluntary).

- It helps readers get through the content with minimal time and effort and no confusion.

- It *looks* clear, as if it won't take much effort or time to read, so it encourages the decision to read.

That last one was confirmed by surveying readers of a sixteen-page monthly newsletter. "I read the newsletter cover to cover right away," wrote many of the respondents. Big deal, you might say; it's only sixteen pages. But to these readers, who regularly reported being overworked, it *was* a big deal. They were amazed to be taking time to read *anything* during a workday, let alone sixteen pages of it. They read it all right away because the content addressed their needs, and the design and writing delivered it clearly. If instead the design or writing had interfered, the reader might have relegated the piece to the "later" stack.

Readers got right into and through the newsletter because it looked as if it wouldn't take up a lot of their time. And *that's* because it avoided common design and writing crimes against reading motivation, such as:

- unclear or inconsistent type

- disorderly layout

- lack of alignment

- lack of grouping

- too many elements

Example of a grid

>> A reasonable exception to matching bottom margins within a page is the use of the "clothesline effect": columns of different lengths that start in the same place. It ensures consistent space between paragraphs and other pictures in the column. And the reader sees extra white space at the bottom as a cue to continue reading the next column.

To pull off the right effect, adjoining columns should show enough of a length difference—at least a quarter of an inch—to make it look deliberate. But they shouldn't show so much difference—more than an inch—that something seems to be missing in the shortest one.

More generous space at the top can help the eye fall into the type at the start of the page. They generally do—and should—match from page to page.

Bottom margins tend to be shallower than top margins but still deep enough to keep the information from looking as if it's falling off the page. The eye's distance from the page bottom—greater than its distance from anything else on the page—reinforces that illusion of gravity. "Big enough" often means the same size as the outer side margin, no less than a half inch. Like those at the top, bottom margins also should match from page to page and generally within a page. (See the sidebar on this page.)

Side margins also should match from page to page. Within a page is a different story. For a print publication that's designed in spreads (such as a magazine with left and right facing pages), add a little more space to the margins on the sides between the pages (the spine or folding side) than to those on the outer (trim) sides. Binding takes up space that can hide any type placed too close to it. So does the publication's natural curve, which gets more pronounced with more pages. Hole punches also can cut into the type. It might make sense for left and right margins to vary even more, leaving extra space at one side of the columns for display type, info boxes, and artwork.

Columns add structure

Consistently used columns help to establish a regular pattern throughout a project. Use as few or as many columns as you need to present the number and combination of words and pictures in the format in which you present. The column count also should match readers' expectations for the format. For example, they don't expect a book to print in five columns, so avoid a five-column structure for a book unless the content absolutely demands it.

From an information-design perspective, columns' presentation matters more than their number. Make sure the layout allows enough space for generous side margins. Avoid letting the sole column on a page take up more than about three-quarters of the page. And, in general, a bit of asymmetry in column placing can fight monotony. Look for it in the other designs you encounter.

As the early part of this chapter recommends, count characters to set legible type. Point size, typeface, and column width affect character counts. So, for example, if you must follow strict type size and face standards, they'll determine the correct column width—when you type 40 to 50 characters of that typeface in that size.

But free will still can reign—to a point—in the column count. For example, although the optimal character count on a page might allow three columns of text, you can choose to forgo one of those columns for artwork, sidebars, or empty space.

For another perspective on columns in use, see pages 48 and 49 of *Editing by Design,* third edition, by Jan V. White.

EXERCISE: Find the grid on three print magazines. With a pen or pencil, draw the grid lines on a few pages in each magazine. Then draw them in your page layout program. Practice creating grids for every project you design.

Grids depend on empty space

A design's empty space is really the grid's key ingredient and secret weapon. It's a valuable, active design element because of all it can contribute to content's digestibility when it's used properly. It adds structure, breathing room, and a sense of order. It helps to show relationships among elements. It funnels readers toward the content. It even helps to protect and isolate content from anything that competes for the reader's attention, both within and outside of the design.

Designers refer to empty space as "white space," even though the space need not be white, only unfilled except for a solid background of white, black, gray, or a quiet color. "White space is nice space," my first art director liked to say. It *is* nice in the right amounts and places. Let's look at what "right" means in white space's various design uses.

White-space placements

Notice space between elements such as photos and the text below it, or between stories. Don't let the space fall where it may. It's common, but not effective, to stretch or shrink space in a column to make everything line up at the bottom of the page. Instead, come up with a standard-sized "spacer," maybe a quarter of an inch, but no less than an eighth. Use the spacer as if it were a chunk of metal holding elements apart (as hot-metal typesetters literally did).

Shrink the space between two items to show they relate to each other more closely than to others. For example, tighten the space between headings and secondary headings, between headings and the text it introduces, and between photos and their captions. Put more space above a subheading than below it. Put less space between two items to show they relate to each other more than they do to others on the page. People expect things that are close in space also to be close in meaning. Such space use sets a standard by which readers recognize and understand a meaningful deviation. It makes pages look planned . . . and stationary, as if the info isn't drifting away from view.

And it helps eyes flow through text. When readers get used to a grid, they don't have to think about where to find things.

Space between paragraphs

Use space between elements as a legiblity tool. For example, avoid letting a paragraph run on and on to complete a single thought (despite what your junior-high teacher might have told you). Paragraphs that run more than about two inches deep look daunting. Their very look can warn the reader to pack an overnight bag before entering; a less motivated reader won't enter at all.

Instead, subdivide that thought in logical places. Try to limit each paragraph to about one and a half or two inches in whatever size, face, and column width you've chosen. Should you signal a new paragraph with an indent or with an extra line space? There are plenty of schools of thought on the topic. Some designers and writers always add the line between paragraphs to inject more white space. Some prefer the indent on the theory that an extra line interrupts reading flow. Others use both at once. (That's the norm for direct-marketing letters, which also lean toward oversized indents to give readers a head start into the full-width column.)

Still other designers and writers sensibly choose one or the other according to the project. For example, you might indent the paragraphs of a publication with at least two columns on a page. The lack of an extra line between paragraphs emphasizes and unifies each column, a subtle prompt to read down it.

By contrast, an extra line space puts a bit more focus on the paragraphs than on the columns. That might be fine on a book or other project with one column and few other elements on the page to distract the reader. The extra line space would help to avoid too much unbroken text. And that's fine as long as you realize that an extra space between paragraphs alone rarely is enough to break up a gray page. You also need contrast, in the form of subheadings, pull quotes, and/or artwork.

Afghani Women Officials Recall Their Life Under the Taliban

Farah Ebrahimi

Among the 15 Afghani officials taking the IMF Institute Macroeconomic Management and Policies course in Tehran in July 2003, four were women. Each held a senior position in the Central Bank of Afghanistan. Three were directors in the Monetary Policy Department and one headed the Banking Institute. Seeing these dynamic women participate actively in the course or walk arm-in-arm from the lecture room to the dinning hall, laughing and gesturing excitedly about their day, I was hard pressed to imagine them as prisoners in their homes only 18 months before. Yet for six years, they, along with all women in Afghanistan, had lived a nightmare under the rule of the Taliban.

I was part of the IMF Institute mission to Tehran and during the two weeks training course, I heard some of the participants' stories. During one of the breaks in the lectures, I interviewed the women, who spoke in Persian. We formed a small circle, and as soon as they began their stories, the circle widened as some of the Iranian women attending the course joined to listen.

The four participants spoke excitedly, interrupting each other to describe the plight of women during those dark years. Although their lives had been profoundly affected by two decades of civil war, they had managed to go to school and hold professional positions, each working at the Central Bank. But when the Taliban took power in 1996, overnight women were stripped of their rights as members of society. They were forbidden to work, to study, to leave their homes unless covered by the *burqa* (a tentlike garment that covered them from head to toe, with a crocheted grille across the eyes) and accompanied by a *mahram*—a male relative such as a father, brother, or husband. Once outside, women were forbidden to laugh or speak aloud since strangers should not hear a woman's voice. They were forbidden to wear shoes with heels since men should not hear the click of a woman's shoe. And they could not enter a store unless to buy basic necessities, and again only when accompanied by a mahram. Any breach of these rules, real or imagined, resulted in swift punishment, always severe and sometimes deadly.

Farzaneh, a petite woman with sweet, sad eyes, told of the loss of her husband and infant son, who, in the early years of Taliban rule, were caught in the crossfire while they were on their way home from the market. Then, almost casually, Farzaneh told of her own brush with death. She had gone with relatives to buy gifts for an upcoming wedding. To see the gift items, she had lifted her veil slightly, since the grill across the eyes makes seeing difficult. But she was seen by a Taliban guard, who immediately grabbed and pulled her into the middle of the street, forcing her to kneel. He then pointed his gun to her head, shouting that he was going to make an example of her by executing her right there. She was saved, Farzaneh said, only after her pleading relatives convinced another Taliban to intervene.

Each woman spoke of depression, but each also spoke with pride of holding clandestine classes for young girls at great risk to herself and family. Zarmina remarked proudly that when schools reopened and girls were tested for placement, her girls had passed their exams and entered the grade appropriate for their age.

When the break was over, the women joined their colleagues for the next lecture. Observing them in the lecture room, I was again impressed by their resilience and found myself sharing in their excitement at being a part of a new era of women living, learning, and working in Afghanistan.

Farah Ebrahimi is Assistant Editor in the IMF Institute.

Left to right: Zarmina Samedi, head of the Banking Institute; Farida Waezi, director of the Central Bank section of the Monetary Policy Department; Farzana Mehraabi, manager of the Balance of Payments Section of the same department; and Farida Ibrahimi, head of the Commercial Bank section of the Monetary Policy Department.

Rebuilding Afghanistan a Brick at a Time

Two decades of war and civil strife and six years under the Taliban have left Afghanistan's economy in tatters and its institutions destroyed. As Abdul Waheed Qadeeri, a senior official of the Central Bank of Afghanistan, explained, restarting the economy requires rebuilding Afghanistan's institutions one brick at a time. Speaking to Farah Ebrahimi in Persian in Tehran in July 2003, Qadeeri described the challenges the country faces, noting the importance of international technical assistance in the reconstruction of post-Taliban Afghanistan.

Rebuilding institutions a brick at a time.

The interview with Qadeeri and other Afghani officials took place during a break in the course Macroeconomic Management and Policies conducted by the IMF Institute in Tehran from July 19 to 30. The course was the first of its kind targeted to Afghani officials, whose participation was financed through the Japanese Account for Selected Fund Activities, and the event was hosted by the Central Bank of the Islamic Republic of Iran. The course, conducted in English with simultaneous translation into Persian, included 14 Iranian officials, in addition to the 15 Afghani participants.

Qadeeri described the Taliban as "antiscience and antiknowledge." "It will take years if not decades to overcome the destruction they caused," Qadeeri remarked. From 1996 till 2001, he noted, no economic documents were created nor data kept on which to base a national budget. And when the Taliban left, they took whatever assets the treasury still had. For all practical purposes, the infrastructure began unraveling 25 years ago. "So when the World Bank or the IMF ask us for information to develop the government finance statistics as a first step toward creating GNP predictions, we have nothing to give them," remarked Qadeeri. We literally have to create our statistics by hand, column by column, item by item.

Until 2002, the Central Bank worked with obsolete cash register machines for its recordkeeping, since it did not have any computers. In 2002-03, the Central Bank received 25 computers from the U.S. Agency for Interna-

12 13

These facing newsletter pages demonstrate appropriate margins. But the spacing still can be improved:

- Reduce the space between the headlines consistently to bring them closer to the stories they introduce.
- Match the spacing below stories, and between text and artwork.
- Break long paragraphs in half, and match the spacing between paragraphs. A skipped line only after the first paragraph doesn't work.
- Use more hyphens and a wider measure for the text wrapped around the photo on the right-hand page. Those extreme gaps ("trapped white space") draw the eye.
- Fit the initial text around the drop cap so the first word reads like a word.
- Tighten the letter and word spacing of the headlines for quicker grasping.

Reprinted by permission of the International Monetary Fund. Newsletter: The IMF Institute Courier, *Winter 2004.*

Whether you indent or skip lines between paragraphs, also pay attention to the paragraph endings. Edit to leave enough words—more than half of the column width—on each paragraph's final line to avoid gaps that distract the eye away from the reading.

Controlling paragraph remainders and beginnings is even more important for paragraphs that end on a different page or column than the one they began on. Bring forward—or leave behind—no less than two or three full lines to avoid a fragment that the reader might overlook.

Also avoid asking readers to do more than just turn one page once to finish what they're reading. Many jumps for one story or jumps over multiple pages interrupt reading flow, give readers a way out, and turn off plenty of readers.

But like many guidelines, the one-jump rule has exceptions, including the cover page of a newsletter that includes three or more stories. (Also see the sidebar on this page.) Most publications go to more than one audience, so an early choice of stories is more likely to provide something for every potential audience. And the story that starts a reader reading right away attracts more powerfully than even a table of contents or a menu on the cover.*

Space between sentences

Put only one word space between sentences. That bears repeating for the organizations and supervisors who still swear by two word spaces after a period or other ending punctuation. Like caps and underlining, the two-space style is a typewriter leftover. Monospaced letters from typewriters might have needed an extra space between sentences. But the proportional text you produce with a computer does not, so double word spaces leave noticeable gaps.

Space between lines of text

How much leading should you use where? Leading, the amount of space between lines of type, is measured from the baseline (the invisible line on which type minus descenders sits) of one line to the baseline of the line above and below it. Like type size, it's measured in points.

Text leading should be open enough so the readers don't lose their place, straying into lines above or below them while trying to focus on one. Adequate leading also keeps lines from "crashing" (touching or overlapping extenders).

> **» Calculated jumps**
>
> Direct-marketing letter writers often plan to break their most compelling sentences in a cliff-hanging place at the page end to encourage readers to continue.

The gray lines represents the baseline. It's what the type sits on, and descenders extend below.

* But also use a table of contents or a menu, because it answers the essential question of any potential reader: "What's in the publication for me?" On the Web, it also eliminates scrolling to find something. For dozens of listings, alphabetical links help people move quickly to their chosen topic (if you use the same topic name that they do, and audience research can ensure it). With fewer listings, you can let them link on the name or the headline.

Too-tight leading can make readers lose their place(especially in wide columns), and lines crash. This is 12-pt. type on 9-pt. leading.

Too-tight leading can make readers lose their place (especially in wide columns), and lines crash. This is 12/9: 12-point type with –3 pts. of leading (a negative number means negative leading).

Too-loose leading emphasizes the background

and de-emphasizes paragraph groupings.

This is 12-pt. type on 21-pt. leading.

Too-loose leading emphasizes the background and deemphasizes text and paragraphs. This is 12/21: 12-point type with 9 points of leading.

But leading also should be tight enough so the background between lines doesn't draw the eye away from the type or disconnect each line from others in its paragraph. The lines in the paragraph must be seen as a unit.

Adequate space means no less than one or two points of leading. For example, you'd refer to two points of leading for, say, 10-point type as "10 on 12" (10 + 2); one point would be "10 on 11" (10 +1). This book is set in 9½-point text type ITC Stone Serif Semibold on 13-point leading. Consider at least an extra point of leading for typefaces with a bigger-than-average x-height and for bold faces; they cover more ground so they can look too dense at an average leading. And for all typefaces, always use enough leading to keep extenders from crashing into those on other lines.

Again, add even more leading to a type column that must be far wider than what's optimal for legibility. Extra leading will help eyes that must travel a great distance across a column find their place on the way back to the next line.

EXERCISE: See the effects of leading for yourself. Type a paragraph, set it in 10-point type, and copy and paste it a few times. Set the paragraphs with different leadings and compare them. You might start with no leading (known as "set solid," 10/10 in this case), then add two points of leading (10/12), then 4 points (10/14). Then really exaggerate the leading differences and notice the effects of various leading amounts on the paragraph's overall density.

Space between letters in text: not too loose or tight
Tracking is the name for adjusting the amount of space between all characters in a continuous section of type over a page or pages. It applies to text, the main body of type—generally 9-point to 12-point—that's meant for sustained reading.

Software programs don't always call it tracking—look instead for "Spacing" in Photoshop, and "Character Space" in Word. But don't look too hard. People often change tracking for reasons that don't serve legibility: They squeeze too much text into a line, paragraph, column, or page, or they expand too small an amount of text to fill the available space. More legible solutions for having too much text are to edit (usually the best idea) or to move extra text to the next page. If you've got too little text for the page, add a pull quote or meaningful artwork. Or consider leaving the space empty and adjusting the layout to make the emptiness look deliberate.

But even tracking is a lesser evil than divvying up a distracting amount of space between paragraphs or other elements, or injecting it in one big blob. Such space becomes an obstacle the eye must leap. It also draws the eye away from the live elements on the page. Trapped white space is *not* nice space.

So save tracking as a last resort, and then use it only with utter restraint. That means if you must turn on the tracking, use the smallest possible increments you can get away with—Photoshop, for example, permits as little as a tenth of a point or pixel. And use it over everything that's visible by the audience at a time. That means a whole page, a whole two-page spread for a print publication, or even a whole document or publication. Print out the pages, and squint as you flip through them to guard against extremes.

Why? Tracking affects the page's "color," the density of the text versus the background. Even nondesigners can tell when a page or section of a page is much denser or lighter than others. If the extreme letter spacing doesn't bother them, the change in pace—more or fewer characters on a line—will. The change in density also makes text look harder to read, so it could discourage readers. And when the text becomes lighter, it also loses contrast against the background, diminishing its legibility.

Shrinking or expanding the size just of the word spaces in one section of text is no more advisable. It also affects the page's color and the audience's reading rhythm, as does changing leading to fit. (See the sidebar in the following pages for more about paper.)

How paper affects text legibility: light reflectance, thickness, flexibility, texture, color

reflectance

Avoid the glare factor when you choose paper that will hold a lot of text. That generally means avoid paper with a gloss coating. Reading from a glare-inducing surface requires squinting or moving the page away from the light. That's too much to ask of readers who have chosen to spend precious time on what you've designed. You'll find uncoated paper used for the pages of most books because it absorbs the light from a lamp or the sun rather than reflecting it back in readers' eyes.

Look around your office or studio for a publication printed on uncoated paper (you're probably printing on it), and one on gloss-coated (shiny) paper. Notice how the uncoated one absorbs the available light and the coated one reflects it—maybe right into your eyes, so that it hurts to read.

absorbency (dot gain)

Uncoated paper also absorbs ink almost as a sponge absorbs water. The ink spreads, so the dots on uncoated paper can also spread. Text type doesn't need enough ink for dot gain to be a problem.* And dot gain is predictable, so printers adjust for the paper and equipment.

Dot gain *can* become a problem on uncoated paper when you're printing photos whose tones muddy up as the dots get absorbed. This doesn't happen on a sheet with coating, which provides good ink "holdout" (ability to hold the ink on the surface). Gloss-coated paper is the best choice for good photos.

Legibility also applies to photographs. Not only must photos be well edited to tell a clear story, they also must print clearly. Stock that's gloss- or dull-coated, with multiple coatings, does the best job of reproducing the dots.

The best paper choice for a project with a lot of text and good photos is dull- or matte-coated paper, which both prevents ink gain and controls glare. These varieties have fewer layers of coating and less or no calendering (machine buffing or polishing of the coated surface) than gloss-coated papers. Dull-coated has better ink holdout (ink doesn't absorb) than matte, whose rougher surface permits more dot gain.

Another option that delivers both sharp photos and glare-free verbal information is a publication designed with two stocks. Annual reports traditionally have combined gloss-coated pages for photos and light text with uncoated financial pages so they're easy to read and write notes on. In annual reports, text tends to support the high-profile photos, rather than the other way around.

thickness/opacity

On any publication, form, or report that's printed on both sides of the sheet, keep what's printed on the back of the sheet from showing through enough to interfere with the reading of the front. That problem is actually *called* "show-through," and the less of it, the better.* The solution is paper that's opaque enough to minimize the effect.

Opacity comes from the fiber count in paper, and paper is measured in pounds. Most situations—pages filled with text—need a minimum of 60-lb. uncoated paper to avoid the battle of back-to-back text, says Kelley Dragonette of Central Lewmar Paper in Jessup, Maryland. A matte-coated sheet might need to be 70-lb. to equal the opacity of a 60-lb. uncoated sheet. That's because a 60-lb. uncoated sheet will contain most of its weight in fiber, where coating will make up some of the weight and reduce

---

*Dot gain on uncoated paper even could improve legibility, according to *Papers for Printing* by Mark Beach and Kathleen Ryan. With low-resolution type, such as from a 300-dpi laser printer, the paper might absorb the jagged edges, making them less apparent.

---

*Some designers have used paper show-through as a design element. John Sayles might have been the first to deliberately design black graphics that would show through his letterhead and envelopes." Many designers followed. Another popular design technique puts a transparent sheet in front of an opaque one to show both pages' contents at once. Of course, neither technique works for extended reading matter.

opacity. Beyond that, the calendering done to some coated sheets crushes the fibers, reducing opacity. If your pages include big, solid sections of dark ink, you might go even thicker.

Paper flexibility also factors into reading ease. Does the paper flop around? Moving content certainly discourages easy reading. (And you can't get away with calling it "poor man's animation.") Or is the paper so rigid that it resists turning or folding? Can it lie flat for hands-free reference if needed? That's a useful quality for a cookbook. (By the way, because cookbook pages often get splattered during use—try reading through dried tomato sauce or cookie dough—if you produce one, you'll be wise to budget for washable varnished pages.)

Another example: The ideal road map would be rigid enough not to flop or fray, and yet flexible enough to be viewed in full size and folded to pocket size.

texture/pattern

Too much going on in the background also makes text less legible. "Too much going on" includes heavily textured paper, whose valleys can hide serifs, thins (in thick-and-thin type), and parts of strokes; a smooth surface is best. It also still might include some recycled printing papers that contain random ink spots and dark fibers. And it includes paper with a pattern built into it, as well as patterns, photos, and solid or graduated color printed behind text.

color

Black ink on white paper gives the best contrast, but ivory or cream paper is easier on the eye. When you have a lot of text to deliver, you'll wisely resist papers that come in bouquets of appealing colors. For signage, black on yellow provides the highest contrast and the most visibility over distance. (And it's fluorescent yellow-green, judging from the change in the colors of those "pedestrian walk" signs.)

How to set display type

Display type refers to headings (headlines and titles), secondary headings (kicker heads, subheads), pull quotes, and sometimes to captions.

Size and weight

Because humans equate size with importance and prominence, it follows that headings (such as article headlines, chapter titles, and category heads) should be noticeably bigger and bolder than text. The size and weight should contrast with text enough that readers notice them first. As usual, what's noticeable and what works depends on the context.

Headlines catch the eye first or just after artwork, so get the message out in a glance with the right size, face, spacing, *and* words. Make sure you include a benefit to encourage people to want to find out more. As to size, you might start by considering headlines that are twice that of the text, smaller if needed for the column width and surrounding elements. For example, typically long heads in a narrow-column design dictate smaller type, while heads in a wide column could go bigger.

As in a good photo, a variety of lights and darks looks interesting. The contrast fights monotony, attracts attention, and helps to lead the eye through a page. Use enough contrast so the reader can easily distinguish the various levels while reading. That might mean changing "one parameter at a time," one of the guidelines in Robert Bringhurst's excellent *Elements of Typographic Style;* it'll probably mean changing at least two parameters.

The guideline wisely advises restraint. A too-big heading, with little relationship to text size, could dominate the text so much that it distracts from reading the text. Also consider when changing, say, just the weight and not the size will do the job.

As for subheadings and captions, same thing: They should contrast with the text, not overwhelm it. Make the differences among various levels of type obvious and memorable but not distracting.

As usual, also consider the medium and the audience. For example, readers often decide whether or not to read a newsletter article by its headline. So it's wise to make those type elements stand out.

About pull quotes

The compelling text bits blown up into the display type known as pull quotes are handy design elements. They break up text with contrast to avoid unending, mind-numbing grayness. They also lure readers who haven't yet committed to reading the full text.

A few guidelines: Make sure the words you choose for pull quotes are compelling; their size alone won't capture someone thumbing through for something worthwhile. And make pull quotes at least 14-point. Limit them to one pull quote per page or spread because using too many dilutes their effect. Also limit them to five lines in a one-column layout, and no more than three lines in a layout with two or more columns—too many lines must be read as text instead of at a glance.

Typeface for display

Contrast figures here, too. Use the same typeface as the text but change the size and weight, or use a contrasting face. A typical pairing is bold sans serif, such as Franklin Gothic, for the heads, with a Roman serif text. In general, sans serif faces seem to reinforce an authoritative heading style. Decorative typefaces such as scripts and Old English do the opposite, so keep such gimmicks out of your information designs.

Style in display type

Style constraints for display type are the same as for text. So you won't want to:

- underline (though an occasional hand-drawn swash might work for a key word in a head)
- outline
- reverse (except for a word or two, maybe for a category heading)
- drop shadow (except on the Web or on slides)
- italicize or
- distort

Type distortion is a drawing-program feature new designers love to play with. But resist the temptation. Distortion not only fails to aid comprehension, it usually hinders it. That's because, almost by definition, it acts in defiance of type's careful design. Stretch, curve, or otherwise torment type at comprehension's peril.

But what if your clients insist that a stretched "STRETCH" would demonstrate what they can do for the readers' budgets? Although verbal clichés can be memorable, graphic ones tend to lose meaning with repetition because readers stop seeing them.

STRETCH

Case in display type

Never set all caps for more than four words. The traditional style caps the first letter of each word except for articles (*an, a, the*) that aren't the first word of the line, and acronyms. Nontraditional "downstyle" capitalizes just the first letter of the first word of each line, plus proper nouns and acronyms. Fewer caps and the familiar sentence structure speed perception.

Standardizing on downstyle also helps to eliminate ambiguity where caps create it, as in "Senators Kill Bill." Readers might wonder, are you talking veto or murder? (*Polish* and *polish* could create similar confusion in a traditional headline. Can you think of other words whose meaning changes with the case?)

Downstyle might take some getting used to, even for informal use; we're familiar with the traditional, formal newspaper-headline style (although some newspapers have adopted downstyle). But its benefits make it worth getting used to. (And if you don't mention it to your supervisors or readers, they might not even notice it; yet they're likely to nix it if you do mention it.)

Alignment in display type

Choose flush-left alignment most of the time. You *can* center a single one-line title on a cover page, a small category header on inside pages, or an invitation. But if symmetry (a highly overrated form of balance) tempts you to center anything else, breathe deeply until the temptation goes away.

For headings and pull quotes that have more than one line, break the lines where you can give readers a complete phrase in each visual "gulp." That's news to those who fill the line before continuing to the next, or who strive for a longer second (or third) line. Instead, put a subject on the same line as its verb, a verb with its object, a preposition with its object.

For example, when you glance at this first line of the two-line headline, you get:

> Democratic senators kill
> bill in late session

It'll take the next word to complete the phrase.

> Democratic senators kill bill
> in late session

 "You are here"

A drop initial cap that begins text is another display element with a meaningful mission. It helps to flag the start of the text, which is useful when many page elements compete for attention. Make the cap big enough to stand out, but not bigger than the heading. Close up the space between it and the word it introduces.

AWARD Award ATLANTA TALENT Talent Teacher

AWARD Award ATLANTA TALENT Talent Teacher

The top line, with no kerning, shows gaps between letters that don't fill up their "boxes." The bottom line squeezes out the gap.

Space between letters

Kerning means changing the space between any two characters in display type that need it (as opposed to tracking, which is changing letter space throughout text). Some characters contain angles that leave a gap when they abut others. With kerning, you can reduce or eliminate the gap. In that case, kerning's value is to make sure words read as whole words. Kerning keeps that extra letter space between, say, the *A*'s and the *W*'s in the word *AWARD* from looking and reading like word spaces. (Kerning's also useful in lowercase, but not needed in sizes smaller than 14-point.)

Examine the difference between the same words set with and without kerning.

You also can kern to add space between characters that might be calling attention to themselves in a word by "kissing" or overlapping. Look again at the word *TALENT* above. The *A* and the *L* appear closer together than the *L* and *E*, which can't close up any more without losing the termination point of the *L*. So, along with closing up the space between the *T* and the *A*, you might want to open up the *A* and the *L* to balance the word and let it be read as a unit.

Space between lines

Inside two-line (or more, if you must) headlines and subheads, tighten the space between lines so they're seen as a unit, but not so much that the extenders and caps kiss or crash.

Tight leading (18/17 or –1 point of leading) visually groups the two lines of this headline without letting them touch, at least for this typeface with average-length extenders. Longer extenders would need extra leading.

One point of leading separates this primary headline from the 12-point secondary one, but not by too much. Both samples above shave a point from the formula for figuring minimum leading between display type lines: Add one-third of the point size of the type on top to two-thirds of the size of the line beneath it.

Marauding elephants damage local buildings

Elephant born in zoo
Crowds expected to visit

That's also true where a headline precedes a secondary head or the text itself. Set some variations in your page layout program until your eye gets used to what looks best.

EXERCISE: In a page layout program, experiment with headings of varying sizes and the amount of space between them. See how little space you can get away with before parts of characters overlap.

If you have more than one heading or subheading in a column, use more space above than below the heading to connect it to the text it introduces.

Placement
Put things where readers expect to find them. Don't let the quest for creativity get in the way of that. So put:

• headlines and titles (close) above the text

• captions (close) below the photo

• pull quotes before their appearance in the text, if possible, for people who have committed to reading the text. Seeing a pull quote after seeing it in text feels redundant (yet rarely is off-putting enough to lose the reader), while seeing it first should intrigue. Put pull quotes toward the trim side of a printed page to attract uncommitted people who thumb through the publication to decide whether they'll read it. (As readers thumb, one hand usually holds the publication's spine and at least partially obscures elements at the fold.)

Respect page balance—and both the committed readers and the browsers—by not placing pull quotes at the very top or bottom of the page, where they'd look too heavy. Also, when a pull quote breaks into a paragraph, place it in the middle of the paragraph, rather than leaving just an easily overlooked scrap above or below.

How to design other style sheet elements clearly
Rules (lines) and ruled boxes
Even with an element as skinny as a rule, use no more weights than have meaning, and use them consistently. In any one publication, restraint and consistency might mean a hairline vertical rule between columns, a half-point rule around photos and info boxes, and a

>> A formula for figuring minimum leading between display type lines: Add one-third of the size of the type on top to two-thirds of the size of the line beneath it. But the formula's only a starting point. According to that formula, a two-line headline would be best set solid—1/3 + 2/3 of its size equals the point size, so, for example, a two-line 48-point headline would have 48-point leading—and that's too loose. The leading for the same headline followed by a 24-point secondary head would be 32, also too loose. Formula's a good start for those who like formulas, but it's too conservative, so tighten beyond its prescription.

2-point horizontal rule to set off pull quotes. Especially avoid inconsistent or fancy box frames that call attention away from their contents.

With rules, go lighter than heavier. There's a fine line (so to speak) between showing enough difference between weights that it's obvious and varying so much that the heavier weight gets horsy. And use finer lines for low-resolution printing or Web sites than for high-resolution, because low-res bulks up everything.

Page numbers

Put them where readers are likely to look for them, probably at the outside lower corners. Make them visible (text size and weight), but not so big that they distract from the content readers used them to find.

Recurring features

When you have elements that recur in a project, make sure they're placed consistently, and record that placement in the design style sheet.

❯❯ Method to their madness? Ads designed by shoehorn

Earlier in the chapter, you saw an ad that used fuzzy type to send a clear message. Now let's look at less clear-cut exceptions to the legible-type rule (and see whether they're really exempt). These include crammed grocery ads that endure in violation of legibility principles. (Caution: *Don't try this at home or at work.* Use these examples as makeover exercises, not as models.)

The ads endure, their sponsors might tell you, because they uphold at least two important principles of another sort: They meet customers' expectations, and they reflect the company image.

For example, Snider's Supermarket in Silver Spring, Maryland, has run a weekly ad in the *Washington Post* for about thirty years. More recently, the store has added a smaller ad in the Sunday paper.

The smaller ad (3⅞ by 5 inches) contains more than sixty products. Product and price type always run in the typeface named Kabel, but that's pretty much where consistency ends. The type gets bigger or smaller, more condensed or more expanded to fit each product's box.

Category groups, such as they are, show another shot at order:

- Most meats and seafood are on the upper left.

- Most fruits and vegetables are to the right.

- Most refrigerated dairy and bakery products are in the middle, set off by lines that are thicker than anywhere else.

- Frozen, canned, and other items are on the bottom, flanked by titled, boxed items that look pasted on by hand.

But groups contain mismatches, which is easy to do because the categories are seldom labeled.

Supermarket ads such as this one, and the one on the next page, look like an information seeker's (and designer's) nightmare. You're seeing the smaller one at the same size it runs in the newspaper. *Exercise:* Before you read about them, see how you can incorporate information design principles to improve it. *Client: Sniders Supermarket. Typesetter: Gordon Hoeft,* Washington Post.

Client: Sniders Supermarket. Typesetter: Allen Coté, Washington Post.

most meats and seafood   most fruits and vegetables

most refrigerated, dairy and baked products

titled, boxed items   frozen, canned, and random grocery items   titled, boxed items

A category "site map" for the busy ad might look like this.

Also chaotic are the reversed boxes scattered everywhere but in the bottom section. The contrast breaks up the copy for navigating, says Gordon Hoeft of the Creative Production Department at the *Washington Post,* who typesets the Sunday ads (and says they used to be even smaller). But it means that new viewers of the ad, at least, will search in vain for meaning. Or maybe the chaos will keep them from searching at all.

Tilted and other unaligned boxes stomp on the information-design principle that calls for lining up every element with something else to help the eye move through information.

Although the ads' direct results are as hard to track as the type ("3-point is the minimum," says Allen Coté, builder of the bigger ad), supermarket co-owner Jerry Snider says he gauges an ad's success by the "movement" of advertised products. And he sees marked-up, torn-out ads in shoppers' hands. Does that mean that customers like the ads? Plenty don't; Snider cites "numerous complaints" such as

"can't read it." But, he says, complainers still show up to shop: "I tell them it must be right, you're here." Once they're in the store, shoppers can see the ad blown up onto letter-size posters displayed throughout the store.

But Bill Simmons, manager of the *Post* production department, says, "We've approached the client about cleaning up the ads . . . with more white space and focus on each product." He says the client declined on the grounds that customers are used to the ads. Forget white space. "Mr. Snider wants everything filled up. You jam-pack it, and you stretch and fill up the space," Coté says.

Snider says the ads look like the store itself. It's "jam-packed, hard to get around, and people complain about that too." Coté agrees: "The aisles are small, like mom-and-pop stores from fifty years ago. You can find everything as long as you don't trip over the boxes in the aisles." Hoeft says the ads work because they're "like a treasure hunt . . . You never know what you're going to find."

That's also the philosophy behind some print catalogs: Scattered products encourage meandering and picking up impulse items on the way to a consumer's goal. Online shoppers, though, demand the grouping they've come to expect on the Web.

What's more, Snider says, the ad's thrown-together look also is meant to convey timeliness and flexibility. The ads are put together just days before they run, so they contain what's actually available, not what the grocers hope will be. (That's similar to the thinking that kept so many subscription newsletters looking typewritten long after desktop computers made the look obsolete. Courier type across the full width suggested hot news typed on the kitchen table, with no production time coming between the sender and the reader.)

Needs research

Formal research among local grocery shoppers would show whether a legible ad—and a more organized store—would attract new customers

The packed ads reflect the store's packed aisles, shelves, even floors and ceilings. (Note the taped-up, blown-up ads.)
Photographer: Ronnie Lipton.

or cause existing customers to spend more. It also would show whether the current ads and floor plan are success-ful (maybe because they suggest low prices, along with the old-fashioned charm and personal service of a long-standing independent store).

The ads seem to argue for the latter, based on less formal research: talking to customers, and traditional wisdom, which Snider boils down in these words: "The best criteria are price and quality. They'll beat a path to your door if you offer value." (An unannounced visit to the store on an average weekday afternoon found a full parking lot and a partly filled overflow lot, if not a beaten path.)

A different, spacious approach
You'll find more white space and emphasis on each product in ads for another food store (which adver-

The store's charm and commitment to service show up in this sign at the store's exit.

Wisconsin Ave. (Rx) • White Flint Plaza • Randolph Rd.   GOOD THRU 7/05/05
Free Parking at All Stores

www.rodmans.com

Rodman*'s ™

50 YEARS OF VALUE AND SERVICE
1955 2005

*DISCOUNT GOURMET (AND OTHER GOOD STUFF)   NOT RESPONSIBLE FOR TYPOGRAPHICAL ERRORS

The 'Ove' Glove
CHAR THE FOOD, NOT THE FINGERS

AS SEEN ON TV

$14.99

Kevlar & Nomex Glove,
As Recommended in
the *Washington Post,*
"Food 101"

COKE 12 PACK
Assorted
Varieties
12oz Cans
2/$5.00

Coca-Cola CLASSIC

Desert Pepper
Salsa
16oz
$2.99
Assorted
Types

Tribe of Two Sheiks
Hummus 8oz
5/$5.00   Assorted
Flavors

CLASSIC HUMMUS

Dirty Potato Chips
Assorted
Flavors
5.5oz
2/$3.00

Haagen Dazs
Ice Creams
Pints
$2.29

Haagen-Dazs

THE CELLAR
PRICES DC STORE ONLY

SEE THU. MONTGOMERY WKLY FOR MD. WINE SPECIALS

BLOCKBUSTERS:
Carlo Rossi 4 LITERS $7.49
Concha y Toro 1.5 LITER $5.99
Lurton *Malbec* $7.99
  Pinot Gris..................................$5.99
Beringer *Pinot Grigio* $4.99

AMERICAN WINE SALE:
Pepperwood *Chardonnay, Pinot Noir,*
  Merlot, Syrah..............................$4.99
Cline "California" *Viognier,*
  Zinfandel....................................$7.99
Columbia Crest "Grand Estates"
  Chardonnay, Cabernet, Merlot......$7.99
Estancia *Chardonnay* $7.99
  Cabernet.....................................$9.99
Ferrari Carano *Fumé Blanc*...........$10.99
Barnard-Griffin *Fumé Blanc*...........$7.99
  Chardonnay.................................$8.99
  Cabernet...................................$12.99
  Syrah..$12.99
  Merlot.......................................$12.99

FRENCH WINE SALE:
La Vieille Ferme *Red, White, Rosé*..$4.99
Paul Jaboulet *Cotes du Rhone*
  "Parallele 45".............................$6.99
Louis Jadot *Beaujolais Villages* $6.99
  Macon Villages............................$7.99

ITALIAN WINES ON SALE:
Mezza Corona *Pinot Grigio, Merlot* ...$5.99
Antinori *Santa Cristina, Orvieto*.......$6.99
Michele Chiarlo *Barbera D'Asti*.........$7.99

ALL WINES 750ML UNLESS NOTED

German Specialties From Hengstenberg

KNAX

"Knax" Pickles XL 57.7oz....$2.99
Mixed Pickles 12.5oz............$2.69
Sweet Red Peppers 12.5oz ..$2.19
Carrot Salad 12.5oz..............$1.99
Celery Salad 12.5oz..............$1.99
Silverskin Onions 12.5oz......$1.99
Wine Vinegars Red,
  White w/ herbs 25oz $1.99
Mustards Hot, Med.,
  Sweet 7.1oz $1.99
Bavarian Wine
  Sauerkraut 24oz $1.69
Red Cabbage
  w/ Apple 24oz $1.69
Sliced Red Beets 12.5oz......$1.49

PRODUCE   NOT AVAILABLE AT WHITE FLINT

TOMATOES		CHERRIES...................$2.79 LB
"ON THE VINE"...........$1.29 LB		GREEN/ WHITE GRAPES
MACINTOSH APPLES.....69¢ LB		(Seedless) ....$1.39 LB
PINEAPPLES (Sweet)...$2.99 EA		TOMATOES Eastern........99¢ LB
NECTARINES................89¢ LB		RED APPLES...............69¢ LB
PEACHES.....................89¢ LB		WHITE CORN ....3/99¢
RED GRAPES (Seedless).$1.39 LB		CANTALOUPES- Eastern..$1.79 EA

• 5100 Wisconsin Ave., NW (2 blocks south from Friendship Heights Metro Station) Phone: 202.363.3466
• White Flint Plaza, Rockville MD (next to Petsmart) Phone: 301.881.6253
• 4301 Randolph Rd. Wheaton, MD (at Veirs Mill Rd.) Phone: 301.946.3100

Another grocery store's newspaper ads feature more space, more order, and photos.
Client: Rodman's. Designer: Tony Julien.

tises in the same newspaper section as Snider's). Rodman's typical ad shows a dozen produce items and two dozen wines grouped in two headlined boxes. It also features another dozen or so items, each boxed individually with a photo.

The individual treatment does more than call attention to each product; it's also a requirement for getting co-op money from the product manufacturer, says Rodman's Steve Schattman.

The ad looks like three or four different ads in one, so a redesign might connect them more effectively by using the same typefaces, headline color, borders, and alignment.

Nope, says Schattman—the ad works as it is. He knows this because he gets a separate sales report on every advertised product. And, like Snider, he cites observational research—seeing the ad in shoppers' hands.

Another metric came to Schattman's attention by accident two years ago when the merchant advertised a line of crab soups. An unfortunate typographical error in the product's first word (yeah, *that* typo) drew "a hundred calls to the office. So somebody's reading it," he says. He also saw a sales hike when the store began running the ads, a switch from only direct mail. (But, he adds, it's hard to attribute the hike just to the new medium, because it also coincided with the store's remodeling.)

The wine section is text-heavy and might be viewed separately from the rest of the ad, as a wine shop within the store would be. That's another case of an ad reflecting a store's layout. But in the hierarchy of the ad, the wine section is less important even though the products are more expensive, says Tony Julien,

the freelance graphic artist who does the ads. It's at the bottom because most people read top left (where the most important item is prominently displayed) to bottom right.

The layout changes a bit from week to week. "I don't want it to be so regimented," says Julien. "I believe in having order and then breaking the order—start off with a structure, then veer off." You can see his philosophy in the way photos emerge from their boxes' boundaries, which adds dimension and emphasis. But never let "veering" sacrifice understanding and meaning. Julien justifies different corner treatments because using all rounded corners would look monotonous. But different corners also call attention to themselves instead of the products within them.

EXERCISE: Compare, contrast, and analyze ads from three different grocery stores in your local newspaper. Redesign one to comply with information-design principles.

CHAPTER 4

How to write clearly

Useful, clear information design begins with the content, and content often means words. The first rule of comprehensible words is clear, concise writing that speaks to the readers' needs, understanding level, and preferences.

In case you think content and writing aren't your problem, please consider this: The practice of information design doesn't let you off the words hook. Think of writing as essential cross-training, because the most valuable information designers develop is skills in both writing and visual design. At the very least, they understand how words, pictures, and design interact with one another.

What's more, these valuable designers work effectively with writers because they have mutual respect for the others' contributions. They see the content as the core of the information-design project, not just as something to pour into their layout. They *read* the content, because they know that's the best—and usually only—way to know how to present it effectively. They develop the confidence to speak up when something's unclear. They recognize good writing, and they aren't afraid to suggest a headline. And the rarest but most valuable designers even write well.

Beyond reading the content in your projects, also read the guidelines in this chapter and in books and Web sites about clear writing. Consider attending technical or editorial writing courses or workshops. And rate the clarity of the writing you encounter every day—in manuals, articles, memos, for example. Then think about how to improve it.

How to write information for your audience

Clear, useful writing begins with knowing the subject at hand, then conveying what's essential about it to the audience. The writing must answer readers' questions clearly, concisely, and in the order readers are likely to have them. So, like good design, clear writing also involves listening to and observing your audience members.

For example, find out what your audience members already know and what they need to know. Such research will help you deliver just the information they need and can understand—and you'll avoid drowning them in everything you've got. Consider your own experience as an audience member. Let's say you've already picked out a computer you want to buy; now you just want to compare prices and guarantees. But the company forces you to plow through a ton of information to find what you need to know, which takes up a lot more time than you wanted to spend.

In this case, clear content probably means almost no writing—just headings, and maybe a price-comparison table. It doesn't mean having to learn about the company, or about the history of computers, or even about the service plan. Make that other information available for people who want it, but keep it from getting in the way of what most people tend to want first or most.

Also find out your audience members' preferred language because of course you can't even begin to connect with your audience members if you don't speak their language. In some cases, that also might mean speaking more than one language within the same project. Some publications accomplish that feat by assigning alternate paragraphs to each language; others assign facing pages.

Still other publications, such as the one in English and French on the facing page, switch languages seamlessly by printing the whole message in one language, then in the other. It avoids favoring either language or cluttering readers' path, because each language comes "first" with its own "front cover." All readers must do to find their preference is flip the book to the other end and upside down. (Readers won't even need to turn the book upside down if one of the languages runs right to left, such as Arabic.)

Listening to your audience might also include finding out their comfort level with professional jargon ("inside" or technical words that are used by a particular group or industry). Guidelines for clear writing often advise against using jargon, but if a professional audience expects it, that's a guideline to ignore. (In fact, ignore or modify *any* guideline that doesn't work for your particular audience or situation.)

But the guideline would've helped in the case of a particular software company. A previous version of its Web site stopped potential

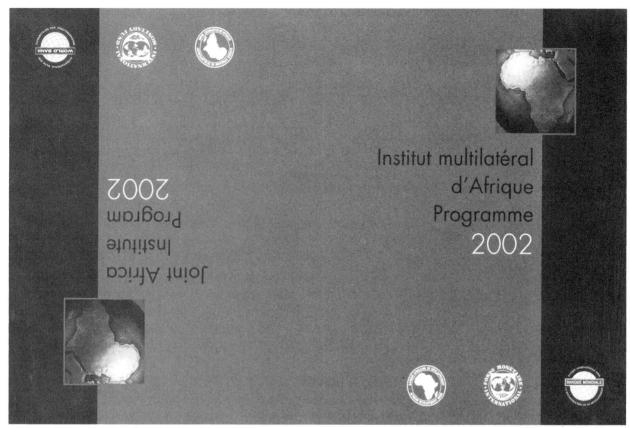

A bilingual publication, shown here with interchangeable front and back covers, serves two audiences without favoring either. Readers have only to flip the book to see the other language. *Reprinted by permission of the International Monetary Fund.*

buyers at the door by asking them to identify themselves as belonging to one of three listed categories, including "enterprise user." Presumably, consumers who are in that category know it, but given the potential overlaps of the two other categories ("home office" and "small business"), other consumers might have wondered whether it applies to them. There was no easy way to find out. But the term is so familiar to the company's employees, they don't see it as jargon.

How do you know what terms audience members use and know? *Ask* them. If you've got a Web site, you can also track the audience's search terms.

How to write information for most audiences

So when you write, combine what you know about your audience with what you know about almost any audience. In writing information, rather than novels or short stories, assume almost all audiences want clarity. That's where these general guidelines for clear writing come in.* Keep them in mind when you read, write, and design.

Favor the active voice

Make the sentence's subject the actor; make it act on the verb. In most cases, also put the stated or implied subject at or near the beginning of the sentence. In the guideline, which is itself in the active voice, the subject is the implied "you" at the beginning: "[You] favor the active voice."

By contrast, the passive-voice version of the same guideline—"The active voice is to be favored"—is indirect and unclear. It takes the emphasis away from the actor; in this case, the passive voice fails to specify *who* should favor it. And it relies on a weak form of the verb.

Use of the passive voice *has been defended* in certain cases, such as when the writer doesn't know who the actor is, when the audience doesn't need or want to know, or when there are too many actors to name (as in this sentence). And organizations tend to use passive voice when they don't want to name themselves as the actor (not that they're fooling anyone): "An additional 125 employees will have to be let go."

A more acceptable reason for the occasional use of passive voice is to focus on the acted-upon or the action, not the actor, as here: "In the study, 2,000 students were injected with the flu vaccine." That construction calls attention to the number and type of test participants. The active form, on the other hand—"In the study, the nursing team injected 2,000 students with the flu vaccine"—calls attention to the injectors.

And always eliminate the newsletter perennial "A good time was had by all." Translate it to active voice this way: "Everyone had a good time."

Show the story, don't just tell it

Better still, make your writing more informative by *describing* the event and letting the readers decide whether it was good. Paint a clear picture

---

* Many of these guidelines are adapted from *Guidelines for Document Designers*, a publication from the Document Design Center. (Why is that sentence in the passive voice? I adapted them, but I hope you infer the "I" throughout the book, except for anything I've attributed to someone else. Explicit references to the author are distracting, as in this case, especially when they begin the sentence.) For more writing wisdom, go to the classic *The Elements of Style* by Strunk, White, and (in later editions) Angell, or to a book on writing for the Web. The more books you look at, the more variation—and often disagreement—you'll find among the writers. Let what's clear to your audience be your ultimate authority.

for readers who couldn't attend, acting as their eyes and ears. To do so, be objective, give details, and maybe add quotes from people who attended.

Favor short sentences

Make each sentence just long enough to make its point. But to achieve the perfect sentence length, you don't have to count words. Instead, watch for sentences that *look* long, and shorten them or cut them into two sentences. If you're still not sure if a sentence is too long, read it aloud. It's too long if you have to take a breath while you read it. We mentally "speak" what we read silently; what daunts the ear daunts the eye and the mind.

(Reading aloud is also a good test of paragraph rhythm; you'll hear awkward constructions, such as too many too-short sentences, which could sound—and be—choppy.)

How to shorten? One way is to use the active voice, as noted above. A few more guidelines also apply:

- Limit the number of asides you insert into sentences (with parentheses like this, commas, or em dashes), especially those that split subject and verb or verb and object.

- Put series items in a bulleted list like this, rather than in a paragraph.

- Divide long compound sentences at the conjunction, or combine the verbs. Compound sentences are two or more long complete sentences combined with a conjunction, such as *and, but,* or *or*. For example, consider this compound sentence: "Find any series items in the paragraph, and put them into a bulleted list to make them easier to browse and possibly to recall." You can separate the sentences after *paragraph*, but here combining "put" and "find" does a better job because the *find* is implied: "Put any series items in bulleted lists instead of in paragraph form, to make them easier to browse and possibly to recall."

Favor simple sentences

Begin most sentences with a subject, verb, and object (like this one; the subject is the implied "you"). You won't insult your audience's intelligence by writing simple sentences (unless they're all in the "see Spot run" category). Your intelligent but busy audience will appreciate sentences that deliver content quickly and easily rather than getting in the way.

Write complete sentences

Short and simple, yes; incomplete, no. You've just read an example of what to avoid: a sentence fragment that's more than a word or two long. Here's another example in the first three words: "Clear information design. It begins with . . ."

This verbless form has little place in informational writing (unless it's a single word, such as *yes, no,* or *alas*) because it tends to leave readers wondering if they missed something. So leave sentence fragments to advertisers, who love them. (Here's the irritating—yet admittedly memorable—tagline of a whole-grain bread brand from years past: "It's not hard. To taste great.")

Favor short paragraphs

If you follow some standard definitions of a paragraph (a complete thought or five-to-seven sentences), you'll produce rambling paragraphs. Instead subdivide it at a logical break so that it extends no longer than an inch and a half or two inches. If that length permits only one sentence, consider shortening the sentence. You also might need to rethink your overall typeface, point size, or column width.

Favor short words

Avoid *indicating* when you can *show* or *point out*; *procuring, obtain,* or *receive* when you can *get*; and *informing* or *notifying* when you can simply *tell*. Every extra syllable and stodgy-sounding word can delay or even interrupt your message's delivery.

Instead of:	Use:
require assistance	*need help*
request	*ask*
provide or *offer*	*give*
regardless of	*no matter what*
necessary	*needed*
allows to or *permits to*	*lets*
the majority	*most* (or often better yet, give the actual number)

Use precise words

How much is *much*? How big is *big*? And how old is *old*? Journalists learn to avoid using relative adjectives, because (being relative) the words mean different things to different people based on their frame

›› Pros and cons of readability formulas

The guidelines in this chapter favor short words, sentences, and paragraphs to help your audience absorb and comprehend information. That's also the operating premise of most of the 200+ available readability formulas. Such formulas include the SMOG (Simple Measure of Gobbledegook) Formula, the Fry Readability Graph, the Gunning FOG Test, the Flesch-Kincaid Formula (available in Microsoft Word), and Forcast (which applies to forms and other materials that don't require sustained reading). Other formulas, including Dale-Chall, Spache, and Powers-Sumner-Kearl, specialize in elementary- or secondary-school textbooks.

The formulas typically measure a writing sample to determine how many years of schooling the reader needs to understand it. Their accompanying guideline often is to write instructional or business reading materials at a lower grade level than the audience can handle. A seventh- or eighth-grade reading level often is considered ideal, even for an audience that's highly educated. To write at that general level, limit words with three or more syllables, sentences with thirty or more words, and paragraphs with more than three sentences (such as this one).

You might run some of your writing through one of the formulas occasionally if you need a reminder to control length, if you want to objectively compare two samples, or if you simply find comfort in numbers.

The trouble with formulas
Using formulas doesn't mean your work is finished, or necessarily even started, because:

- short is no guarantee of clear. Take the word *rue*. With only one syllable, it's a darling of most of the formulas, but more readers understand its longer synonyms (*regret, mourn*) than the word itself.

- few of the formulas measure more than length. But at least one does: the Clear Language and Design Reading Effectiveness Tool from the Toronto East End Literacy Project also addresses less quantifiable issues such as tone, structure (subheads), and appearance (space, legibility, alignment, graphics).

- formulas aren't considered highly accurate or consistent. Reading analysts often apply three or more to the same copy and average the results.

- most attempts to quantify or categorize an interactive process such as reading fail to consider variables beyond reading level. So combine any such findings with better ones from comprehension testing and interviewing actual audience members. (Uh-oh . . . eight words of three or more syllables in this bullet point.)

You'll find another good adaptation of the SMOG readability formula, but without the tone and design features, at www.med.utah .edu/pated/authors/readability.html. You'll also find more about the relative merits of the formulas in an article by Keith Johnson on his Web site: www.timetabler.com/reading.html.

of reference. For example, people tend to expand their perspective of *young* as they age or *fat* as they expand; consider the newspaper article about four dancers the writer referred to as "middle-aged" even though one of the dancers was twenty-nine. Clarify your meaning with a number (the actual age or the weight) or a comparison to something your audience understands ("the length of two train cars placed end to end"). Or show a clear illustration, diagram, or photo of the object next to something that's understandable to your audience.

Instead of:	Give:
few, fewer	a number or percentage
more	"
less	"
some	"
many	"
most	"
much	"
several	"
small, tiny, minuscule	a size, height, weight, depth, dimension, or comparison to a universally familiar object
light, thin, skinny, scrawny	"
big, large, huge	"
heavy, portly, fat, obese	"
shallow, deep	"
short, tall	"
light, dark	a comparison to a universally familiar object
beautiful, pretty, ugly	"
good, bad, awful	"
average, normal	"
young	an age or age range
middle-aged	"
old, elderly	"

Also make sure you know the precise meaning of the words you use. Often-confused words include:

• *While* (meaning "during the time that") and *although* ("despite the fact that"): "*Although* you had your cell phone with you, I took messages *while* you were out."

More examples. Which of these adjectives would you use to describe this circle: big, medium, or small? Now ask six people, and note their answers and how they differ. Turn the page.

- *Since* ("between then and now") and *because* ("for the reason that"): "You've remained a member *since* 2002 *because* you follow our bylaws."

Use only essential words

Weigh every word for its value to the sentence; kill any words that don't contribute. So avoid redundancies (such as "future" or "advance" plans), and strip wordy sentences to the bone. For example: "~~You want to make sure that you evaluate~~ weigh every ~~single~~ word ~~you write~~ for its ~~intrinsic~~ value to the sentences ~~you write in your projects~~; ~~eliminate~~ kill any words that don't contribute ~~meaning to the sentences~~."

Use clear words

In general, use familiar, simple words except where only more complicated words will do. And avoid technical terms and industry jargon unless your audience expects them.

Sometimes you need jargon to tell your audience members you speak their language. But even in that case, your audience probably also includes newcomers to the industry or the materials. For those readers, define the terms in a glossary. By pulling the definitions out of the text, you help people who need the definitions without forcing people who don't need them to trip over them. In print, put the glossary near the text, on every page the terms appear. On a Web site, link those terms to their meaning.

Use terms consistently

Wherever you refer to a thing, refer to it by the same word. Switching to a different word (maybe for the sake of variety) might cause the reader to wonder whether the meaning changed, too. A case in point is the Washington, D.C., parking ticket. One side instructs recipients, "Write your tag number and the ticket number on your check or money order to ensure proper credit." So if you want to avoid a fine, you'll look on the other, filled-out side for that very "ticket" number. But there you'll find only a "citation" number.

Nor will you find your "tag" number, only a "license" number. But unlike the citation number, at least it's yours. So you probably won't mistake it for the vehicle identification number, which also is on the ticket. Such differences won't challenge people who read English fluently. But not every driver is fluent, especially in Washington, which boasts one of the most diverse populations in the United States.

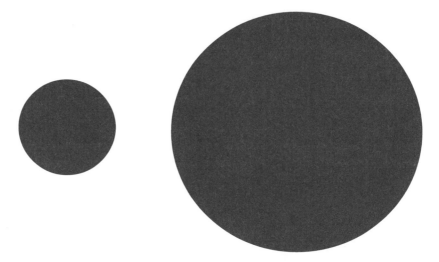

Now which adjective would you use to describe the same circle?

Of course the answer's relative. The response differs according to each person's mental picture of the word, as well as the shape's context.

The moral of the story is at least twofold: Use terms all audience members are likely to use, expect, and understand, and use them consistently.

Use the same construction for the same kind of info

Known as parallel construction, this guideline applies to situations such as items in a series. Present each item in the same way. So consider a series of bulleted items or subheads (as in this chapter) that each begin with an imperative verb—*use, limit, favor*—and have a direct object. Construction would cease to be parallel if, say, one of them began instead with its gerund form, as in *limiting*.

Favor personal pronouns and use them consistently

Begin to convey the idea that you think of audience as individuals, rather than as a faceless crowd, by calling audience members "you." You might also help to encourage the audience to think of your client in human terms, not a giant depersonalizing megalith, by referring to the organization (when it makes sense to refer to it at all) as "we." Better still, you might refer to the writer as "I" along with the writer's name as signature or byline. You'll often help to establish a sense of accountability by substituting "we" or "I" in articles or letters.

Write compelling headings and captions

Make every heading tell readers why they should read what the heading introduces. Give it a verb and a "what's in it for me?" benefit. And underscore every piece of artwork with a caption that connects the artwork with the corresponding text. These high-profile elements will encourage your audience to read the text.

Keep a positive, courteous tone

Avoid issuing commands in writing to your audience unless it's essential to do so for safety, regulatory, military, or legal reasons. For example, avoid saying "don't" as in "don't do this or that," or telling audience members what they "must" or "must not" do. Especially avoid the authoritarian tone that so many companies use with their employees. To paraphrase the Golden Rule, communicate with others—your members, customers, clients, employees, colleagues, or constituents— as you would want them to communicate with you.

Avoid burying verbs in nouns

Ironically, the term for nouns made from verbs—*nominalization*—is itself a nominalization. (But *nominalize* isn't much of a verb, which is why you don't see "avoid nominalizing" in the heading.) Buried verbs often depend on passive or helping verbs, as in "The *decision* of the boss was to hire her."

Instead, use the verb: "The boss *decided* to hire her" or (depending on the point of the sentence) maybe simplify further to "The boss hired her." You can usually identify verbs masquerading as nouns when you see these endings: *-sion, tion, -al, -ance, -ence, -ment, -ure.*

Avoid long strings of nouns

A sentence such as "The New York design publication budget planning subcommittee meeting came to order on Thursday evening" uses up its noun budget in one sentence. "What noun goes with what?" confused readers might wonder, because the string hides their relationships. Take the nouns apart for readers, as in (depending on the meaning): "The New York subcommittee met on Thursday to plan the budget for the design publications."

Place modifiers where they make sense

Let's define a misplaced modifier by example: "While driving to the vet, Mark's dog jumped out of the car." Such structures change meaning and amuse readers to distraction. In this case, the dog seems to be driving, because she, not Mark, is the subject. So make it clear who's doing what: "While Mark was driving to the vet, his dog jumped out of the car."

Follow other grammar rules (but not out the window)

Go ahead and split infinitives ("to boldly go . . ."). You probably work with or for at least one grammar stickler. But there's no need to sweat the small and ridiculous stuff or engage in great debates about commas and such. You can go along with the editorial stylebook or the sticklers unless their rules sacrifice clarity (what's grammatically correct isn't always what's *clear*).

In general, put punctuation and words where they contribute to clarity, and remain consistent at least within a project. (Unless your audience is made up of writers and editors, they're not likely to recall if you use the serial comma from project to project.)

Use punctuation to support, not interfere

Avoid ending punctuation except question marks (where they're needed) in headings. In particular, avoid exclamation marks everywhere. Content rarely demands the implied excitement or warning that the marks convey. (If you find any in this book, consider whether they belong. If not, do as the book says, not as it does.) In most cases, let the power of the words and the typography do the job.

Put the numbers with the name in phone words

Speaking of words, here's a related idea: If your business or client uses a phone word, such as 1–800-BUY-BOND, to make the phone number more memorable, also include the numbers it corresponds to. Although a well-chosen phone word is easier to recall than a phone number, it's harder to dial because of the design of most phone keypads. There's typically only one large number but three or four smaller-sized capital letters to a key on the phone keypad. Test it yourself by using only the phone word the next time you want to call a business that has one.

(A phone keypad designed for phone words—which would exist if everyone used alphabetical phone addresses—would feature a full-alphabet keyboard, such as a Blackberry's. Or, building on the model of a traditional stationary phone keypad, it might take up more space with three or four smaller alpha keys directly beneath each number key.)

CHAPTER 5

How to use
color meaningfully

Color might be the least understood design element. So many producers of materials that are meant to inform use color just to decorate. That might be enough to get attention for the materials. We notice color; most sighted people, even color-blind ones, can see at least some color. And we tend to like it. So color decoration might cause us to look at something, but it won't fulfill its potential to send its message. What a waste.

Instead, if you can use color for a project, harness its attracting power. Make a color plan to help you nonverbally deliver information about the projects' elements. Because we humans notice patterns, and especially differences within patterns, use color consistently. And break that color pattern only to signal a change in meaning. Color can:

- show differences
- show similarities
- help readers find things
- encourage readers to move through information
- help readers recall information
- emphasize something
- play something down
- convey meanings—inherent, assigned, or both

Color can show differences

A different color for each bar in a graph (or each heading on a Web page or manual) clearly shows that the bars (or headings) represent different categories. And a different color and headline for each brochure in a series clearly shows that the brochures are about different topics. At least those examples are clear as long as the colors look obviously different. Subtleties have little or no place in color choice in information design.

Colors owe their degree of visual differences to factors both stable and shifting. Those factors include:

• the distance between the colors on the color wheel—those that are at least a color or two apart tend to contrast more than direct neighbors (see more about the color wheel in Chapter 1)

• the colors' background and viewing environment (what's within the page and outside of it, plus lighting, etc.)

Color can show similarities

For a graph that uses color as a code, readers can tell by the key (sometimes called a "legend") what the graph bars stand for because the colors repeat next to the explanation. And within a Web site, manual, or other publication, the use of the same color for all the elements within a category show they belong together.

For example, a Web site's menu bar might include these categories: "About us" in blue, "Publications" in red, "Archives" in green. Clicking on "Publications" brings the viewer to a page in which all the subheads and accents also are red. That extended color serves to subtly reinforce the category and distinguish it from others.

To do the job effectively, the color should match exactly everywhere it appears; any obvious variations might cause the reader to wonder whether something has changed. And as in the guideline above, a color works best to connect elements in a category when it most clearly differs from colors used for other categories.

You can even use matching colors to link different kinds of elements, such as photos and type. In a magazine, ad, or brochure with a prominent photo, pick up a color from the photo to repeat near the accompanying text. For viewers who look at artwork first or only, connecting the colors is a subtle, nonverbal way to reinforce the connection between the two and to use the power of the photo to help lead the reader into the text. (See Color Plate 13.)

You can see the same philosophy at work in the Web site for the spread's photographer (www.jillwachter.com). On the home page, a photo against earth-tone horizontal bars dominates white labels that link to eight categories of photos. (See Color Plate 14.) Mouse over one name and the others fall away, obscured by a solid band of each file's signature color (usually the dominant color of that file's photos). (See Color Plate 15.) The technique's a simple and effective way to tie interest in a photo to what it accompanies: text, or in this case the Web site and the other photos.

Color can help readers find things

Extended use of a color also tells readers they're in the right place. For example, match the color of a chapter title in the table of contents to the title's appearance in the chapter to speed readers to their chosen chapter. Repeating the title's color on the chapter pages' edges reinforces that destination; the color shows up even on a closed book to direct readers' eyes and fingers.

Color can encourage readers to move through information

Use the same color for the same kind of information in a project to help lead readers through the information. Such color use creates a visual rhythm that readers can recognize and follow, and that helps to unify project parts. For example, you might use one color for the horizontal bar at the top of every page, category headings, thin lines between columns, bullets, and marks that end an article. Consistent color also gives clues about the kind of information, distinguishing, say, a category heading from a headline in another color.

Color can emphasize something

Bright colors do tend to emphasize best, but only when used sparingly and not drowned out by even brighter ones or the background. You'll interfere with emphasis if you use too much of one color or too many colors the way you will if you use too much bold, all-cap, or italic type. The same caveats apply to the emphasizing power of warm colors (red, orange, yellow). Those colors seem to advance toward the viewer, but only as effectively as they contrast with and dominate the background.

The amount of contrast depends on the colors, the environment in which the colors are viewed (for example, the lighting, production quality, medium, and competing images and colors), and the viewer's ability to perceive color. Picture the powerful effect of a photo that's all black-and-white except for the model's red lips. The emphasized element provides a strong nonverbal clue to the message.

Even all black-and-white or other monotonal schemes can draw attention away from colorful neighbors, such as in a magazine article, poster, ad, or especially a Web site. Color's free on the Web, so Web designers tend to overdo it. A black-and-white site can refresh weary Web travelers. Yet it also lacks the value of color as a tool to organize info.

But don't expect hues to show magnitude, says information designer Richard Saul Wurman: "Green is not more or less than red; blue is not more or less than purple." To show magnitude, use degrees of hue, or intensity: "Dark blue is more than light blue; dark purple is more than light purple. And lighter blue can be colder . . . or a higher magnitude of cold than dark blue. Once you set up a pattern of light-to-dark color, you can show magnitude. But color itself has nothing that says cars are green and bigger cars are another color." (Showing more of something and using a bigger image are other ways to visually communicate an increase in magnitude, he says.)

But a strong color such as red when it's used with weaker colors or black can *emphasize* something; it suggests a magnitude of importance, Paul Mijksenaar says. He describes a form on which red emphasizes the items people must fill out, compared with the rest of the information that prints in black. But, he adds, you'll lose the power of red by placing it among other bright colors.

Color can help readers recall information

Readers must notice elements before they can recall them. So color that calls viewers' attention to them also encourages recall . . . *if* you limit the number of colors. We become familiar with a color that's used consistently, especially when it's appropriate. Consider what pink would do to the authority of the stop sign—an example that Spiekermann and Ginger use in their book *Stop Stealing Sheep*. The powerful red contributes a lot to the sign's impact; it would even if you could separate the color from its (inseparable) association with the shape and the word. And even a strong blue would carry less authority.

Color can play something down

Dark cool colors (blue, green, purple, blue-gray, and the non-color black) seem to recede into the background. So to keep from fighting nature, consider *using* them for the background.

But here again, color effects are relative. For example, when the background is white, it's usually better to put text in a dark high-contrast cool color than in a warm color. So darkening text isn't playing it down so much as giving it equally legible treatment.

Color can convey meaning

Choose colors that acknowledge any obvious meanings where not doing so would mix your message. For example, Color Plate 16 shows *inherent* meanings. Green logically represents replanted forests, and red represents fire-damaged land.

But when colors fight nature, as in Color Plate 17, something probably will look wrong even to readers who can't explain what it is.

Another example of inherent color is the use of red for hot-water taps and blue for cold. That's a natural choice because of the association of red with fire and the warm part of the spectrum and blue with ice and the cooler part. The fact that the red used to label taps tends to be stronger than the blue doesn't mean that the hot-water tap is more important than the cold-water tap, just different, Mijksenaar says. But the added strength might help to convey the greater risk of hot water over cold.

You can see *assigned* color meanings in the map that divided the United States into blue (Democrat) and red (Republican) states. You also can see assigned meaning in most of the colors that help to distinguish restaurants from shops, hotels, and parks in Wurman's early Access city guides. Only the use of green for parks adds inherent meaning. Readers who notice that meaning will find it easy to link that color to its category without memorizing the code.

Language also figures into assigned meanings, as you see in expressions such as "in the red," which means "having a deficit." So designers of materials for financial services traditionally have steered clear of the pure color. But when mixed with enough reliable blue, red turns into a fiscally acceptable burgundy. On the other hand, although "in the black" means "solvent," black's rarely chosen for those materials (except when budget demands it), probably because of its more common association (in Western nations) to mourning and loss.

More about culture: Test to avoid negative associations of various colors in the cultures for which you're designing, then test again. An international bank designed a newspaper ad around cultural response to color as part of a campaign to show how well the bank understands its local community: "In Korea red is an unlucky colour," the 48-point, full-width headline reads (in black). So the bank's logo and the ad's notched border ran in blue instead of its typical red (in modern defiance of the traditional ban on red for banks, mentioned in the paragraph above). (See Color Plate 18.)

Actually, red is considered unlucky in Korea primarily for names of living people (or entities), and the bank's name prints in black. It's also considered unlucky for personal letters (which are like ads, the advertiser might argue). But red is considered so lucky in other contexts that it's in the Korean flag and the national costume, according to media specialist Sammy Kim and her colleagues in the Korean Embassy's cultural office in Washington, D.C.

Such potential missteps are easy: Most colors have multiple, sometimes contradictory meanings, and those meanings can vary by the viewer's culture, sensitivity, and awareness level. For example, in addition to growth, green's psychological associations include the environment, the traffic light that signals "go," money, and jealousy. So psychological associations "matter less than where you use the color, how you use it in relation to the meaning of the information, how much of it you use, and its noticeability (i.e., darkness/lightness contrast)," according to *Color for Impact* by Jan V. White.

EXERCISE: Discuss (on paper or in a group) what each of these colors reminds you of: red, orange, yellow, green, blue, violet, brown, tan, gray, black, white. What are the emotions, other traits (positive, negative, and contradictory), and even phrases you associate with each?

EXERCISE: Find at least three other examples of inherent color meanings and three other examples of assigned meanings.

How to treat that first or second color

More colors don't necessarily translate to more clarity in information design projects. Plenty of projects say everything they need to say by using just black ink or black with one high-contrast color. But although projects can live without color, few projects of any description can live without contrast. Elements such as bold type, screens, and line art help to balance visual tone.

To use color articulately, start planning your projects in black-and-white, adding only as many colors as the message demands. A corollary to the "don't decorate" rule: Limit the number of colors to those that mean something, while resisting the temptation to "paint" pages because it's fun. And when the message does demand color, one emphatic color added to black often is enough to do the job.

Take care in choosing that second color. A strong red often works if it contrasts well against the background—as it does on a white page or screen.* Use red's eye-attracting properties for accent elements—such as arrows, bullets, checkmarks—near black type, but not for text. Higher-contrast black against white works better than any text color.

Dark tones—of blue, green, brown—come close to black for legible text but don't match it. Although they contrast pretty well against white, they look so similar to black that they fail to draw the eye. What does draw the eye is a dynamic, bright color that's different enough from black that it registers as different, such as teal, green, cranberry or blue. (Dark tones can be useful as black alternatives in one-color printing, though, because they add color, especially in screens.)

But here's the trade-off: Although bright color calls attention to itself, it's usually not the right choice for type, and never the right choice for text type, because it gives less contrast against a white back-ground than black or even dark tones. Compensate for that reduced contrast in display type by darkening the color, simplifying the type, or increasing the type size. Similarly, if you use color to emphasize some type within a section of black type, you'll probably need to enlarge the color type to make it look as big as what surrounds it.

EXERCISE: This very second-color dilemma came up in the design of this book. Because of its limited number of four-color pages and art examples that communicate best in a strong—bright—second color, the first choice was red. But the design includes screened boxes, and many reds screen to (undesirable) pinks. A red on the orange side would work better, went the discussion, or maybe a bright green. But a color that's bright enough to work for the accent won't hold enough contrast against white paper for legibility. You're looking at a compromise. Analyze the second color's benefits and drawbacks. Which color would you choose?

In any case, avoid most yellows against white for type, because they're almost invisible. A cookbook's creators learned the disappearing-yellow lesson the hard way—the color made every recipe title nearly

---

* . . . and if the viewer can see the contrast: Most color-blind people—about 1 in 12 men and 1 in 200 women—see red (and green) as brown.

disappear. But yellow worked as a clue in a *Washington Post* article about the cookbook's color blunder. The article's secondary headline reads, "*The Gourmet Cookbook* weighs 5½ pounds, has 1,200 recipes, cost millions to produce and took 3 years to compile. There's just one problem." Art director and designer Kathy Legg told the story nonverbally by putting the word *problem* in yellow.

Color hazards also can challenge newsletters whose design style sheets call for a different second color for every issue without imposing some limitations. For example, a semimonthly 12-page government newsletter accidentally sacrificed its headlines to yellow ink. And a monthly newsletter for a technical lab eventually painted itself into a corner with *pink* as one issue's second color. Limiting the second ink to high-contrast (and *professional*) colors and limiting the number of issues before second colors could repeat would've prevented both unfortunate cases.

Another way to prevent the problem is to avoid changing the second color in every issue and just stick with one that works. But a changed second color helps readers distinguish between issues. That's useful for publications that have a high frequency (at least weekly) or that readers tend to keep beyond the following issue's arrival.

Good color codes go beyond color

Other projects' messages need a bigger color vocabulary or code, a system of colors that represent categories in a project (for example, in the airport, red for Terminal A, green for Terminal B, and so on). Understandable color codes give readers nonverbal clues for quick entry into the content's meaning. They might even feel a welcome sense of insider connection with the content providers.

Let's look at how a poster/brochure milks color as an informative code. The piece looks like a map, folds like a map, and depicts a geographic area like a map (see Color Plates 19 and 20). But unlike a map, it doesn't show how to get from here to there; it never intended to. Instead, it shows the density and variety of UCLA's contributions to Los Angeles County. In doing so, it also replaces "thick reports that no one wants to read," creative director Gregory Thomas says.

A visual code assigns a different color and geometric shape to each of six project categories. For example, purple triangles represent "Business & Economic Development Projects" scattered around the county; gold diamonds represent "Student Sponsored Projects." The symbols define themselves nonverbally—one symbol in each category "explodes" into an outline of the same shape and color, but about seven times its size—so viewers don't need the tiny legend in the lower right-hand corner to find out what the symbols represent.

Communication doesn't end there. The outline frames a photo of that category in action, such as musicians to illustrate "Arts & Cultural Projects." A caption labels each photo with the name of the project category and the number of projects—and icons—in the county and on the "map." And a screened-back spotlight effect connects the exploded views with the icons. The spotlight is a typical design device for linking an exploded view, or detail, to its place in the big picture.

Two of the colored shapes add culturally assigned meaning, which is as memorable to people within the culture as inherent meaning is. Health services get a blue cross, which might remind you of a certain health insurance company if you live in the United States or Canada. And youth education and training programs get a five-sided red icon that resembles a little red schoolhouse.

The colorful icons crowd the map in the location of the projects, with some icons overlapping each other, like so much confetti. The effect shows viewers—even before they read—that the school's doing a lot, in a lot of places. Vibrant and visually arresting colors reinforce both the attraction and the meaning. "We try not to use any element unless it has a very specific meaning," Thomas says.

The color and shape codes carry over to the poster's flip side. This lists projects' names and contact info under their appropriate headings. Each heading (and project name) prints in its iconic color next to its coordinating colored icon.

One element's meaning doesn't come across without verbal aid: the dotty graphic "halos" around the geometric pictures. They're meant to enhance the shapes and reinforce the idea of data dissemination, Thomas explained. But that meaning isn't obvious, and they add clutter and distract a little.

What's more, the halos attach to and downplay the icons they surround, the way a low-res screen blurs the type printed on it. Of course that's more pronounced when the icon they surround is circular.

Although the dots' drawbacks outweigh their benefits, those benefits are still worth noting: They reinforce the icons' color, help anchor the icon (not that they especially need anchoring), link the panels, are smaller than the circular icons, and add some visual excitement.

(And a note about the need for consistent terminology: On one side of the sheet, the categories are called "programs"; on the other, they're called "projects." If there's a reason for the dual terms, it's not clear to audience members, who—if they notice—might wonder about the difference.)

Other color-code guidelines
Use fewer colors to make them more memorable

Although color can help your readers to recall information, don't expect them to remember a code of more than three or four colors (or more than four of *anything* for that matter). "If you need more than four colors, you'll simply defeat the reader," Burkey Belser says. "Let's say you take a dictionary and you put the *a*'s in red and the *b*'s in green, up to twenty-six different colors. The only thing you'll accomplish with that is make it more colorful."

Baja Fresh, a fast-food restaurant, uses only three colors in its coding to track each order's progress and speed. The restaurant color-codes pending food orders on a computer screen that's visible to the cooks. The screen shows all undelivered orders as rectangular boxes framed in the thick diagonal black-and-white stripes of warning signs at construction sites. As an order approaches the maximum number of minutes from order-taking to delivery, the box's background color goes from white to yellow to pink.

At many restaurants and cafés, the use of only two colors clearly reminds servers which carafe holds decaf coffee—usually the one with the orange rim, as opposed to the brown-rimmed one for regular coffee. (Some servers also use a design system to remind them which customer takes which kind: The paper coaster under the coffee cup shows the printed side up for regular, down for decaf.)

Color coding can be an effective wayfinding tool, but only if it's easy to use. It isn't at the entrance to Washington Dulles Airport, where drivers pass four signs, one for each terminal. The signs, in two rows of two, give color-coded terminal numbers above a list of as many as eight airlines in each terminal. So passengers who don't know their terminal number (it's not on their tickets) face these daunting tasks: While driving at 40 or 50 miles an hour, they must scan each list quickly enough to find their airline name, then connect it with the terminal color and number above it. The color and number are all they see from then on, no names, so passengers who miss any of the steps are out of luck. Now they must guess (maybe having to drive all the way around and start over). Or they pull into the first terminal they come to and hope the traffic-directing officer will guide them before shooing them off.

Houston International Airport also uses a different color to identify each of its five terminals in signage, and the color code helps,
says a security officer working there. When she directed traffic at the
airport, motorists would ask her which terminal they needed. "I would
say A or B; they would say, 'Which color'? I realized it was easier for
them to see the color than the letter because they were driving." (But
what color can't do is to imply an order, as letters can. Drivers would
expect to come to A before B.)

Again, though, drivers had to ask, so that suggests a need to rethink
at least the presentation of the color code. If they have to find the
right terminal from a list of corresponding airlines, they're better off
with a series of signs, one for each terminal and its contents. And they
need more than one sign for any terminal that includes more than
four or five airlines.

Nameable colors are more memorable

For code colors to be memorable, viewers also "must be able to name
them." So stick with the basic four or five easily named colors, advises
Wayne Hunt in "Basic Principles of Wayfinding," in *Designing and
Planning Environmental Graphics Design.* He refers to colors in wayfinding systems, but the advice applies to other information-design
projects.

Make code colors equally strong

Design systems of colors that have the "same difference": different
hues of equal strength and contrast show that the categories are
different but of equal importance. Varying strengths, on the other
hand, seem to put emphasis on the items with the strongest colors.
Equivalent colors also impart equivalent legibility, especially at a
distance. You can see color parallelism in use in the signage for the
city's downtown area (see Color Plate 21).

. . . but not for the airport terminals (see Color Plate 22), where
colors of different contrast level identify some terminals more powerfully, and at greater distances, than others. Notice which colors look
strongest, which look weakest. And the weakest colors get even weaker
when the sign's farther away, which could pose a problem in an airport.

Build in redundancy for viewers who don't get the code

In his book *Don't Make Me Think,* Web site usability consultant Steve
Krug writes in praise of Amazon.com's color-coded tabs. A different
color distinguishes each category from the rest consistently wherever

it appears. He approves of color coding "as long as you don't count on everyone noticing it."

Krug's observations of users over the years tell him that "as many as half of all users aren't very aware of color coding." In fact, he reconsidered later, even that figure is "probably pretty liberal." Whether people notice color coding has so much to do with "context and implementation . . . that a supposed 'stat' might be comforting, but it certainly wouldn't be useful."

So because you know at least some members of your audience probably won't notice a color code, make it explicit by being redundant. Reinforce the code with labels or graphics. That's the case in the menu bar on United Nations Habitat's Web site (see Color Plates 23 and 24), where color plays only a supporting role. So viewers don't have to memorize a color for it to lead them into the link, reinforce the choice, and distinguish this choice from the last one.

Redundant color coding helps to organize Wurman's book *Understanding Healthcare* into three categories—"Understanding Yourself" (gold), "Understanding Them" (blue), and "Making It Happen" (green) (see Color Plate 25). Effective redundancy starts in the heading that introduces the code in the infographic table of contents: "This book is divided into three color-coded sections," it states in 18-point (gray) type.

Instead of labeling the colors, the heading shows and immediately reinforces the colors in the topic lists. Throughout the book, the colors help identify each section. They're the background for the questions in the top right, and screened behind the "action items" at the bottom of most pages (see figure at right). Because the corner color "bleeds" (extends to the edge of the page), you can see it even when the book is closed. That's when it's most obvious that there's less distinction between the blue and the green (the smallest sections) than the gold (biggest) and the blue. (Also see Color Plate 26.)

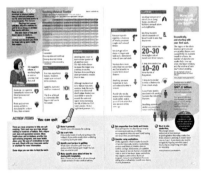

Labeling in *Understanding Healthcare*. Designer: John Sotirakis, Agnew Moyer Smith, Inc. Art director: Richard Saul Wurman. Production designer: Lorea Burnett Appel.

Be redundant even without color

Color budgets aren't a given, so it's a good thing you can do a lot with just black and grays. One thing you can't do with black and grays alone, though, is to show off citrus fruit. The photo in the ad on the facing page, which ran in black-and-white in some newspapers, shows more than one type of fruit. Removing the fruits' labels (just for this book) shows the power of color as well as other distinguishing design elements.

FLORIDA° FRESH CITRUS

BETTER THAN EVER!

Help stifle the sniffles. Vitamin C supports a healthy immune system.

Available at your local grocer now!

www.floridajuice.com

©2004 Florida Department of Citrus

Guess which type of citrus fruit is which in this ad. Color—and labels—would help a lot, but in their absence, which other design elements give you clues to the fruits' identity? The ad ran—with labels we took off to make the point—in black-and-white in some publications, and four-color in others. *Photography: The Food Group for the Florida Department of Citrus.*

EXERCISE: Before you turn the page, notice your first impression and analyze the ad. Also try to identify each fruit. What are the clues? (Turn the page to check your answers.)

EXERCISE: Now show the unlabeled ad to a dozen colleagues to get their reactions. Note the results, identifying the participants by gender, age, culture, and diet (citrus eater or not).

FL☀RIDA FRESH CITRUS

BETTER THAN EVER!

Help stifle the sniffles. Vitamin C supports a healthy immune system.

Grapefruit

Tangerines

Oranges

Available at your local grocer now!

www.floridajuice.com

©2004 Florida Department of Citrus

Check your answers on this actual, labeled ad and see Color Plate 27 for the ad that ran in color. *Photography: The Food Group for the Florida Department of Citrus.*

Confirming the need for labels or color, a few of the participants in my informal test misidentified at least one of the unlabeled fruits despite the information conveyed by size and shape. Labels plus color, as in the color version of the ad, let readers perceive at any level, although no test participant needed the labels on the color version. It's a tribute to the ad that it worked so well in black-and-white, but for pure informative as well as emotional impact, it can't hold a candle to the color version, which went to newspapers with color food sections. (See Color Plate 27.)

(A testing note: Many tests include at least one participant whose responses challenge the test, and this was no exception: One person identified a fruit in the unlabeled mix as a cantaloupe. But it's too easy—and flawed—to discount such findings, or to write off the participant. In fact, the cantaloupe finder is highly intelligent, just perhaps not fully attentive . . . common among busy or distracted audiences. You'll be wise to assume the same of your audiences. Assume it even if your test participants don't demonstrate it. In their desire to please, participants often behave more attentively and cooperatively than they would if they weren't being observed.)

Section III: picture design

How to Design Meaningful Graphics

CHAPTER 6

How to make pictures that inform

Graphics—photos, illustrations, diagrams, maps—add to, replace, reinforce, explain, and illustrate words. Reduced to their simplest, most familiar visual language, lines and curves, they can communicate almost instantly, more quickly than words do. And readers (of printed documents, not necessarily Web sites) often look at them before anything else and use them to decide whether to read adjacent text. But that doesn't mean pictures only have to show up to be effective.

Used to their full potential, graphics help to eliminate any possible wiggle room in the words. When we read descriptive words, we form a picture in our minds, but it's rarely the same mental image as another reader's. It might not even be the same as the writer's. (It's similar to seeing a movie after reading the book, and disagreeing with the casting based on what you had envisioned.) And we had to read first to get any picture.

But with a clear graphic to go with the words, we see the same picture as the writer right away. And we get some meaning even before, or without, reading anything.

Photos in information design must be clear.* They must:

* be in focus
* *have* a focus (give the right amount of detail, not more or less than the reader needs)
* mean something
* show what you're telling
* tell what you're showing (include legible and consistent captions, titles, and labels)
* appear close to where you talk about them
* point readers into the text

---

* Substitute the word *pictures* or *graphics,* and these principles still apply.

Photos must be in focus

Informative pictures are sharp—shot well and produced in high resolution. (That's true unless what's being conveyed *is* the absence of sharpness, as in the difference between one camera's output and another's.) They have contrast that supports the focal point. For example, if the photo is meant to show a remodeled building entrance, it won't inform if the entrance is in shadow, is fuzzy, or blends in with surrounding details.

Photos must have a focus

Don't let the camera or photo frame decide what ends up in a picture. Edit the photo to include no more or less than the reader needs. Charts, diagrams, and illustrations work similarly: Also limit their information so the reader can focus on the important points.

As discussed in Chapter 1, the camera lens picks up everything within its range. So a typical point-and-shoot photo includes too much

Hidden in this photo is an apt illustration for a (hypothetical) story: A town follows (and covers up) the letter, but not the spirit, of required bilingual voting signs. But the busy background competes with the sign that should be the photo's focal point. *Photographer: Ronnie Lipton.*

detail. Viewers can get lost in it, admiring the scenery without a visual clue to show *why* they're admiring it or what they're supposed to notice. Even a well-composed photo can hold distractions for info seekers.

Such sightseeing trips might be desirable for vacation or wedding snapshots, but not for photos that viewers depend on for information. So eliminate the guesswork with a strong focal point and no elements in the foreground or background that compete with it.

If you can, start with a photo that cuts to the chase, one that has what master photographer Henri Cartier-Bresson called "the decisive moment." Like a good sentence, a good photo is "built with a subject, verb, and object," photojournalist (and the author's husband) Jeff Young says. And, Young says, a good photo favors storytelling over clichés. For example, instead of one more shot of a person accepting an award, show what she did to win it.

If you can't take or direct an ideal photo, crop or silhouette* it to keep only what tells the story. And check the remaining background for signs of ambiguity by asking other people what they see in it. (See Color Plates 28 and 29.)

For example, a tight crop or silhouette of a marker between Canada and the United States could illustrate relations between the two countries. (See the photo on the next page.) The editor/designer could make an editorializing political statement by leaving in (and mentioning in the caption) the fence and the shadows on the U.S. side, or even the comparative condition of the foliage.

A crop showing only the shadow of the shooter could tell another story, if only a warning in a photography guide to make sure you're out of the frame when you shoot.

Crop out the background and emphasize the message. *Exercise:* How might you crop the original photo to show the presence of voting places in residential areas? (And what would you crop, no matter what the story, to eliminate a weak area in the composition?)

EXERCISE: Find the story in a photo of your choice, and crop to emphasize the story.

1. Crop with Post-it notes for print photos or a photo-editing program for digital ones.

2. Trace the crop onto tracing paper.

3. Briefly describe the story the cropped photo illustrates.

4. Write a benefit headline for the story the cropped photo illustrates.

5. Find two different crops/stories in the same photo, and repeat the process for each.

---

* *Cropping* is a form of visual editing in which you cut from a photo any elements that distract from the story you want to tell with the photo. *Silhouetting* is a form of visual editing in which you cut the photo subject out of its background and horizontal borders. A variation is a partial silhouette, in which you cut out only the part you want to draw attention to, such as a mortarboard that looks as if it's thrown out of a photo of a cheering graduate.

How many stories—and their corresponding crops—can you see in this simple photo? *Photographer: Jeff Young.*

Photos must mean something

Designers add pictures for many reasons, which unfortunately don't always include reader comprehension. For example, people who write proposals with imposed page limits often try to replace text with as many graphics as they can, because pages with graphics aren't counted in the total. The skewed thinking is that more pages translate to a stronger proposal. But most of the time (and especially to the people who must read all the proposals), puffed-up documents actually seem to hide a lack of good ideas. You're more likely to impress your readers with muscular proposals—clear, meaningful images (along with tightly edited text).

Too much info can plague other forms of infographics as well. In a bar graph, for example, cluttered increments draw attention away from the trends. The nature of a graph, you'll see later in this chapter, is to encapsulate information, not list it all as you would in a table.

Photos must show what you're telling

Words in Western languages all look pretty much the same (just ask someone who can't read one). They're formed by letters that give no clues to their combined meanings. For example, words with *m*'s in them don't form a different category of meaning than those without them. Words come in different widths, but the widths don't relate to meaning.* Pictures, on the other hand, can illustrate meaning in a glance, and they should.

Photos must tell what you're showing

Include captions, labels, and titles that compellingly connect the picture (along with the reader) to the text. A name under a person's photo is better than nothing, but it's not enough. Tell the readers not just who this person is but why they're looking at him.

Consider a photo that goes with a story about a new human-resources manager. The name alone under the mug shot gives readers some information to go with the text. But it's not likely to lead the reader into the text. Neither is adding the person's title. You want a caption you know your readers will care about (because you know your readers), such as "Karen Williams, the new human resources manager, will help approve promotions" (or "pitched a no-hitter at the last company picnic").

Most photos and pictures need captions because they're highly visible. People will look at them, at least in print, so use that attention to get people into the story.† Every diagram needs a title and labels. Make them legible and consistent.

The nonverbal messages—the stair walker next to the gutted escalator—reinforce the verbal message and maybe even make it redundant. Crop here (with Post-it notes) to eliminate useless areas and tighten the focus on the message.

---

* For example, the word *narrow* is wider than the word *wide; short* is longer than *long.* So typographers and designers sometimes manipulate words so they look like their meaning (*w i d e*). Have fun with these kinds of effects, but keep them out of your information designs. They tend to call too much attention to themselves and to writing that didn't do its job. Communicate more clearly—and elegantly—with a picture and words that illustrate what's wide.

† Online pictures get less attention because of the way Web sites traditionally have used them, as background, and the way people have used Web sites, as informational sources. So for informative pictures to take up valuable Web space, they'd better look as informative as they are . . . and even more stripped down. Use a caption, title, or label (or not), depending on how close the photo is to text and whether the audience needs an explanation.

Connecting the dots is tougher than it should be

In the booklet in Color Plate 30, inconsistent labeling is just one of the obstacles in the path between the illustrated diagram and the text. On the illustration of a neuron, clearly numbered labels identify the parts and those numbers show up where the parts do in the text. But in text, the numbers reverse out of gold circles, while on the diagram, the numbers print in black. That might force a reader to hunt to confirm the connection.

The number circles also interrupt the text, forcing readers' eyes to leap over them. To add to the potential confusion, the same text panel includes a second set of the first three numbers representing a different type of information (the three classes of neurons).

And the numbers run out of order in the text. For reading comprehension, it makes more sense to put them in order there, instead of on the diagram. If the numbers are needed, and that's iffy, it would be clearer to use them more like bullets or a glossary instead of putting them in text. Or omit the numbers and maybe add a brief definition with each diagram label.

Another visual element that looks like a color code but isn't: The gold of the circles matches the gold of the neuron, even when the numbers flag a neuron part that's shown in red or blue. The various neuron colors remain consistent throughout the diagrams.

(On the cover, though, the title colors suggest other meanings: Gold is for living neurons, black is for dying ones, and red, as the last line—"of a neuron," seems to have a stronger link to the red support cell of a neuron than to the neuron itself. See Color Plate 31.)

It also would make sense to illustrate the boxed facts that are reversed out of navy blue, as in, "It would take 30,000 neurons just to cover the head of a pin."

Back in the first spread, notice the challenges to legibility and meaning posed by type sections on inconsistent backgrounds. The word *architecture* in the title of the first inside spread straddles white and two colors, seeming to emphasize the part of the word that's higher-contrast black on white.

All the text on a pink background suffers from diminished legibility, compared with panels of text on white. It's even worse when a paragraph runs into and out of the two tones.

Why does a bird lead into the introduction panel? (See Color Plate 32.) It's a fair question, which isn't answered until the third paragraph (research into birds' learning behavior inspired breakthrough research on the human brain). The image seems out of place and not likely to tease readers into reading to uncover its mystery.

As a general rule, include no illustration that "doesn't extend the information in print and no print unless it further explains an illustration," Richard Saul Wurman says. "Pictures have to extend words . . . nothing is just illustrated."

Pictures must show up close to where you talk about them

At a minimum, "close" means on the same spread. Support readers' desire to connect related info by putting it on the same page as its text, and if you can, next to, above, or below it. If you can't put them on the same spread, provide enough info in the caption to satisfy readers where they happen to be, and point to the text's location. (You're right if you noticed this book's design violates the guideline. A limit on four-color pages with plenty of art that demanded four-color printing dictated that art be separated from the text. My apologies.)

Pictures must point readers into text (if they point at all)

Some photos and drawings have an inherent direction. For example, a profile of a person or vehicle in motion favors one side. (See Color Plate 33.) If the picture has a direction, it's like an arrow that can point where you want it. Place directional photos so they point toward the text, not off the page. The eye tends to follow the direction to its natural conclusion.

Two Gestalt grouping principles might apply:

- *Common fate.* People see elements going in the same direction as being related. That suggests enough awareness of a perceived direction to follow it.

- *Good continuation.* People see elements that are arranged in a line as a group, even if the line contains gaps. That suggests they'll mentally fill in the gap between a direction and its object.

To flop or not to flop

If you can't move the photo to take advantage of its natural arrow, maybe you can flop it. (Flopping, as the name suggests, means turning the negative around to make it point in the opposite direction.) Or maybe you can't. Some organizations' strict photo-accuracy policies don't allow flopping. And some photos suffer from a direction change, including military insignia, police badges, buildings, hair parts, wedding rings on hands, or anything with type (unless you lift the type up in a program such as Photoshop and replace it after flopping).

CHAPTER 7

Design, label, and caption diagrams clearly

Of course diagrams can break up text, relieving otherwise uninter-rupted, sometimes daunting text columns. But although useful, the passive ability to take up space is the least of their benefits. Among the myriad active roles they perform, charts, graphs, maps, and process drawings can

- compare numbers
- plot locations
- clarify relationships
- show trends
- quickly and sometimes dramatically answer questions for the reader

When the situation calls for a diagram, a well-designed one communicates more clearly and memorably than text alone can. It communicates on a different level than words do because it *shows,* it doesn't just tell. Good writing creates images in readers' minds; diagrams, like good photos, bring the images into focus. Unlike most photos, diagrams also can bring *numbers* into focus.

A graph is "a shorthand means of presenting information that would take many more words and numbers to describe. A graph is suc-cessful if the pattern, trend, or comparison it presents can be immedi-ately apprehended," according to *Graph Design for the Eye and Mind* by Stephen Kosslyn.

When readers see it before text that describes it, a good diagram might provide an overview that draws them into the text to learn more. When they see the diagram after reading, it can deepen under-standing by (depending on the situation):

- adding depth with the visual perspective
- eliminating wrong impressions
- improving information recognition and recall

Those benefits would be reason enough for you to get familiar with diagrams' various forms. But the least talked-about yet perhaps most valuable role of diagrams in the communication process is this: The process of creating a diagram encourages the creator to intensively analyze the data. In fact, the process almost demands that the creator consider the data more deeply and more from the reader's perspective than might be the case with text alone.*

In fact, the process of planning or redesigning a diagram, approached with full respect for the reader, often sends the conscientious writer back into the text. It can point out content flaws such as the absence of appropriate emphasis or the presence of inappropriate redundancy (for example, where the text should stop and the graphics take over) or fuzzy thinking in general. (In some cases, it might even guard against fuzzy diagrams, which complicate or distort info instead of clarifying it.)

The thinking that leads to a clarifying diagram includes the search for the right kind of diagram. We'll look at the most common variations, which ones work when, and how to make them clear.

Where to begin

Kosslyn's book distinguishes between quantitative and qualitative visual displays. Quantitative displays show measurements and quantities. They include:

- graphs, including pie "graphs" (the term Kosslyn recommends instead of "pie *charts*" because they're quantitative)
- maps, because they imply measured distance between geographical points

Qualitative displays show processes and relationships among people and categories. They include:

- organizational ("org") and flow charts, and family trees
- process diagrams, such as the illustration that identifies the various parts of a piece of equipment in its operations manual

All diagrams share the need to answer a primary question for the reader. The question itself helps determine the right diagram for the

---

* The standard disclaimer applies: *Every* information design project, regardless of its components (text alone or text with graphics), should begin with the deepest level of analysis.

purpose, so begin by identifying the question. For example, looking at the classic example of sales figures by months, you get the main question just by restating the problem: "How do sales for each month compare with sales in other months?"

Text alone would make the answer tough to compare and harder to recall: "In January, sales totaled $112,000; in February, they rose to $130,000; in March, they dropped to $97,000 . . ." As the example shows, the best the text can do is to point out whether each amount is more or less than that of the months before and after it.

Rather than a forced march through the months, text would more logically interact with a comprehensive graphic by reinforcing the high- or lowlights, as in: "September showed the biggest sales income, posting almost 20 percent more than May, its closest neighbor, and almost twice as much as lowest-reporting July."

To fine-tune the kind of diagram and its details, fine-tune the question. Maybe the audience wants to go further, asking the question, "What are the best and worst months?" In that case, a vertical bar graph might answer best by calling quick attention to the extremes in bar heights. If the difference between the tallest and the next tallest bars isn't pronounced enough to be obvious but is important to convey, an element such as a different, stronger color would help emphasize it.

Why vertical rather than horizontal bars? As a convention and in general, quantity tends to be on the vertical (y) axis of an L-shaped graph, and time on the horizontal (x) axis. People associate height with quantity, and width (reading from left to right for a Western audience) with time.

Why not a line graph, with plotted points on the graph connected by a line? A line graph answers a different question: "What is the sales trend over twelve months?" The bar emphasizes individual months as compared with every other individual month, where the line emphasizes the year's pattern.

A pie graph is the wrong choice in this case. You might argue that a pie shows parts of a whole, so each month could be a pie slice, showing how the year's sales divided up by month. It certainly could, but with clutter and commotion. Besides, twelve slices is at least twice as many as most pie graphs can comfortably contain.* (See Color Plate 34 for an unusual pie graph example.)

Looking at trends, both the diagram and the text might be in percentages instead of numbers. A table—which you might think of as

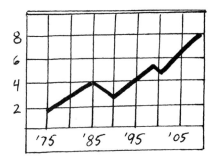

A vertical bar graph. *Adapted from "Uses and Misuses," by Nigel Holmes* (Designer's Guide to Creating Charts & Diagrams).

A line (also known as "fever") graph. *Adapted from "Uses and Misuses," by Nigel Holmes* (Designer's Guide to Creating Charts & Diagrams).

* Here's a communication principle to trump all others: When following any principle would interfere with clarity, go with clarity. For example, limiting pie slices makes sense unless the point *is* the clutter, such as a market that has become fragmented (an example from Kosslyn's *Graph Design for the Eye and Mind*).

a combination between text and a diagram—lists the data without the extraneous words in between. For example:

Jan	$112,000
Feb	130,000
Mar	97,000
Apr	125,000
May	141,000
June	117,000
July	85,000
Aug	114,000
Sep	168,000
Oct	136,000
Nov	119,000
Dec	123,000

A table will provide the most accurate portrayal of the data. But you can't compare data as vividly with a table as you can with a graphic display, and although a table reflects a pattern, graphs show the pattern more quickly. In a table, your only emphasis tools are color, weight, or extra space; graphs add hierarchy based on size.

Some of the varieties, boiled down:

• Bar graphs visually represent each month's sales and how each compares with the others. They clearly show the relative amounts in chronological order, with an emphasis on the amount of sales and the highs and lows. But should the bars run vertically or horizontally? When time is one of the comparisons, tradition says run time increments across the bottom, on the x axis (but, again, defy tradition when it's clearer and more meaningful the other way). Kosslyn recommends putting the most important part of the data ("the major independent variable of interest") on the x axis as a default. But, he says, "there are situations where horizontal graphs make more sense, e.g., if the labels are too long to fit in a vertical format."

• Line graphs emphasize trends more than they do individual points.

• Pie charts, meant to show only how parts relate to the whole, work for this example only if you add the months' sales figures (to equal 100 percent), and convert each month's figures into a percentage, or pie slice, of the whole. But even then, the large number of slices and the closeness of some of the months' results, would recommend another type of graph.

Add a second product to the graph with a line or bar in another color. Or use stacked bars to show readers how the sales of each product compare *and* combine. At least that's the idea. As always, don't assume what readers will understand. Sketch your best, clearest diagram of the material and then make sure you test it for clarity.

EXERCISE: A report on a salary survey needs diagrams to help convey the results. Respondents represent twelve main categories of industry and about as many job titles. The diagrams need to show them all because respondents measure the info's effectiveness by how clearly they can "see themselves" in it.

Come up with a graph or table to answer at least three of the following numbered questions. For the purpose of the exercise (only!), you can make up the data. As you analyze, consider in which cases you might

• answer the "how much" question with a percentage instead of the actual quantity

• combine any two questions in one graph or table

• use a solid bar (in bar graphs) or maybe substitute an icon

Throughout, put yourself in the place of the reader to consider which questions might provide you with the most support in asking for a pay raise. For example:

1. How many respondents have which job titles?

2. How many respondents make how much?

3. How does the staff size affect salary scale?

4. Which job titles make how much (overall, and by gender)?

5. How does geographic location affect salary scale (overall, and by gender)?

6. How many respondents got a promotion (overall, and by gender)?

7. How many respondents got how much raise?

8. How have respondents' salary scales changed in the past five years, compared with the national average of workers' salary scales (overall, and by gender)?

9. How does the size of the organization affect salary size?

10. How do the number of years on the job and number of years in the field (usually different figures for respondents) affect salary scale?

EXERCISE: Collect comparative data from your daily life and the lives of those around you, then determine the best way to depict it. For example, you could track, record, and plot how long it takes you to travel the same commute over a week. Or you could track:

• the price of a gallon of gas over the past two months

• the amount of time you spend in meetings compared with other work tasks

• the number of songs you download in any given week

You also could compare attendance levels at work or in your classes, as observed over two weeks. Or track and compare what time in the day your colleagues showed up over the course of a week.

Find logical increments

After you choose the right diagram format, you also need to analyze the data to find workable increments to plot. For example, working with the numbers set on page 182 (leaving off the thousands)—112, 130, 97, 125, 141, 117, 85, 114, 168, 136, 119, 123—let's first arrange them in hierarchical order, then find equal increments that encompass them.

At least at first, the twelve-number set from 85 to 168 suggests ten increments of 10, from 80 to 170. But consider whether that many increments will clearly portray the situation, and how much space the publication allows. If a small space dictates fewer increments, you can add precision by labeling the graph with the actual numbers represented (but added labels can diminish the power of the graph, according to Kosslyn).

More increments would be more precise—19 increments of five—as long as the extra height wouldn't negate the benefits. Or you could go in the opposite direction, and still get across the differences among the numbers with six increments of 20, or even five increments of 25.

Notice how using fewer increments minimizes the differences between the numbers so they might distort the message. So might this: Viewers might not notice that none of these increment sets starts from zero. For ethics and clarity, make clear when numerical data doesn't start at zero. (A little diagonal or curved-line symbol often isn't prominent enough; add words.)

More about avoiding distortion (keeping out the riffgraph)

Graphs work so well to convey a quick impression that they can just as quickly convey the wrong one, by plan or accident. Information can get easily distorted in graphs because of what viewers take for granted, Kosslyn says. We expect more (bigger, wider, taller, steeper, or more voluminous) of any element in a graphic to mean a greater quantity. We also expect elements that *look* less to *be* less, and those that look the same to be the same.

Make clear and meaningful graphs (and detect deliberate distortions in other people's graphs) with the help of these guidelines:

• Write a title that's more like a headline than a label to make clear the point of the diagram. A headline form, preferably with a verb in it, better reflects the fact that a diagram is meant to answer a question.

• Start the scale at zero or visually shout the fact that it doesn't. (Again, although a small diagonal or curved line drawn through the scale is a conventional way to show it's truncated, readers don't always notice the symbol.)

• Use equal increments within a graph. If you don't, readers who fail to notice the inequality will register the wrong impression.

• Use equal scale increments on adjoining related graphs, or the reader's likely to assume that the scale used on the first one applies to the rest.

• Make labels and other type legible and consistent. Favor a clear typeface that's big enough for your audience to read easily. Shoot for the same minimum size—9-point—as for text, or the biggest you can fit in the tightest spot. And use a clear sans-serif typefaces for graph labels, although serif and sans-serif typefaces are equally legible for

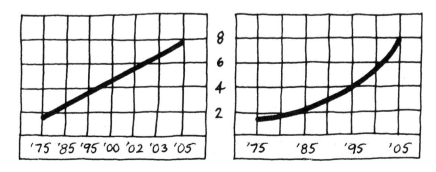

Use equal increments within each graph (and equal scales on parallel graphs). Although the two graphs show the same figures over the same time frame, the unequal increments on the left-hand graph incorrectly suggest a direct trip, while the equal ones on the right show an accurate gradual trend. *Adapted from "Uses and Misuses," by Nigel Holmes* (Designer's Guide to Creating Charts & Diagrams).

Where's the firehouse? Too many details on the left-hand graph get in its way. The right, reduced to its essence, makes the way clearer (only Harvard Square's prominence, by arrow and bigger type, might now interfere). *From* Graph Design for the Eye and Mind *by Stephen M. Kosslyn.*

text. But for labels, especially in smaller sizes and with numbers, serifs can clutter the field. And sans serif labels also help to distinguish themselves from serif text (but they're also a good choice with sans-serif text).

- Speaking of numbers, make sure readers can tell the difference between, say, an *8* and a *6*, a *3* and a *5*, or a *4* and a *1*. Such figures are tough to tell apart when they're set in type that's too small (in point size or x-height), too detailed (such as italics or serifs), either too light or too bold, or on tinted backgrounds. In the "Lap Lane Availability" table in this book, the number (of lanes) is one point bigger than the word *lanes*; the numbers are more important, and it was hard to distinguish the numbers at a smaller size. They also made time increments bigger to fit bigger labels throughout the table.

In fact, too-small labels are one of the most common problems Kosslyn reports seeing in graphs. Perhaps even more common is "packing too much information in a single display." To save your displays from such reader-unfriendly afflictions:

- include only what clearly and quickly answers the readers' question

- make keys* concise and simple enough for easy recall. And put them close enough to what they describe that they can be seen in the same visual field, instead of far enough away to force readers' eyes from the graph. If readers don't bother to make the trip, they can get the wrong impression. Or if the keys contain too many definitions, readers must make the trip more than once to read the graph. (Such a key probably means that the graph is too complicated and might need dividing in two.)

---

* Sometimes also known as "legends," keys identify what symbols or colors represent in graphs.

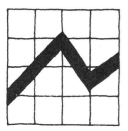 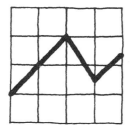

Too-thick fever lines . . .

- avoid lines in line graphs that are so thick that they obscure the reference points

- avoid graphics that look three-dimensional for the same reason. In a bar graph, for example, the appearance of dimension often makes it hard to tell which line is being measured.

- make icons a consistent size. For example, let's say you want to compare the number of cups of coffee bought by graduate students versus undergrads in a year at one university. So you draw a coffee mug as an icon to fill the bars of your graph. Use one size of icon to represent an amount that makes sense for the data, maybe 1,000 cups. Then stack the icons to show more or less quantity—three mugs for 3,000 cups, and so on. If instead you changed the mugs' proportions— stretching the mug to show more cups—you'd distort the difference.

- make icons easily discernible, logical, and understandable at the sizes at which they'll display

- make colors and patterns that symbolize data clearly distinguishable from each other

- limit the number and complexity of patterns to keep diagrams from looking like patchwork quilts and readers from confusing and forget-

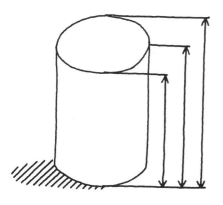 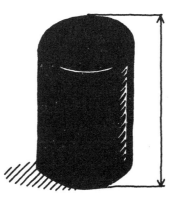

. . . and bars that look three-dimensional hide the data points. *Both sets on this page adapted from "Uses and Misuses," by Nigel Holmes* (Designer's Guide to Creating Charts & Diagrams).

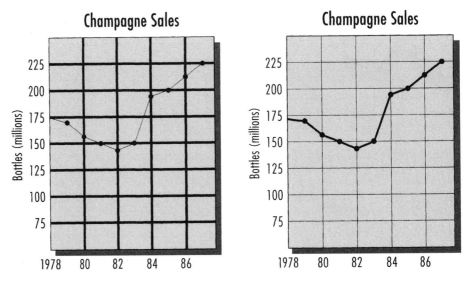

Avoid grid lines that overpower the foreground, as on the left. On the right, the "fever" line dominates the grid, as it should. *From* Graph Design for the Eye and Mind *by Stephen M. Kosslyn.*

ting them. We can't reliably or comfortably hold more than three or four pieces of data in short-term memory. The optimal number for patterns might be smaller still if they ask viewers also to recall detail, not just major differences.

- use background lines or a grid if they're needed, and only as many and as thick as you need to serve as reference points. As always, the background must never intrude on the foreground.

- put related information close together, especially in a table. Readers should be able to easily scan from one column to the next without risk of connecting unrelated items

- avoid pies when you want to compare more than five or six parts, or those of very different proportions

- when you use a pie graph, put the key categories in the same order they appear in the pie to help readers make sense of them

- you can follow convention by starting the biggest slice of the pie graph at the circle's top center (at 12 o'clock) and proceeding clockwise to the smallest slice. But readers aren't likely to know the convention. And although it would seem that the big-to-small-slice sequence works because it emphasizes the biggest, it's possible that readers' familiarity with a clock face makes it more natural to read small to big. Either way, it makes sense to start at the noon position, choose an order, and be consistent about it.

EXERCISE: Analyze the "Car Markets" pie graphs to discover where they failed to answer the implied question (and ask colleagues what they think the implied question *is*): "How does the Italian market compare to the total European Community (EC) market for these car makers?" Note any navigation and accuracy problems within the "Car Makers" section. (Also note how overly complicated graphs make it tough to catch mistakes in them.) What form of diagram would work best in this case? Sketch it.

The "Revenues and Employees" pair of pie graphs on the next page work better because of a closer correspondence between sections, and fewer sections. (Again, though, depending on the point, another form of diagram, such as a bar graph, would more efficiently show a correlation between number of employees and amount of revenue.)

Here are some general guidelines for tables—verbal, numerical, or mixed:

• Put columns close together so they're easily read across a row (but not so close that they seem to run together). For example, the columns in the "Calendar" table on page 191 could have lost a quarter of an inch and still left a pause after the first column's widest item. And you can improve the copy by trimming it and imposing parallel construction. For example, only one listing ("Memorial Day Weekend," next to last) says "closed for"; some other listings say

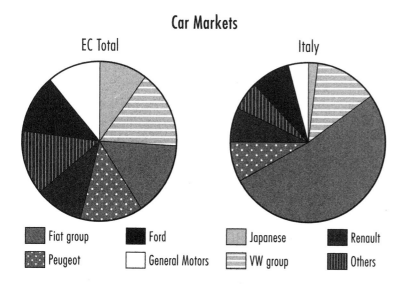

Car Markets

EC Total   **Italy**

Fiat group Ford Japanese Renault

Peugeot General Motors VW group Others

Too many slices, all those patterns, and tedious eye tracking discourage recall (in these diagrams that were designed to show what not to do). One graph with eight bars divided in half—for the EC and Italy—would be clearer. *From* Graph Design for the Eye and Mind *by Stephen M. Kosslyn.*

Revenues and Employees per Region of Electrotechnical Corporation

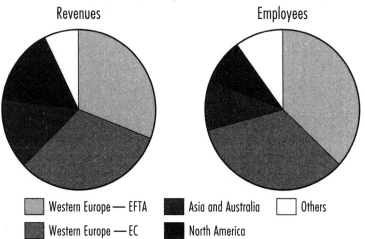

With just five slices and sequential shading, from light to dark, this pair's much easier on the eyes and brain. *From* Graph Design for the Eye and Mind *by Stephen M. Kosslyn.*

Calendars rarely get the care of other types of communication because they're often inherited or thrown together at the last minute. That's in indirect proportion to the amount of attention they receive from readers, who'll be grateful for the effort you spend to clarify them.

"break." They should be consistent. And won't readers assume classes resume at the end of the "closed" period without stating it? Also, because other listings say "closed" or "break," it's unclear whether school is closed for "Martin Luther King Birthday" and "President's Day." (See sidebar.)

- Reinforce horizontal tracking by adding fine lines between rows, a pale screen or color behind alternate rows, or extra space after every third row, suggests White's *Editing by Design,* third edition.

- Line up columns on the left, except for numbers, which should line up by decimal (whether decimals are shown or just implied).

- Put headings in bold to contrast with the table's data.

Groceries	Price
tomato sauce	2.49
milk	1.83
lemon	.35

- Consider the meaning of line weights: Make them as lightweight as visible between rows, noticeably heavier to separate categories of rows or the headings from the rest.

CALENDAR 2004-2005

EVENT	DATE
In-Person Registration	Saturday, May 15, 2004 10:00 am – 3:00 pm
In-Person Registration Dance Supplies, Etc. will be here to sell dancewear.	Saturday, August 28, 2004 10:00 – 3:00 pm
In-Person Registration Dance Supplies, Etc. will be here to sell dancewear.	Friday, September 10, 2004 5:00 – 9:00 pm
Classes Begin	Monday, September 13, 2004
Thanksgiving Break	November 22 – November 27, 2004
Nutcracker	November 27, 28, 2004
Classes Resume	Monday, November 29, 2004
Winter Break Classes Resume	December 20, 2004 – January 2, 2005 Monday, January 3, 2005
New Student Enrollment	Saturday, January 8, 2005 10:00 – 3:00 pm
Martin Luther King Birthday	Monday, January 17, 2005
President's Day	Monday, February 21, 2005
Spring Break Classes Resume	March 25, 2005 – April 4, 2005 Monday, April 4, 2005
Recital	Saturday, May 28, 2005
Closed for Memorial Day Weekend Classes Resume	Saturday, May 28 – Monday May 30, 2005 Tuesday, May 31, 2005
Last day of classes	Saturday, June 18, 2004

Help the eye connect the columns in this calendar in a ballet school's program booklet by taking out space between the columns and editing the first column for consistency. Horizontal dotted lines already help. *Client: Ballet Royäle Institute of Maryland. Design firm: Design Army. Creative directors/Art directors: Pum Lefebure, Jake Lefebure. Designer: Dan Adler. Programmer: Tim Madle. Copywriter: Howard Kaplan.*

Diagrammatic case studies

Bar graphs compare "cases"

No lines, scales, or axes muddy up the bar graphs on the annual report spread shown in Color Plate 35. Careful readers who check "cases docketed" bars for meaning will note more difference between the second and third bars (although they represent less numerical difference) than between the first and the second bars. Or, if they expect consistency among the graphs, readers might reasonably question the proportions of the end bars compared with their neighbors, which would have to be almost twice as tall to share an implied scale.

Fortunately in both cases, the big red numbers are likely to speak more loudly than the bars. But if readers miss the smaller type for the year, they might mistake the bar on the right of each graph for the current year instead of a five-year average. Although annual reports often try to put a positive spin on things, that potential mistake doesn't seem like a deliberate distortion because a bigger number isn't always better in the third column ("cases pending end," which means pending by the end of the year, not the end of pending cases, the text explains).

The graph format continues through the report. On a previous page (see Color Plate 36), readers might wonder about the numerical breakdown under the red numbers. Then they have to figure out that the number before the slash represents "mediation" cases and the one after it represents "ADR" cases, as hinted at in the title. Both are in white (reversed) type, which is weak against the gold ink. It will be clear only to readers who've seen and understood the shorthand before or who read the text before examining the graphics.

Unclear diagrams meet goal

Graphs and pictorial tables abound in a brochure from a design firm that wants to show how it can help law firms recruit students. The diagrams don't communicate clearly, but they're not meant to, says Burkey Belser of Greenfield/Belser Ltd. Their goal is more to impress than to inform. (See Color Plates 37, 38, and 39.)

The designers chose graphic design over information design, and form over function. They meant these charts to be "irreverent and appealing. It's in fact pretty difficult to pull information from those charts," Belser says. "I could have conveyed that information much more efficiently than we did. So we chose to be inefficient in order to be creative" in a style students would appreciate. The designers wanted to show the audience (law firms) "ways to present themselves (to law students) that they never thought about."

The graphic style and samples of recruitment work for clients are intended to distinguish the design firm's work from law firms' typical recruitment materials: dense "stuff that students just toss in the trash can as soon as they get it." To show what the law firms' materials *could* look like, the booklet's light tone reflects the design firm's understanding of college students, the audience's audience. Anyway, he adds, "the key information's in the headline."

But even within that context, the designers didn't have to sacrifice the *graphic* information. For example, let's look at the decision tree chart. (See Color Plate 37.) The "tree" becomes the playing surface of a pinball machine whose pins and levers represent students' deciding factors. The factors seem to be arranged in order of importance to students, but not consistently. Students rated the levers at the bottom as more important than what's immediately above them, serving the graphic's theme more than its content.

Nor is color used consistently for the top percentages and graphics. But it's *almost* consistent, so to show the 21-percent category, using pink (the color for factors with secondary priority), instead of higher-priority blue, seems like a mistake. Another inconsistency: The factors that counted least are yellow, but their percentage figures are pink. (Maybe yellow numbers would seem too relatively important because, of the three colors, yellow contrasts most against the background.)

EXERCISE: Analyze the pinball diagram in Color Plate 37 for ways to enhance the information's clarity, then redesign it.

Graphic table tells who, what, how many

Firms typically display client lists and other self-promotions on their Web sites. Potential clients can use this info to help them answer questions such as:

- "Do they have experience doing projects like mine?"

- "Whom did they do them for?" ("Do they have experience working with companies like mine?" "Have they worked for any well-known companies?")

- "Can they handle a range of projects?"

But lists can get repetitive, so many firms group the type of projects under category heads. Clients who want, say, a Web site can click on that heading to see what other sites the firm has designed. One firm went farther, as you can see in Color Plate 40. A matrix shows the firm's clients and the project or projects—ID (identity: logo, stationery), Web site, collateral (brochures, ads), or system (combinations of the preceding)—the firm designed for each. Dots alone simply and nonverbally convey a lot of information without repeating the common elements.

Each project type has its own column and color for its heading and related dots: lightest cream for systems, lemon for ID, marigold for Web, and pumpkin for collateral. On the left, the client names are in white. After the first screenful, the list of names is beyond the reach of the project-type headings. Instead of repeated headings cluttering the top of each new screenful, the headings show up on their side at staggered intervals to aid column identification.

The dot colors reinforce the categories for those who notice and recall them, at least until you mouse over the dots. At that point, dots turn white with butterscotch circles around them. The dots are live, so clicking on them answers another important question from the audience: "What do the projects look like?"

Distinguished by shape

A series of diagrams made of the simplest geometric shapes helps to describe how an investment firm screens financial products. The screening process is the star of the firm's capabilities brochure, because the audience identified "'a consistent process' as the most important element when choosing investment managers," writes Kate Dautrich at Carla Hall Design Group.

The simple diagrams also help sales people convey the process in person. A circle, triangle, and square each represent a different part of the screening process. The designers chose "very primary shapes that would clearly be differentiated from one another," creative director Carla Hall says. At least two of the shapes also reflect what they symbolize. The "thematic screen" seemed more circular, and the "quantitative [screen] starts from the bottom up, so we've got a nice triangle pointing upwards."

The master diagram on the first page (on the facing page) introduces each screen and its shape, then combines it with the other two on its way toward client portfolios. In this case, the graphic approach

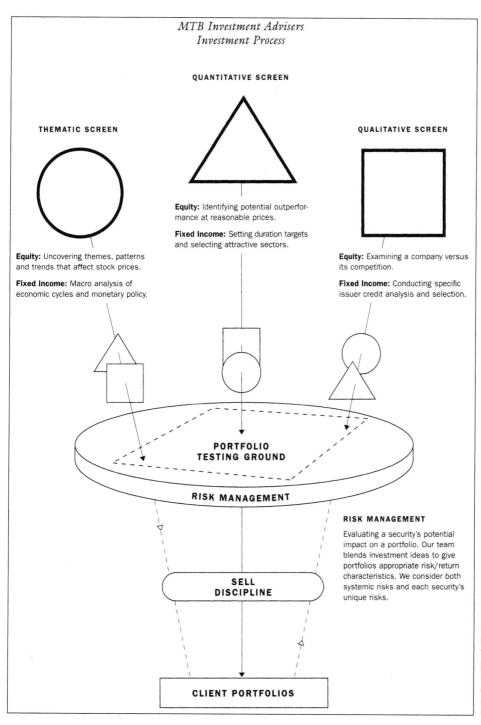

MTB Investment Advisers
Investment Process

QUANTITATIVE SCREEN

THEMATIC SCREEN

QUALITATIVE SCREEN

Equity: Identifying potential outperformance at reasonable prices.

Fixed Income: Setting duration targets and selecting attractive sectors.

Equity: Uncovering themes, patterns and trends that affect stock prices.

Fixed Income: Macro analysis of economic cycles and monetary policy.

Equity: Examining a company versus its competition.

Fixed Income: Conducting specific issuer credit analysis and selection.

PORTFOLIO TESTING GROUND

RISK MANAGEMENT

RISK MANAGEMENT

Evaluating a security's potential impact on a portfolio. Our team blends investment ideas to give portfolios appropriate risk/return characteristics. We consider both systemic risks and each security's unique risks.

SELL DISCIPLINE

CLIENT PORTFOLIOS

In one of a series of investment brochures, three geometric shapes correspond to as many types of processes for screening potential investments. © *M&T Investment Group, all rights reserved, used with permission. Design firm: Carla Hall Design Group. Art director: Jim Keller.*

works for the sophisticated audience: institutional investors, who don't need the level of verbal explanation that less knowledgeable investors would, the designers say.

The designers intend transparent vellum paper on the first and last pages to introduce the shapes, but also to reinforce how transparent the firm is making the process, subtle though it is. "It's a subliminal emotional thing; some people might recognize that," Hall says.

It's tough to count on audience members drawing that or perhaps any other conclusion from such a subtlety. So make explicit any messages that your information design must convey. But Hall also says she mixes the emotional and the intellectual in designs because "people perceive communication from so many different levels." And it's typical to have to reach a wide range of people with any project. "You have to be sensitive to your audience. I am always putting the designers who work with me in the shoes of who is going to read this."

In choosing colors for any project, the designers first look at the competitive environment and the project's relationship to other work by the same client. For this business-to-business brochure series, the designers chose sophisticated-looking cool metallics to contrast with the brighter palette for materials that go to the company's retail audience.

Other diagrams in the brochure use different shapes to distinguish other services. The one on page 197 holds an overview of the services in a process diagram, which looks like an organizational chart with flow.

Universal nonverbal messages in the chart include:

• solid lines to solid arrows: a direct path

• dashed lines to open arrows: optional or secondary paths

• starting at the top, ending at the bottom: orderly direction, with arrow direction reinforcing starting and ending points

• big caps above a section: headings of the categories they introduce

• smaller upper- and lowercase type enclosed in a shape: identifies only the object that encloses it

• a second color (when visible to the viewer and used consistently): reinforces common elements, in this case everything that isn't an upper- and lowercase label.

• different shapes: different services

"Planning Services," on another page in the brochure, contains another organizational/flow-chart look (see the next page). In this case, the format's familiarity could delay readers' understanding of the

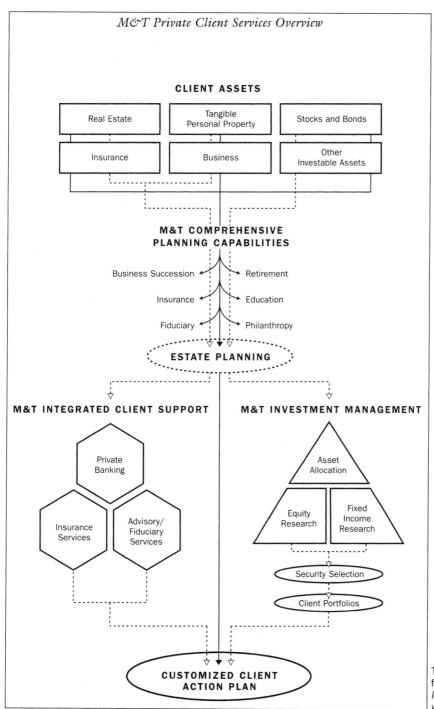

M&T Private Client Services Overview

CLIENT ASSETS

Real Estate	Tangible Personal Property	Stocks and Bonds
Insurance	Business	Other Investable Assets

M&T COMPREHENSIVE PLANNING CAPABILITIES

Business Succession ← → Retirement

Insurance ← → Education

Fiduciary ← → Philanthropy

ESTATE PLANNING

M&T INTEGRATED CLIENT SUPPORT

- Private Banking
- Insurance Services
- Advisory/ Fiduciary Services

M&T INVESTMENT MANAGEMENT

- Asset Allocation
- Equity Research
- Fixed Income Research

Security Selection

Client Portfolios

CUSTOMIZED CLIENT ACTION PLAN

content. The arrow direction, dual headings, and the space between the two "columns" are the first nonverbal clues that the diagram compares opposite situations. A subtle second color, another clue, takes a back seat to the blue that's shared between columns for headings and backgrounds.

One exception: In the bar at the bottom left, the brown dominates as the highest-contrast element on both pages. The diagram meets the designers' complex challenge: to graphically compare a hypothetical estate with and without estate planning. And they did it with space for legible type, and with only two colors plus black.

EXERCISE: Sketch a different way of showing the comparison, focusing on the nonverbal signals without losing any needed verbal ones. The point is to encourage estate planning without overselling. As the original recognizes, a credible tone is essential.

Working within the same data constraints, analyze the problem, get feedback from people around you, and incorporate it into a revised design.

Chart freedom

An art director agreed to do the statistics-filled magazine for a sailing association on one condition: total creative freedom, every designer's dream. The client agreed. Let's see whether the art director used that freedom to the reader's advantage.

The previous magazine, for the German section of the International 14 World Association, offered plenty of room to improve. It was a "horrible, boring design . . . like a cheap Xerox-copy thing," says art director Lars Harmsen. Charts were "just one Excel sheet followed by another."

Harmsen reduced and grouped poor provided images, and found good photos to blow up to full-page size to add drama. (See Color Plate 41 and the spreads on page 201.) Why talk about drama in an information-design book? Knowing the readers also means giving them an emotional connection to the material. And this audience, often passionate about the sport, would appreciate dynamic images more than just dry results, he reasoned.

Emotional connection, along with a budget only for black-and-white interior pages, also is Harmsen's reason for breaking rules. He threw out the typeface-restraint rule he learned in graphic design

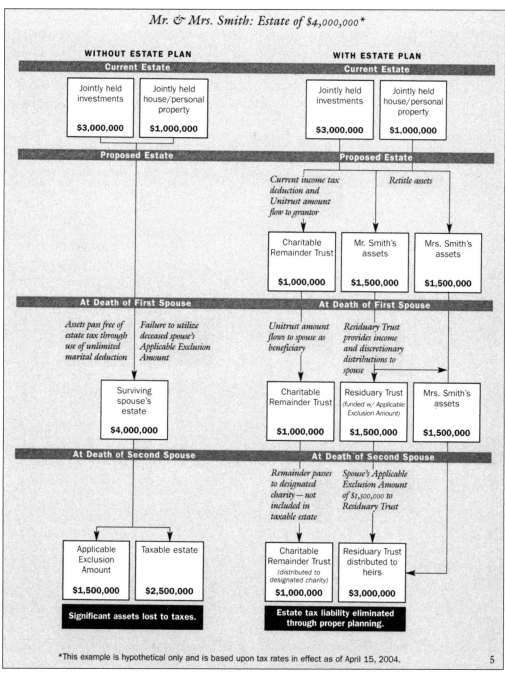

Mr. & Mrs. Smith: Estate of $4,000,000*

WITHOUT ESTATE PLAN

Current Estate

Jointly held investments	Jointly held house/personal property
$3,000,000	**$1,000,000**

Proposed Estate

At Death of First Spouse

Assets pass free of estate tax through use of unlimited marital deduction   *Failure to utilize deceased spouse's Applicable Exclusion Amount*

Surviving spouse's estate
$4,000,000

At Death of Second Spouse

Applicable Exclusion Amount	Taxable estate
$1,500,000	**$2,500,000**

Significant assets lost to taxes.

WITH ESTATE PLAN

Current Estate

Jointly held investments	Jointly held house/personal property
$3,000,000	**$1,000,000**

Proposed Estate

Current income tax deduction and Unitrust amount flow to grantor   *Retitle assets*

Charitable Remainder Trust	Mr. Smith's assets	Mrs. Smith's assets
$1,000,000	**$1,500,000**	**$1,500,000**

At Death of First Spouse

Unitrust amount flows to spouse as beneficiary   *Residuary Trust provides income and discretionary distributions to spouse*

Charitable Remainder Trust	Residuary Trust *(funded w/ Applicable Exclusion Amount)*	Mrs. Smith's assets
$1,000,000	**$1,500,000**	**$1,500,000**

At Death of Second Spouse

Remainder passes to designated charity — not included in taxable estate   *Spouse's Applicable Exclusion Amount of $1,500,000 to Residuary Trust*

Charitable Remainder Trust *(distributed to designated charity)*	Residuary Trust distributed to heirs
$1,000,000	**$3,000,000**

Estate tax liability eliminated through proper planning.

*This example is hypothetical only and is based upon tax rates in effect as of April 15, 2004.   5

In the same brochure, a organization-chart-like graphic compares a couple's finances with and without estate planning. © *M&T Investment Group, all rights reserved, used with permission.*

school (and you learned in this book). Chart headings get as many styles as headings, where consistency would better show their parallel structure.

Different words present enough diversity for any project, and too many typefaces often only interfere. So here you have another example of where graphic design and information design can part company (although Harmsen, like most graphic designers, would choose a consistent style sheet in most cases).

The only possible defense of diverse headings in this case: If readers are more interested in one heading than the others, and if the

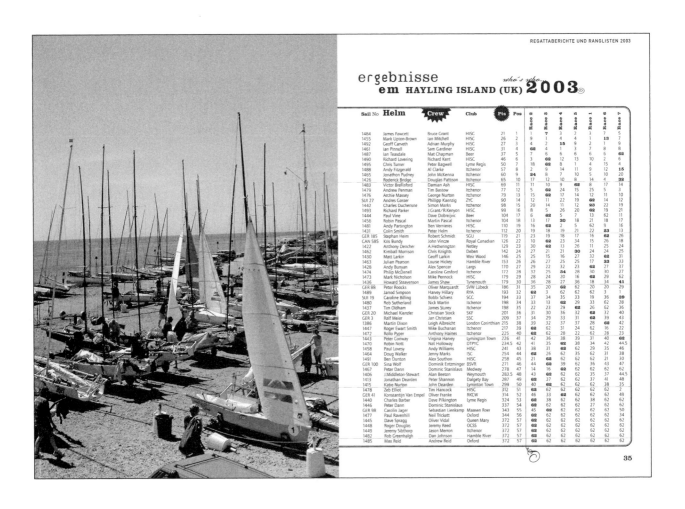

headings are consistently inconsistent from chart to chart or magazine visit to visit, a nonverbal flag might help readers find the info they want. Harmsen explains that the heading diversity also shows that the magazine is "about sport, fun, and lifestyle," not about the economy. But if you're just trying to find someone's ranking. . . .

Inside pages, all in budget-friendly black-and-white, show race results. The style of the results is more consistent than that of the headings, at least usually—but in one chart, the number *62* in bold stands for unfinished or unstarted races. In another, those races are shown between parentheses, with no bolding.

Lower-Quality photos get reduced and grouped; good ones get featured. *Design firm: Magma [Büro für Gestaltung]. Art direction: Lars Harmsen.*

german open 2004 *to win or to loose*©

Platz	Segelnr	Steuermann	Club	Vorschoter	Club	Punkte	Race 1	Race 2	Race 3	Race 4	Race 5	Race 6	Race 7	Race 8	Hull	Mast	Main	Jib	Gennaker	T-Foil
1	GER 91	Voss, Oliver	TSVS	Holscher, Jens	KYC	9,0	1	1	3	1	1	1	1	[dnc]	Bieker3	CST11	Alexander	Alexander	Moritz Delta	Jason King
2	GER 185	Heim, Stephan	SGU	Schmidt, Robert	SCAW	14,0	2	2	1	3	2	[5]	3	1	Ovington3	Bieker	North	North	North	Heim
3	GER 88	Roocks, Peter	SVW	Klinger, Ole		22,0	3	3	2	[8]	4	3	5	2	Bieker3	CST	Moritz Delta	Moritz Delta	Moritz Delta	Heim
4	GER 32	Jahn, Bernd	SGU	Braun, Ludwig	SGU	28,0	[13]	5	7	2	3	2	6	3	Ovington3	CST	Alexander	Hyde	Alexander	
5	GER 180	Reinsch, Axel	SVS	Schulze, Jörn	NRV	31,0	5	4	4	4	8	[14]	2	4	Bieker3	CST3	Alexander	Irwin	Irwin	
6	GER 20	Kienzler, Michael	SKF	Stock, Christian	SKF	35,0	4	6	5	5	5	6	4	[dnf]	Ovington3	CST	North	Hyde	North	
7	GER 44	Fackelmann, Claudio	Wind Club	Rübel, Frank	Wind C	55,0	6	8	[17]	6	6	8	8	13	Bieker3	CST	Alexander	Alexander	Alexander	Chris Turner
8	SUI 20	Billing, Caroline	SCC	Fischer, Claude	SCC	70,0	11	7	6	9	9	15	13	[dnf]	Bieker3	CST	Irwin	Irwin	Irwin	
9	GER 81	Holste, Olli	WSCW	Teichmann, Thilo	WSCW	72,0	7	9	11	11	7	[16]	11	16	ICE		Pinell	Pinell	Pinell	
10	AUS 365	Schenk, Dominik	SVM	Schenk, Lukas	SVM	76,0	16	12	10	[dns]	13	13	7	5	Jason King	CST	Irwin	Irwin	Irwin	
11	GER 9	Böhme, Tobias	WCL01	Hövel, Stefan	WCL01	80,0	9	13	14	17	[19]	11	10	6	Ovington 1	CST	North	Hammerlindl	North	
12	GER 96	Kulenkampff, Jens	RR&ZV	Kamke, Stefanie	RR&ZV	83,0	12	10	13	[dnc]	11	12	17	8	ICE	CST	Irwin	Hyde	Alexander	
13	GER 154	Hölter, Sönke		Gräpel, Sven	SVSt	85,0	10	[17]	9	7	14	17	16	12	ICE	Willets	Moritz Delta	Irwin	Irwin	
14	GER 100	Wolf, Sina	BSVR	Entzminger, Dominik	BSVR	85,0	[19]	11	8	12	17	18	9	10	Ovington 1	Willets	Batt	Batt	North	
15	GER 69	Weininger, Johannes	WC01	Sitton, Felix	WC01	98,0	[18]	14	18	14	16	7	15	14	Ovington 1	Willets	Batt	Hyde	Batt	
16	GER 86	Frick, Kai	ESC	Kopp, Tilmann	ESC	99,0	20	16	15	15	12	[21]	14	7	Börresen	Super Spars	HR	Hammerlindl	Batt	
17	GER 41	van Empel, Konstantijn	RKCW	Kleinevoss, Steffen	PSVK	106,0	15	[20]	19	13	15	9	20	15	Bieker 2	CST	Hyde	Hyde	Hyde	
18	GER 97	Scheulen, Lutz	RR&ZV	Koch, Stephan	RR&ZV	107,0	14	15	[dnf]	18	20	19	12	9	Morrison 8	CST	Batt	Batt	Moritz Delta	
19	GER 21	Heilmann, Andreas	STSG	Claudius, Tobias		109,0	8	[dnf]	dnf	10	10	4	19	dnf	Morrison 8	Willets	Batt	Batt	Batt	
20	DEN 21	Humpel, Peter	TTYC	Wilfert, Klaus	TTYC	117,0	[21]	18	16	20	21	10	21	11	Ovington 2	Angel	Hyde	Hyde	North	
21	GER 66	Wieland, Marcus	WVF	Dalgarno, Craig	MRSV	122,0	17	19	12	16	18	22	18	[dnf]	ICE	Willets	Moritz Delta	Moritz Delta	Moritz Delta	
22	GER 163	Henßen, Gerd	ASV Aachen	Braunschmidt, Inken	ASV Ki	166,0	24	21	[dnf]	22	24	24	22	dnf	Howlett1 b mod.	CST	Batt	Batt	Batt	
23	GER 31	Wolff, Thomas	SUCÜ	Liekmeier, Laura	SGÜ	169,0	26	[dns]	dnc	19	23	20	23	dnf	Ovington 1	Willets	Hyde	Hammerlindl	Hyde	
24	GER 192	Jordan, Helmut	YSCC	Jordan, Fiona	YCSS	175,0	22	[dnf]	dnf	21	22	23	dnc	dnc	Ovington 3	CST	Hyde	Hyde	Hyde	
25	DEN 20	Roering, Julian	SVW	Roering, Jana	SVW	190,0	25	[dnp]	dnc	24	25	dnc	dnc	dnc	Ovington 1	?	North	North	North	
26	AUT 2099	Müller, Alexander	YCRHd	Heim, Thomas	YCRHd	191,0	23	[dnf]	dnc	23	dnf	dnc	dnf	dnf	Howlett1 b	Proctor	Hyde	Hyde	Hyde	
27	GER 80	Mutz, Jan		Renz, Heike		203,0	[dnf]	dnc	dnc	dnc	dnc	dnc	dnf	dnf	Howlett1 b	?	Hyde	Hyde	Hyde	
	GER 89	Hauck, Caroline	WCL01	Linke, Riko	WCL01		[dns]	dnc	dnc	dnc	dnc	dnc	dnc	dnc	Hammer	Proctor	Hyde	Hyde	Irwin	

38

39

Challenging chart

On the last page of a program booklet, color, pattern, and shapes turn a course schedule table into a chart. Color Plate 42 shows the whole page reduced, so you can see the layout; Color Plate 43 shows a detail from the first six months, so you can see the type as the audience did.

The page takes on a big job, giving at least nine categories of info: course names, numbers, quantities, language, months, dates, durations, format, and even location. Can one chart do all that effectively?

EXERCISE: Analyze the course schedule's strengths and weaknesses from the perspective of someone who has signed up for classes. Focusing on clarity, what can you improve?

Of course the first step for any project like this would be to interview the staff and the audience, and you can't do that here. But you can show it to people around you to watch their reactions.

Table of contents isn't parallel

The design of the events calendar's contents page (see Color Plate 44) raises questions because of the nature of its content and because it doesn't follow parallel (design) construction. Before you read on, examine the table of contents for any potential confusion for readers (who are county residents).

Lack of parallel construction is the main confusion factor: All but one of the listings are months, yet you find that out only by reading the words. The page would communicate more clearly if it used different type styles or a subheading over the months to show the difference between the two categories.

And although it's a table of contents, some people might see the numbers that come after months as dates instead of page numbers. The confusion becomes even more likely when you turn to the actual listings (see Color Plae 45), where numbers in the same style and color now do mean dates.

Putting the months after the page numbers in the table of contents would be clearer. So would taking out the unneeded ending page number. That and reducing the numbers also would help to deemphasize the numbers and make them look less like dates.

Readers also might wish for a number color that contrasts better against white than gold—such as red—and for more help with navigat-

Table of Contents

Calendar Legend

$ Fee/Admission

H Handicap Accessible

H* Limited Handicap Accessible

TBA To Be Announced

The edition of the calendar that came out the year after the one in Color Plates 44 and 45, lost the color and some of the emphasis on the page numbers, making them look more like page numbers.

MAY continued

18 Jazz at the Center with John Eaton and Friends
Pianist John Eaton will be joined by Tommy Cecil on bass and Chuck Redd on vibraphone and play tunes by Kurt Weill, Vernon Duke and others. Tickets are $30, discounted to $25 for senior adults and students, and $20 for JCC members. To purchase tickets call the JCC Box Office at 301-348-3872. JCC of Greater Washington Kreeger Theatre, Rockville, 8 p.m., $, H, www.jccgw.org.

18 CHI Centers' Annual Meeting
Annual meeting and awards ceremony of CHI Centers directors. Hillandale Center, Silver Spring, 7:30 p.m.-9 p.m., H, 301-445-3350, www.chicenters.org.

19 BSO at Strathmore, SuperPops: Swings
Jack Everly, conductor and Ann Hampton Callaway, vocalist. Music Center at Strathmore, North Bethesda, 8 p.m., $, H, 301-581-5100, www.strathmore.org.

21 National Philharmonic's Choral Masterworks, "RAVISHING RHYTHM"
Voices of superb soloists and the expansive strength of National Philharmonic converge for Orff's pulse-pounding Carmina Burana. Music Center at Strathmore, North Bethesda, 8 p.m., $, H, 301-581-5100, www.strathmore.org.

22 Maryland Classic Youth Orchestra
Olivia W. Gutoff, conductor; Chris Allen, conductor; Scott Herman, conductor; David Levin, conductor. The pieces include Beethoven, Egmont Overture, Op. 84a; Dvořák, Symphony No. 9 "From the New World." Music Center at Strathmore, North Bethesda, 2 p.m., $, H, 301-581-5100, www.strathmore.org.

27 Blessing of the Animals
Pets of all kinds and their owners celebrate and are blessed by an ecumenical group of clerics. Animal Exchange in Rockville City Centre, Rockville, 4:30 p.m., H, 301-424-PETS, www.424PETS.com.

27-30 Potomac Memorial Day Tournament
Potomac Soccer Club hosts a soccer tournament for local, regional and national competitive soccer teams. Maryland SoccerPlex, Germantown, 8 a.m.-5 p.m., H, www.mdsoccerplex.org.

28 & 29 Hometown Holidays
Celebrate Memorial Day weekend in Rockville with an arts festival, Taste of Rockville kid activities, Ride for Rockville, free concerts by national recording artists including Hootie and the Blowfish, fireworks and more. Rockville Town Center, Rockville, Saturday 11 a.m.-10 p.m. and Sunday 11 a.m.-5 p.m., H, 240-314-8600, www.rockvillemd.gov.

30 61st Annual Rockville Memorial Day Parade
The event begins at 9:30 a.m. with a traditional wreath-laying ceremony. The parade begins at 10:30 a.m. which includes an exciting variety of drill teams, marching bands, majorettes, and community floats. N. Washington Street, Rockville, 9:30 a.m.-12 noon, H, 240-314-8620, www.rockvillemd.gov.

30 Home Front Street Cars
Recall the role of transit industry during wartime. National Capital Trolley Museum, Silver Spring, 12-5 p.m., H*, 301-384-6088, www.dctrolley.org.

JUNE

TBA Appraisal Clinic
The West Howard Antiques District is sponsoring its annual appraisal clinic. A local "antiques road show" with a two-day appraisal event to benefit The Children's Inn at NIH. West Howard Antiques District, Kensington, Weekend: Saturday 10 a.m.-5 p.m. and Sunday 12-5 p.m., H, 301-530-0175, www.westhowardantiques.com.

1- 7/3 Once on This Island- by Ahrens & Flaherty
An enchanting Caribbean-flavored musical from the writers of "Ragtime" exploring the life-changing consequences of romance between people from different worlds. Round House Theatre, Bethesda, $, H, 240-644-1100, www.roundhousetheatre.org.

Inside the updated calendar, dates and page numbers look identical. They shouldn't, yet they're still clear because of their position. But page borders—the only part of the page that doesn't inform—inappropriately scream for attention.

ing content. Tomato red's already on the cover and the edges of left-hand pages (see Color Plate 45). Right-hand page edges get the gold, alternating for no good informational reason. And the gold edges fail to give enough contrast to the page numbers reversed out of them.

Alternating colors could help in two conditions: if the colors corresponded to alternate months in the table of contents and on the actual pages, and if research showed that readers look for what's happening during a particular day, weekend, or month.

Research is important because effective content and design depend on finding out how people need and want the info. Will people search by date or by category, say, all events in the performing arts (or some other criterion we'll find out from the audience)? If by date, the contents page has it mostly right.

The following year's calendar on pages 203 and 204 avoided the whole color question—and expense—with black-ink-only interior pages. In that edition, page numbers are only slightly more prominent than the contents. Left alignment further helps to emphasize the contents, and ellipsis points (the dots connecting categories to page numbers) make the numbers look more like pages.

But the page borders add clutter without information. Instead they could serve as tabs visible from the closed book to show where each section starts.

CHAPTER 8

Clear forms improve users' experience

"Not another form!" Forms, as certain as death and taxes because both need them, are widely despised. That's true even (or especially) when they stand between you and something you want, such as a job, a tax refund, redirected mail, or essential insurance coverage. Common problems with forms people must fill out every day—from the point of view of those doing the filling out—include finding it hard to know:

• where to begin and end

• how to navigate the rest

• what to fill out and what not to

• what's related, what's not

• how to fill it out correctly

• why to fill it out (inspiring thoughts such as "Do they really need this or do they just like to bother people?")

• which form to fill out under which circumstances (even more despised than filling out a form at all is filling out the *wrong* form)

Reasons for those problems include:

• lack of clear, brief instructions when they're needed

• lack of logical sequence

• lack of grouping of related questions

• excessive, useless or outdated questions

• more than one title or a hard-to-find one

• inconsistent, ponderous, and incomprehensible language

• different styles of type (and other graphic elements such as line and box weights, screen percentages, and colors) for similar kinds of information

- illegible type
- type that doesn't change size or weight to emphasize what should be emphasized
- lack of alignment
- lack of planning for how the form will be treated, such as
  - filling out with various computer programs, systems, or browsers, or by hand with pens or pencils
  - printing, photocopying, scanning, or faxing
- prime space devoted to "for office use only" sections
- lack of planning for processing and incorporating the form's data

In addition to frustrating and alienating the audience, poorly designed forms add to the burden of the organizations that issue them. They force employees to:

- make errors in processing and using the information
- spend too much time helping confused audience members and correcting their errors
- deal with the consequences of uncorrected errors

But careful design, based on close attention to each form's various audiences and systems, reduces or eliminates the frustration that gives forms a bad name. So every time you're asked to design or redesign a form, think of it as an opportunity to perform a public service, to reflect well on the organization, and even save time and money for all concerned.

How to do all that? The process of designing a form is similar to that of any information-design project: It must start, says Janice Redish, information design consultant and first director of the former Document Design Center, by analyzing:

- the form's overall purpose
- the purpose of each question in the form
- the people who must fill out the form (their needs and skills, and the context in which they'll fill out the form)
- the people and systems that will process and use the data on the form. (Ask questions such as "What's the form's life cycle?" "Who gets the form after it's filled out?")
- any constraints

Boiling down the questions, they're the same as for any information-design project, Redish says:

* What are we trying to do here?
* Who's the audience and what should we keep in mind about them?
* What's the scenario? What do I expect the audience to do?

The last question is especially important to bring to meetings with clients. For example, Redish says, if clients expect the audience "to read every word of [the form] and you know very well that people don't do that," you need to find out early so you can move the team toward appropriate expectations.

Part of looking at the purpose of a new form means asking, "Why do you think you need a form?" says Carolyn Bocella Bagin, an information designer and consultant who also directed the Document Design Center. It incorporates a way of measuring its success: "How will you know if it works?"

Asking the right questions while planning a form, Redish adds, "makes you understand the dimensions of the problem and therefore how it has to be solved."

Also ask the right questions *on* the form. Analyze every question. Find out why each item exists, who uses it, and how it's used, because you'll often find wasted items, Bagin says. People might say, "Sure, it's used," but not be able to say how or by whom. "A lot of people assume that because it's on paper, it must be used," or they think, "If we don't use it now, maybe we will."

To help organizations evaluate questions in intended or existing forms, Redish designed this matrix for form projects.

Include how the organization that issues the form will collect, process, and use the information entered into it. For example, will the form require staff retraining or new equipment?

You can and should question every item on every form you design; you will if you use this form. © *Janice (Ginny) Redish, used with permission.*

question #	data	who uses it?	for what?	is it needed?

When you create a form, it's useful to ask questions because that's what forms do. A form is like a conversation, according to "Designing Usable Forms: The Three-Layer Model of the Form," an article by Caroline Jarrett, a usability consultant. Redish adds that the analogy is true even when the questions in the form look like labels, as in "number in household" versus the more conversational "How many people live with you?" (The latter format works better for typical consumers, she says.)

Jarrett's three-layer form model suggests attention to the form's:

- *look.* For example, Jarrett advises the use of headings and color to group related questions, and a legible typeface. Beyond that, consider such issues as the amount of space needed to write or type—give enough to fit in the amount of info, but not so much that people think they haven't answered sufficiently. Another Redish tip that's geared to Web-based forms, but just as valid in print: Make clear which questions people have to fill out.

- *content.* Word the form's questions so the audience will understand them, Redish says.

- *task structure.* This refers to the relationship between the people who fill out the form and the organization that issues it. Looking at the form's task structure can help you decide what information you need on the form, and what you don't. For example, avoid asking people to fill out info you already know about them. And make clear what you want people to do with the form after they've filled it out.

A taxing case study

Bagin worked with the U.S. Internal Revenue Service (IRS) to redesign tax forms that include 941: Employer's Quarterly Federal Tax Return. At the time of the redesign, about 6.6 million employers used the form to report wages and collected taxes, she says.

The goals of the revisions, according to Bagin, were to:

- make the form easier for small-business owners to fill out themselves
- reduce the number of errors they make
- reduce the number of errors internal processors make

EXERCISE: Before reading about the changes on page 214, compare the previous one-page form on page 211 with the two-page revision on pages 212 and 213.

Form **941**		**Employer's Quarterly Federal Tax Return**			

Form **941**
(Rev. January 2004)
Department of the Treasury
Internal Revenue Service (99)

Employer's Quarterly Federal Tax Return
► See separate instructions revised January 2004 for information on completing this return.
Please type or print.

Enter state code for state in which deposits were made **only** if different from state in address to the right ► ⌷⌷ (see page 2 of separate instructions).

Name (as distinguished from trade name)   Date quarter ended

Trade name, if any   Employer identification number

Address (number and street)   City, state, and ZIP code

OMB No. 1545-0029

T	
FF	
FD	
FP	
I	
T	

If address is different from prior return, check here ►

IRS Use

1 1 1 1 1 1 1 1 1 1   2   3 3 3 3 3 3 3   4 4 4   5 5 5

6   7   8 8 8 8 8 8 8   9 9 9 9   10 10 10 10 10 10 10 10 10

A If you **do not have to file** returns in the future, check here ► ⌷ and enter date final wages paid ►

B If you are a seasonal employer, see **Seasonal employers** on page 1 of the instructions and check here ► ⌷

1	Number of employees in the pay period that includes March 12th . ►	1		/////
2	Total wages and tips, plus other compensation (see separate instructions)		**2**	
3	Total income tax withheld from wages, tips, and sick pay		**3**	
4	Adjustment of withheld income tax for preceding quarters of **this calendar year**		**4**	
5	Adjusted total of income tax withheld (line 3 as adjusted by line 4)		**5**	

6	Taxable social security wages	**6a**		× 12.4% (.124) =	**6b**	
	Taxable social security tips	**6c**		× 12.4% (.124) =	**6d**	
7	Taxable Medicare wages and tips . . .	**7a**		× 2.9% (.029) =	**7b**	

8	Total social security and Medicare taxes (add lines 6b, 6d, and 7b). **Check here if wages are not subject to social security and/or Medicare tax** . . . . ► ⌷	**8**	
9	Adjustment of social security and Medicare taxes (see instructions for required explanation) Sick Pay $ _____ ± Fractions of Cents $ _____ ± Other $ _____ =	**9**	
10	Adjusted total of social security and Medicare taxes (line 8 as adjusted by line 9)	**10**	
11	**Total taxes** (add lines 5 and 10)	**11**	
12	Advance earned income credit (EIC) payments made to employees (see instructions) . . .	**12**	
13	Net taxes (subtract line 12 from line 11). **If $2,500 or more, this must equal line 17, column (d) below (or line D of Schedule B (Form 941))**	**13**	
14	Total deposits for quarter, including overpayment applied from a prior quarter	**14**	
15	**Balance due** (subtract line 14 from line 13). See instructions	**15**	
16	**Overpayment.** If line 14 is more than line 13, enter excess here ► $ _____		

and check if to be: ⌷ Applied to next return **or** ⌷ Refunded.

- **All filers:** If line 13 is less than $2,500, **do not** complete line 17 or Schedule B (Form 941).
- **Semiweekly schedule depositors:** Complete Schedule B (Form 941) and check here . . . . ► ⌷
- **Monthly schedule depositors:** Complete line 17, columns (a) through (d), and check here. . . . . ► ⌷

17	**Monthly Summary of Federal Tax Liability.** (Complete **Schedule B (Form 941)** instead, if you were a semiweekly schedule depositor.)			
	(a) First month liability	(b) Second month liability	(c) Third month liability	(d) Total liability for quarter

Third Party Designee

Do you want to allow another person to discuss this return with the IRS (see separate instructions)? ⌷ **Yes.** Complete the following. ⌷ **No**

Designee's name ►   Phone no. ► ( )   Personal identification number (PIN) ►

Sign Here

Under penalties of perjury, I declare that I have examined this return, including accompanying schedules and statements, and to the best of my knowledge and belief, it is true, correct, and complete.

Signature ►   Print Your Name and Title ►   Date ►

For Privacy Act and Paperwork Reduction Act Notice, see back of Payment Voucher.   Cat. No. 17001Z   Form **941** (Rev. 1-2004)

A U.S. tax form lacked alignment and consistency, making it harder to pay taxes than it should've been.

Form **941 for 2005:** **Employer's Quarterly Federal Tax Return**

9501

(Rev. January 2005)

Department of the Treasury — Internal Revenue Service

OMB No. 1545-0029

Employer identification number ☐☐ – ☐☐☐☐☐☐☐

Name (not your trade name)

Trade name (if any)

Address

Number   Street   Suite or room number

City   State   ZIP code

Report for this Quarter ...
(Check one.)

☐ 1: January, February, March

☐ 2: April, May, June

☐ 3: July, August, September

☐ 4: October, November, December

Read the separate instructions before you fill out this form. Please type or print within the boxes.

Part 1: Answer these questions for this quarter.

1 Number of employees who received wages, tips, or other compensation for the pay period including: *Mar. 12* (Quarter 1), *June 12* (Quarter 2), *Sept. 12* (Quarter 3), *Dec. 12* (Quarter 4)   1

2 Wages, tips, and other compensation   .   .   .   2

3 Total income tax withheld from wages, tips, and other compensation   .   .   .   3

4 If no wages, tips, and other compensation are subject to social security or Medicare tax   .   ☐ Check and go to line 6.

5 Taxable social security and Medicare wages and tips:

		Column 1		*Column 2*	
5a	Taxable social security wages		× .124 =		
5b	Taxable social security tips		× .124 =		
5c	Taxable Medicare wages & tips		× .029 =		

5d Total social security and Medicare taxes (*Column 2*, lines 5a + 5b + 5c = line 5d) .   5d

6 Total taxes before adjustments (lines 3 + 5d = line 6) .   .   .   6

7 Tax adjustments (If your answer is a negative number, write it in brackets.):

7a Current quarter's fractions of cents .   .   .   .

7b Current quarter's sick pay .   .   .   .   .   .

7c Current quarter's adjustments for tips and group-term life insurance

7d Current year's income tax withholding (Attach Form 941c) .   .   .

7e Prior quarters' social security and Medicare taxes (Attach Form 941c)

7f Special additions to federal income tax (reserved use) .   .   .

7g Special additions to social security and Medicare (reserved use)

7h Total adjustments (Combine all amounts: lines 7a through 7g.) .   .   .   7h

8 Total taxes after adjustments (Combine lines 6 and 7h.)   8

9 Advance earned income credit (EIC) payments made to employees .   .   9

10 Total taxes after adjustment for advance EIC (lines 8 – 9 = line 10) .   .   10

11 Total deposits for this quarter, including overpayment applied from a prior quarter .   .   11

12 Balance due (lines 10 – 11 = line 12) Make checks payable to the *United States Treasury* .   12

13 Overpayment (If line 11 is more than line 10, write the difference here.)   Check one ☐ Apply to next return.   ☐ Send a refund.

Next ➡

For Privacy Act and Paperwork Reduction Act Notice, see the back of the Payment Voucher.

Cat. No. 17001Z   Form **941** (Rev. 1-2005)

The IRS commissioned a clearer redesign that expanded into a second page. Find and evaluate the other changes. *Client: Internal Revenue Service. Design firm: Center for Clear Communication, Inc. Designer: Carolyn Boccella Bagin.*

Name (not your trade name)　　　　　　　　　　　　　　Employer identification number

Part 2: Tell us about your deposit schedule for this quarter.

If you are unsure about whether you are a monthly schedule depositor or a semiweekly schedule depositor, see *Pub. 15 (Circular E)*, section 11.

14 ☐☐ Write the state abbreviation for the state where you made your deposits OR write "MU" if you made your deposits in *multiple* states.

15 Check one: ☐ Line 10 is less than $2,500. Go to Part 3.

☐ You were a monthly schedule depositor for the entire quarter. Fill out your tax liability for each month. Then go to Part 3.

Tax liability: Month 1 ☐

Month 2 ☐

Month 3 ☐

Total ☐ Total must equal line 10.

☐ You were a semiweekly schedule depositor for any part of this quarter. Fill out *Schedule B (Form 941): Report of Tax Liability for Semiweekly Schedule Depositors*, and attach it to this form.

Part 3: Tell us about your business. If a question does NOT apply to your business, leave it blank.

16 If your business has closed and you do not have to file returns in the future . . . . ☐ Check here, and

enter the final date you paid wages ☐ / /

17 If you are a seasonal employer and you do not have to file a return for every quarter of the year . . ☐ Check here.

Part 4: May we contact your third-party designee?

Do you want to allow an employee, a paid tax preparer, or another person to discuss this return with the IRS? See the instructions for details.

☐ Yes. Designee's name ☐

Phone ( ) – Personal Identification Number (PIN) ☐ ☐ ☐ ☐ ☐

☐ No.

Part 5: Sign here

Under penalties of perjury, I declare that I have examined this return, including accompanying schedules and statements, and to the best of my knowledge and belief, it is true, correct, and complete.

X

Sign your name here ☐

Print name and title ☐

Date / / Phone ( ) –

Part 6: For paid preparers only (optional)

Preparer's signature ☐

Firm's name ☐

Address ☐ EIN ☐

☐ ZIP code ☐

Date / / Phone ( ) – SSN/PTIN ☐

☐ Check if you are self-employed.

Page **2**　　　　　　　　　　　　　　　　　　　Form **941** (Rev. 1-2005)

Here's page 2 of the redesign.

The first changes you might notice overall are:

• the shaded background that highlights the white answer boxes. The feature, borrowed from Australian forms, solves a problem, says Bob Erickson, senior technical adviser for the IRS's Tax Forms and Publications. When the background also was white in the form's previous version, "people were leaving key boxes empty." What's more, the agency's research showed that "people really like" and understand the shading.

• more space (it took a second page to do it)

• a clearer path

• an absence of clutter

Other improvements include:

• logical groupings, which make:
    • related items look related
    • optional items easy to skip
    • the form look simpler and more accessible

• space for identifying the quarterly period in which the form is filed (the absence of such a feature in the previous form led to many errors)

• compatibility with new scanning equipment that's expected to reduce the numbers of errors made with manual processing

• prominence for questions that used to be "hidden"

About borrowing from Australia: The IRS regularly looks at other countries' experiences to guide its forms design. You'll do well to follow suit. Check similar and even not-so-similar projects for elements worth testing and adapting for your own purpose.

How to evaluate a form

The tax-form project demonstrates steps you can use to evaluate an existing form.

• Interview experts on the topic.

• Review error reports and outside critiques.

• Question each item.

• Design, redesign, and revise.

>> Design in the real world: Can't always get what you want
Design often involves compromise and working within constraints. You'll have to fight some constraints, but accept others. For example, although Carolyn Boccella Bagin, the tax form's redesigner, would have preferred a different typeface (such as CG Omega for its "contrast between weights"), she chose Helvetica from a limited list of typefaces supported by IRS systems:

Franklin Gothic: Bold, Demibold
Helvetica: Roman, Italic,
    Bold, Bold Italic, Black
Helvetica Neue: Roman, Italic,
    Bold, Bold Italic, Light
Helvetica Condensed:
    Normal, Bold, Black
OCR A: Normal
Tekton: Normal
Symbol: Normal
Times-Roman: Normal,
    Italic, Bold, Bold Italic
Universal-Greek with
    Math Pi: Normal
Universal-News with
    Common Pi: Normal
Zapf Dingbats: Normal

Before the next round of revisions, the IRS did line-by-line, one-on-one testing with ten to fifteen taxpayers, says Michael Chesman, director of the Office of Taxpayer Burden Reduction at the IRS, which oversaw the project. In the final phase of testing, the IRS asked participants to use the form to do tasks such as looking up answers to questions.

No form is an island you can change without also changing the systems around it. In the IRS's case, that means as many as "fifty different [computer] systems. It's a two- to three-year exercise" that involves a team of fifty to a hundred people, with no more than three forms in major revision at any given time, Chesman says.

The IRS also consults with external software developers to find out details such as "how many inches of space a box needs or if you can use alphanumeric characters in a box," Erickson says.

Extensive research before the redesigned form's release is a predictor of its success, but it's no guarantee. The IRS measures success by feedback from the public and its customer account services departments, and error reports. "These are living, breathing documents, and Congress changes tax laws every six months," Erickson says.

So far the form, released just a month before the interview with Chesman and Erickson, has received "more mixed reactions" from the public compared with Form 1065, another IRS revision. Some complained about the additional page to print out. And despite the clutter of the old form, complainers were used to it, Erickson says.

All revisions require a learning curve, Chesman says, which people who aren't professional tax preparers object to more than the pros do (probably because for them, the learning curve's longer). For the 941 form, that could add up to a lot of objections: "More than 50 percent" of people who fill out that form by themselves are not professional tax preparers, he says.

Look inside, not just out

Identifying the audience, an essential information design principle, applies to internal audiences, not just external ones. For example, because the two pages of the form could get separated within the agency, the form asks for the employer's identification number on each page to help reunite separated pages.

The agency decides which of its 550 forms to revise next based on such factors as the number of people who must file it, the number of errors reported, and taxpayer feedback, Chesman says. The 1040's form, "on the horizon," might use some concepts by Karen Schriver, whom a newspaper reporter challenged to improve the form for an article titled "Making 1040s a Bit Less Taxing."

The eventual official revision won't include Schriver's choice of typeface, Serifa, which, again, IRS systems don't support. It *will* reflect extensive research into the people and systems with which the form must interact (which, being a challenge that came from outside the agency, Schriver's project does not). It also will reflect "two major pieces of tax legislation" Congress passed "very late in the year," months after her work on it.

CHAPTER 9

How to help people find their way clearly

To help your audience get from here to there, a worthy goal for every information-design project, you have to know where "here" is for the audience. That's as true for a Web site, manual, or proposal as it is for a traditional wayfinding format such as a map, floor plan, or sign. And "here" refers as much to audience members' knowledge, background, and skills as it does to their physical location.

In this chapter, we'll look at some wayfinding case studies and apply their principles to other kinds of projects. The goal of each design is to help people navigate, whether on foot or wheel or by hand and eye alone. Notice how the designs demonstrate useful information-design principles . . . and when they don't.

In the traditional sense, navigating or "wayfinding is the science of organizing and defining a sequence of posted messages to make a building or space as self-navigable as possible," according to "Basic Principles of Wayfinding" by Wayne Hunt in *Designing and Planning Environmental Graphics Design*.

Expanding the concept of "space" to include any information-design project, the key words in the definition are "as self-navigable as possible"—design that's so logical and intuitive that people can find their own way to their goal or destination, easily and without frustration.

To find the appropriate design, Hunt advises, look at:

- the number of first-time visitors
- how urgently they need the services they're seeking
- how many destination choices they have
- what the visitors' emotional and mental conditions are
- how complex the route is
- what level of distraction the environment contains

Your task in each case begins with learning about your audience, so you can give the audience just what it needs, no more and no less, in a form they can easily understand. That involves finding out what the audience needs overall, and releasing it in digestible chunks. Show people where to start and how to navigate from there, using type and pictures that stand out clearly against their background and the design's environment.

Editing the viewer's experience

The audience's needs lead John Grimwade, graphic arts director at *Condé Nast Traveler* magazine, in creating informational graphics that "edit the experience for the viewer." For example, he does tour maps to guide his readers through "formidable" places such as London's Victoria and Albert Museum (V&A): "You can stagger out of there several hours later feeling as if you've really had enough." So for V&A and other museums, he did a pull-out pocket guide to a comfortable hour's worth of highlights. (See Color Plates 46 and 47.)

Tell just one thing, not everything

"One problem with the Information Age is that everybody wants to tell everybody everything they know," Grimwade says, citing the "megagraphic" trend in newspapers. Such graphics aren't selective. Instead, he says, he wishes they'd "tell us the one thing we really want to know." As an example, he cites a graphic of a new baseball stadium that includes even where and how the seat cushions were made, when all readers really want is the seating plan.

How can you design selectively? If you can't test, at least put yourself in the viewer's place. It might help if you've been there. Grimwade notes that after visiting, say, the Vatican, "the worst thing is . . . when someone says, 'You went there and you didn't see the Raphael room?' Or 'You went to the V&A and you didn't go to the cast room?' People are going to tell you you're mad; you feel like an idiot." So he designs the guides to call attention to what the writer and he deem to be the best sights.

From his travels, Grimwade also knows to show people what to avoid, not just what to see. Instead of giving a comprehensive account, "you really wish [a guidebook] would say, 'Don't bother with this; it's going to take you hours, and it's not one of the best things in

Barcelona.'" A sight's very presence in a guidebook without a caution implies it's worth seeing, which could lure travelers away from more worthwhile stops.

Walk the walk: "You are there"

Take literally the idea of putting yourself in the viewer's place. Walk the site to record things such as doors that don't open and where the staircases lead. Take photos or videos and make notes or comments on them as you go.

Another thing you'll find out by walking the site is that aerial views of buildings don't do much for people who view them on the ground. You'll help to orient people if you make tall buildings seem to project vertically, as if they were three-dimensional and the viewer were facing them.

Vertical projections also work for non-wayfinding maps, such as the one Grimwade did for a feature story about the rebirth of lower Manhattan. To reinforce the 3-D look and to help anchor the buildings to the background, he used shadows, tinted light enough that they don't look like objects or hide the objects they shadow. (See Color Plate 48.)

Guiding graphics principles

Grimwade recommends more ways to improve all of your graphics, wayfinding or not:

- Show people where to start. Every graphic should include a way in; the more complex the graphic, the more explicit the starting point must be.

- Work within and around your medium's constraints. For example, on the Manhattan map, Grimwade drew the buildings at an angle to keep them out of the magazine's wide gutter.

- Standardize on what few universal signals exist, such as a red line. "Everybody understands that an arrow [or line] . . . that stands out from everything else must be the track you're supposed to be on." He also includes numbered sequences and lines that lead from a graphic element to a piece of text on the short list of universal nonverbal signals.

- Use graphics techniques to show useful details. In "Designing Dubai," an infographic for a feature story about a long-term development project (see Color Plate 49), Grimwade showed blown-up sections of the whole area with:

- a tinted-spotlight effect that connects one of the tree-shaped island groups to its smaller place on the map

- a box connected by a lead line that shows the layout of the exclusive end of the "palm frond"

- Use sans-serif type for graphics because it's "cleaner . . . more informational and business-like," and more legible, especially at small sizes, Grimwade says. Another benefit of sans-serif on graphics: It looks different from the serif text, so there's less chance that readers will confuse them.

- Use graphics to do what photos can't, or can't do well. For example, illustrations with translucent layers that build in "X-ray vision" (such as the layer for the third level of the V&A museum, shown in Color Plate 46) can enhance the feeling of being there for the viewers by showing what's inside or behind something.

What's the question?

Think of questions the infographic should answer. To guide you toward the goal, also come up with a working headline if you haven't been given one.

Wayfinding systems exist to answer a question for the viewer that usually begins with: "How do I get to . . . ?" Although it might seem obvious, often the question and its answer are smothered by too much information, which can result in a cluttered design.

Modify the question or add new questions based on the user's needs or preferences. For example, some Web sites that give driving directions also give users a choice of routes, such as the fastest or the most direct, or ones that avoid highways. So appropriate variations on that question might include "How long will it take to get there from here?" and "Which or how many landmarks will I pass on the way?"

The Dubai illustration mentioned above began with a list of Grimwade's and the writer's questions:

- Where are the islands in relation to the city and the airport?

- How big are they?

- What are they?

- What do they look like up close?

Favor accuracy and authority over flash

For Grimwade's drawing of the latest passenger aircraft developments, he says, "we went out of our way to get the exact cross-sections of all the aircraft and to make sure the air-craft were correct." The "unspec-tacular" look of the drawing ("placid, potentially boring side views . . . and no tricky perspective") reinforces that credibility, as opposed to "a lot of wild graphics," whose very visual "language somehow implies they might be wrong," he says. "As soon as the planes are all flying in formation from some vanishing point, you start to create a showbiz look that I think readers flag as, 'Well, this is all very wonderful, but is it correct?' [and] 'what is it telling me?'"

Speak with a hierarchy of color and weight

Layer color strengths, type weights, and line weights in a hierarchy, with the strongest and boldest reflecting the highest priority, which people understand. Avoid "fruit salad," a term coined by one of Grimwade's former art directors to mean throwing in too many colors.

More color advice: Grimwade likes pastel backgrounds for showing off details, type, and red accents. On those backgrounds, black type is legible even when it's small, and lines and labels can stand out. Black on white gives the best contrast, "but if you've got a graphic like a floor plan, you're going to need a color in there somewhere," he says.

On the V&A plan Grimwade used sumptuous colors instead of pastels because they looked more like the museum, although he recon-sidered that decision as he spoke. If the "plans were pastel-colored, those numbers would be standing way off of that background instead of being pulled into them."

More about constraints . . . and compromise

In the words of *MIT—A Framework for Campus Development: Wayfinding and Signage,* a standards book by Joel Katz Design Associates (JKDA), effective redesign involves give-and-take: "Any comprehensive wayfinding program in a long-evolving environment represents, at best, the most appropriate compromise between the theoretically most effective wayfinding techniques and the limits and constraints imposed by bricks and mortar, planning, culture, departmental prerog-atives, use habits, audience attitudes, and a multitude of cost-related factors."

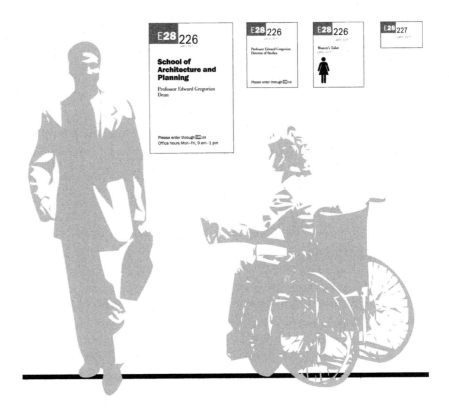

Designing from the viewer's perspective includes varying sign heights for all potential viewers, no matter how they get around. *Design firm: Joel Katz Design Associates. Client: Massachusetts Institute of Technology.*

For a MIT wayfinding-redesign project, studies and surveys identified three major audiences with different levels of navigational habits and needs:

• faculty members and graduate students, who typically learn to find only what they need

• staff members, who learn more about the campus overall

• undergrads, who learn the most

Each group also includes newcomers, who need at least basic wayfinding. And needs can change, as they probably will in this case: Planned construction of more grad housing is likely to expand grad students' campus scope.

The designers' proposed system of signs and maps accommodates wayseekers' diverse needs and tendencies, including how they travel (car, subway, bus, bike, wheelchair, walking; see art on facing page), and whether they're entering or leaving campus versus crossing it.

Use "heads-up" orientation

Signage should show wayseekers which way they're facing, not just where they are. Heads-up rather than north-up orientation on stationary maps makes it easy to relate the map to the environment. (See Color Plates 50 and 51.)

Heads-up orientation also can apply to a portable map. For example, look at Joel Katz Design Associates' flippable 8-by-36-inch map at right that shows construction on Pennsylvania's north-south U.S. 202. It works whether drivers are traveling north or south, because it has two sets of type, one north-up, the other south-up. Drivers might only have to turn the map upside down to orient the map for their route and to read the changes that apply to them.

More lessons taught

The MIT system also demonstrates other orientation and information-design guidelines you can use in your projects, such as:

- *point buildings up.* Like *Condé Nast Traveler's* maps, MIT's maps help to orient viewers with a vertical projection of a landmark: the tower building. (See Color Plates 50 and 51.)

- *include other landmarks.* At MIT, river orientation also helps on wall signs that identify the building. (See Color Plate 52.) Signs give the building's name and number (beginning with the letter code related to compass direction on campus (plus M for "main"). The north-pointing arrow reinforces the compass-point meaning of the letters.

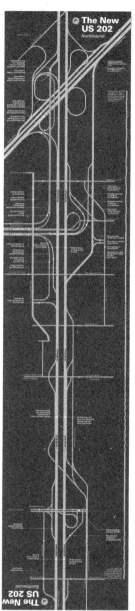

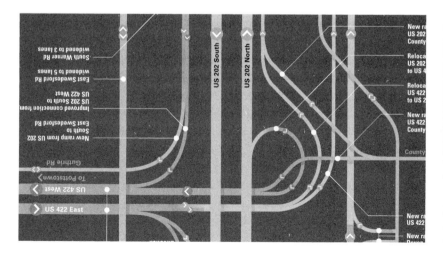

You can turn this map in whichever direction you're headed on this north-south highway because the type also runs both north and south. Here you see both an overview and a detail. *Design firm: Joel Katz Design Associates. Client: Pennsylvania Department of Transportation.*

You can see the heads-up principle violated in the north-up maps to nearby attractions placed on kiosks near the Capitol in Washington, D.C. It's the same map in every kiosk, but the kiosks' orientation is random. So although the *icon* of the Capitol is at the left on every map, the *building* is behind the viewers of some of the maps.

This disorienting map could be fixed by rotating the stationary kiosk to match the landscape. But it would be better to begin by drawing the Capitol, the neighborhood's major landmark, in the heads-up orientation, then placing the kiosks to reflect it.

Another time no one bothered to find out where the audience stood: The sponsor's Web page for an *information-design* meeting clearly directed attendees to the correct subway stop. After they left the train, though, things got trickier. "Look for the 7th St. exit," read the directions. But at the time, the underground signs pointing toward the two exits offered no such option, only "Arena Chinatown" or "Galleries." An incorrect choice would take visitors a block out of their way.

So whether you're creating signage or directions, there's no substitute for a visit to the site. And, for repeated-use directions, such as those on a Web site, visit periodically to check for any changes that need building into your design.

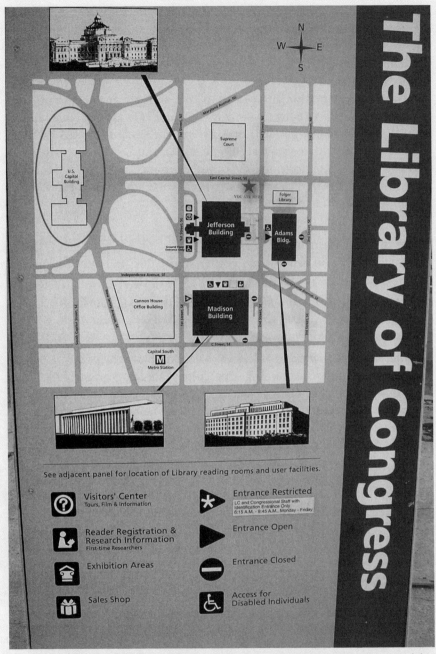

The problem with this map kiosk is that the Capitol—the landmark the map shows to your left as you face the map—is really behind you. *Photographer: Ronnie Lipton.*

- *make it easy to know "you are here."* When a map includes a "you are here" notation with a symbol, make the symbol an arrow or a triangle, never a circle, Katz says. (See Color Plate 53.) As "the only nondirectional geometric form," a circle "gives no clue as to which way you're facing or even if what you're facing is behind you." (But with heads-up orientation, the shape choice becomes less important.)

- *connect below with above.* For underground transit systems, design signs that help orient riders to what they'll find above ground. In the MIT stations now, for example, subway riders come up without knowing which direction they're facing, Katz says.

- *plan wayfinding components at "decision points,"* the places where wayseekers need to decide which way to go next. To do that, you first have to find the decision points. The designers of the MIT system identified both primary and secondary ones by observing pedestrians and noting "forks in the road."

- *fill in any important gaps.* "People can see only a little bit of geographic reality at one time, whether [it's] part of the body, a city, or a transit system," Katz says. And yet they need to "make decisions on things that are part of those systems that they can't see."

- *eliminate unneeded detail.* In some cases, extra detail doesn't help. For example, a passenger on a subway or a plane doesn't need the level of navigation details that the driver or pilot does. So it makes sense to leave them off of the navigation system you design for the passenger, Katz says.

- *be consistent.* As usual, a consistent design style sheet helps tie the system together and inform viewers nonverbally. That applies to elements such as:

  - *color.* For example, at MIT, main campus info is white on purple; east campus info is white on green; wheelchair info is white on blue. Color, borrowed from the familiar traffic-light code, also helps to show drivers where to park: Green signs point to parking areas, and red ones (with the universal symbol of a diagonal slash through the word *parking*) imply "forget about it."

  - *type.* Numbers for buildings are bolder than the letters for campus sections so they stand out. And the wide bottom on the numeral "1" in ITC Franklin Gothic keeps viewers from mistaking that frequently used number for any other.

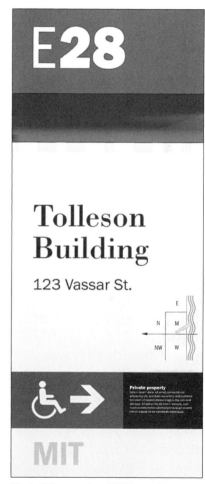

The building number ("28") stands out from the "E" (for the East part of campus), and the wide bottom on the "1" in ITC Franklin Gothic (as in the street number) makes the number clear.

• *hierarchy.* The overall design plan also ensures consistent placement of similar information and a hierarchy of information (campus section, building number, room number and "contents").

Must-haves for wayseekers on the Web

Finding one's way around a Web site shares a lot of challenges with finding one's way around a bigger space on foot. To demonstrate that, let's apply wayfinding-design essentials from the MIT standards book to Web sites. Essentials include:

• *a sense of place:* knowing you're in the defined environment (logos and consistent style)

• *locating:* finding on the map where you want to go (menus and links that include what you're looking for in the words you're looking for)

• *directing:* finding how to go where you want to (for example, clicking or mousing over, direct route or not)

• *identifying:* recognizing when you get there that you've found the place you were looking for (confirming and matching headings, consistent style)

• *accessing:* getting accommodation for your needs, as in type that's clear enough to read (or hear, for those who can't see). (The MIT system builds in accessibility with features such as directions placed at the right height for a person in a wheelchair and type that gets bigger as it gets higher up on the sign.)

The value of symbols in wayfinding

When their meaning is clear and their design simple, symbols have these advantages over words. They:

• speak to people of any language

• are compact, so they work in a much smaller space (as on a mobile phone)

• are recognizable over longer distance (as with traffic signs)

• can be read quickly

On floorplan maps reduced to small sizes for a museum guide (see Color Plate 54), Bureau Mijksenaar used legible icons of a clothes hanger, beribboned gift box, and coffee cup (along with the more common wheelchair-access and restroom symbols). The symbols *look like*

On a banner and a sign, icons stand for the museum's main exhibition spaces. Look closely under the sign for the hanging icons. They're clear in person. *Design firm: Bureau Mijksenaar by, Client: Teylers museum.*

the hanger, box, and coffee cup that they are. Now consider whether what they *stand for* is universally understandable.

More symbols, as icons on banners and signs for the museum's shop, reinforce the museum's and the shop's five main collections: a book for books, a shell for fossils and minerals, a gauge for scientific instruments, a frame for paintings and drawings, and a coin for medals and coins. They nonverbally tell visitors that when they see the symbols again inside the museum, they'll know where they are.

Back up nonverbal symbols if the audience needs it. The designers of Dutch Airways' signs added verbal meanings to the pictograms for new or infrequent passengers, who might not recognize or understand symbols for lockers or baggage claim, Paul Mijksenaar says. At Schiphol Airport in Amsterdam and at JFK, Newark, and LaGuardia Airports in New York and New Jersey, the use of fifty to sixty different symbols demands words even more, he says.

Numbers, color, and photos help to flag "here'"

Unlike outdoor maps you can see earlier in this chapter, the Teylers Museum guide doesn't use vertical projections to show visitors where they are on an aerial-view map. It relies instead on numbers, whitening, and photos. (See Color Plate 55.)

Each panel of the guide focuses on one or more exhibition spaces. The panel contains numbered illustrations of the objects contained in that space, along with its location on the floor plan. The numbers correspond to signs throughout the museum. What's more, a photo shows what the featured room on the floor plan looks like, so people entering the room have instant visual confirmation that they're in the right place.

Still another hint for museum visitors: The featured room in each panel is white on the floor plan; the other rooms are gray.

Each panel also contains a timeline of the objects in the space. That element would be appropriate for almost any museum, but especially for one so old; Teylers was founded in 1784. Time also factored into the signage, which uses different materials to distinguish between original and new parts of the museum: cherry signs and brass arrows for the old, silkscreens on wall and stainless-steel arrows for the new.

Show time, not just distance, when it counts

Schiphol Airport, which tests every three months to see whether people can find its gates, expects a success rate of 93 to 94 percent. But as important as finding the gate is getting there on time. At this "huge airport . . . it takes 20 minutes to walk from the entrance to the end of the concourse," Mijksenaar says. So to the signs directing passengers to gates, the design firm added the number of minutes to walk there.

The walking times show up in white in the terminal letters. (See Color Plate 56.) "That's a big advantage [if you're a passenger] because you see the information where you expect to see it," Mijksenaar says.

In addition to helping passengers make their flights, the walking times also help them spend more time—and potentially more money—in the shops and restaurants instead of at the gates; people can stay longer in the retail space if they know exactly how far they are from the gate.

In proposal at the time of writing, the designers also created a corresponding Personal Indoor Navigator, or PIN. The PIN would give travelers personalized information about their location at Schiphol Airport downloaded to their PDAs through the local Wi-Fi network. For example, one screen in Color Plate 57 shows bars and restaurants within a five-minute walk of the user; the one in Color Plate 58 shows the distance and routes to other airport services.

For signage the firm developed for JFK, Newark, and LaGuardia Airports, color coding reduces the number of signs that passengers have to read and makes the system self-selecting. The idea is that passengers can look for only the colors they need at any given time.

To make sure people notice and understand the codes, the designers also developed signs to help passengers recognize the existence and the meaning of the color system: black type on yellow (the highest-visibility combination) for flight info; yellow type on black for airport facilities; and white on green for exit, ground transportation and parking signs. The sign reads, "This airport has a color-coded signing system" (although just "signs" would be clearer), and gives a sample of each color and its corresponding location below it:

This airport has a color-coded signing system

Follow yellow signs when flying	**Follow black signs for airport services**	**Follow green signs when leaving the airport**
• Ticketing	• Restrooms	• Ground transportation
• Baggage	• Phones	• Parking
• Gates	• Escalators	
• Check-in		

Consider environmental context

Black on yellow makes a highly visible combination for signs and posters. High visibility is especially useful for an airport, a cluttered environment that needs a visual "shout" to compete with it. In fact, although white backgrounds tend to work well for text, on signs and posters, it takes a color or black background to stand out against common backdrops such as light or white walls, windows, or cloudy skies, Mijksenaar says.

If you can't design from scratch, you can add a border to set off a sign or poster from its environment. It's a quick method, but often less effective because a border that's strong enough to set off the content can distract from it.

Wayfinding or anatomy? Project combines them

How does a heart work? The task of "explaining how things work, how things move, and how you move is the same whether you're an individual on a bus or a platelet in a bloodstream," Joel Katz says. Both demand "simplicity and clarity so people can understand" them.

Katz took the analogy steps further when a subway map actually inspired his first heart sketch (for Richard Saul Wurman's book *Heart Disease and Cardiovascular Health*). The heart, he says, is like "a subway network with part of the tracks above the heart, part below in a circle around the heart." Trains travel from station to station, emptying or loading passengers (oxygen) depending on where they are in relation to the terminal. (See Color Plate 59.)

Although Katz liked the subway-inspired heart, he replaced it with a more conventional version (see Color Plate 60), because the original "so contradicted every picture that anyone had ever seen of the heart, I decided . . . it would destroy the credibility of the book."

The final version jibes with "a universal principle that's very resonant with me," Katz says: In maps and diagrams, "balance clarity and simplicity and logic" with what's familiar and expected. Readers try "to make sense of what they think they know, and what they've seen, and how they want to learn. That's just human factor stuff and you've got to respect that."

What remained less conventional for a medical illustration is the valentine shape of the heart. The illustrator used the shape to tip off viewers that he took license with how things really look (to show more clearly how they work). That's a Katz tenet: Give viewers a clue that a diagram is deliberately not anatomically or geographically precise. He builds in clues by "regularizing." For example, he might use pure geometric shapes that don't appear in the actual place or straighten naturally curvy lines whose curves don't inform.

In the final illustration (Color Plate 60 again), the subway analogy still kind of applies. The oxygen-spent blue blood travels from the upper and lower "tracks" through the blue side of the "terminal" to the lungs. There, oxygen replenishes the blood, turns it bright red, and sends it through the red side of the heart before it continues through the body.

Similar to the concept of regularizing, at times you might have to distort reality to make a legitimate point. For example, Color Plate 61 shows a street scene as it might look through an X-ray (assuming you could X-ray a street scene and see through metal). It illustrates an article about how security surveillance invades our daily life. To convey the information, it was more important for the illustration to *look* right than to *be* right, writes illustrator Mirko Ilić.

A place to park, but no place to start

In all environments, getting to a destination isn't the same as getting there without frustration. Consider the plight of drivers facing a self-service parking-fare machine (see Color Plate 62). They have to figure out how much money buys how much time (if they have to pay at all), where to put the money, how to get the ticket showing they've paid, and where to put that. That's a lot to ask of drivers, especially those facing poorly designed machines in Amsterdam.

The instructions on Color Plate 63 lack a clear hierarchy of weights and placement, so they also lack a clear path through the info, and enough relationship between the instructions and the coin and ticket areas. The instructions themselves aren't clear (or bilingual—English-speakers get only the basic instructions, not the fees for how much time, or the times when parking is free).

Is the paying driver meant to start reading from the upper left? That's customary in ambiguous data displays and the equal widths of the three columns weigh against any other plan. But the driver might pause to wonder whether the middle squared-cornered column has the edge over its rounded-cornered neighbors. Or do the color, extra space, and bold headings in the middle and right-hand columns demand first attention? The design doesn't make it clear.

In Bureau Mijksenaar's redesign of the instruction panel (see Color Plate 64), clarity prevails. Parking rates, times, and days are at the top because they apply to all three columns. The two wider outside columns now are parallel: Left is for payment in cash, right is for Dutch bank cards. The right column, unlike the rest of the redesign, is in Dutch only; Dutch bank card holders know Dutch, the designers assumed (or maybe just hoped: Having two extra steps in the bank card column leaves no room for a second language).

The yellow section connects the middle column's options—hourly or daily—to the first step in both payment options in the surrounding columns. And that column's vertical indent and smaller type shows its subordinance to the other columns.

The yellow also keys to the color of the button for the first step. Other steps start with circles in the color of the object used to perform them. Again, colors are intuitively chosen: a green button to get the ticket that shows you paid for parking, and red for the knob that you can turn to cancel the payment process.

Step numbers are now prominent; and all type is high-contrast and set in Meta because "it is a relatively tight typeface without being condensed," writes project leader and designer Rijk Boerma. That means it fits more characters on a line without looking squeezed. The uppercase size of the main heading is 4.9 mm (about 20-point; the secondary heading is 3.19 mm (about 14-point), with body text at 2.45 mm (about 10-point).

Only the text-display area was redesigned, because that was the scope of the project. "The overall integration of operation, information, and display . . . could have improved the ease of use considerably," Mijksenaar says.

Analyzing an information system

Here's a map convention used in a different form of graphic, a kind of photographic table (see Color Plate 65). (Take it as another example that it's useful to notice all forms of information design and when they can play a different role.) To show who's who among conference speakers in a brochure from the American Institute of Graphic Artists, the designer filled a grid with their tiny photos, each about a half-inch square. With no space for captions, he listed their names in three columns on the facing page. The "numeric-alpha" code in front of each name links to the corresponding speaker's map-like coordinates on the photo grid.

There, letters run in alphabetical order left to right across the top, and numbers run in sequential order down the left side. In the text columns, speakers are listed alphabetically by last name. Alphabetical order avoids the perception of favoritism, and in this case, it works for readers who are looking for a particular name. It would work better if it extended to the code, with the letter coming before the number. Viewers are likely to look first for guidance at the top of the photos, not on the left side. Not only are the side numbers a bit hidden near the spine of the thick brochure, but there's a reason we say "alphanumeric." A1, A2, etc. seems more familiar than 1A, 1B, etc. Still, although the order isn't intuitive, it takes only a moment to figure out.

Readers who work backward from the photo grid to match a face with a name hit a longer learning curve. That's where organization by name instead of coordinates (AI, A2 . . .) gets in the way. Readers must scan the three columns until they spot the right coordinates.

The design could serve all readers, no matter where they start, by putting the names *and the pictures* in alphabetical order, so the coordinates also run in order.

The designer might argue the photos wouldn't look as interesting that way; presumably he arranged photos by color, contrast, size and direction to create a pleasing look. And especially when the audience is designers, that's a legitimate argument. The designer (and audience) also could justify the arrangement as kind of a connect-the-dots game, rather than as a quick-search feature.

One more informational feature worth keeping: Numbers that follow each name refer to the pages where readers will find that speaker's bio and session description.

Two actual maps in the same brochure minimize details to show how the conference hotel's location relates to the city's tourist attractions. One page marks the hotel by name, red dot, and street on a DC map with a mileage scale. A red rectangle and a reference to the brochure's next spread represent the tourist area. (See Color Plate 66.)

That next spread blows up the area detailed on the previous spread, but here the area's limits aren't clear. That suggests that the map is designed for planning a free afternoon rather than for wayfinding, especially on foot. (See Color Plate 67.)

Besides color and minimalist style, the presence and angle of Connecticut Avenue are the only elements shared by the two maps. (Can you find the street on both?) More minimalism: Only the placement of the street names show the location of the streets, without the traditional lines drawn. It looks good, and although you notice the lines' absence, an experienced map reader can work around it.

But lines and their intersections can be useful for following along while moving. That's another clue the map wasn't designed for real-time navigating, as-is: no scale, which a visitor needs because the proportions of this map are different from those of the map on the previous page.

Watching the signs

You probably depend on signs more than you're aware in the course of a day. That might mean the signs are working, giving you the information you need without frustrating you. Start paying attention if you don't already. Look for information gaps, places that need signs and existing signs that need improvement, and think about what they need to say.

For example, if you lived in the Washington, D.C., area, and you needed to find out when to leave your place to reach an unfamiliar destination on time, you might go to the "trip planner" on the Washington Metro Area Transit Authority's Web site (see Color Plate 68). You'd plug in your starting point and destination to get the time, bus number, subway trains and stop, and arrival time. (Also see Color Plate 69.)

EXERCISE: Notice the signs on the shops when you walk in a commercial area, and whether you'd have to walk toward the street to see the shop's name. Signs should be visible to pedestrians, not just car and bus riders.

EXERCISE: The next time you travel or commute, photograph the directional and informational signs you'd need if you were a first-time visitor. Evaluate the signs' usefulness based on placement (are they where you need them to be?), clarity of content (appropriate language and amount), legibility, and visibility (language, structure, colors, type size and style, sign size, symbols, etc.).

Navigating a Web site

Something has to be done when a Web site's biggest audience has trouble finding what it needs on the site. Beyond providing resources, the Web site for UN Habitat, an agency of the United Nations with a mission to improve cities, needed to raise the organization's profile and attract funding. Changes, driven by interviews with internal stakeholders and external partners (the biggest audience), along with information-design principles, include:

• rewriting to succinctly state what the organization does and to eliminate what's unclear. For example, in the menu bar, what's the difference between a "campaign" and a "programme," and will all who enter the site know? More visitors are interested in what's going on in a specific place, it turned out, so "countries" replaces both in the menu bar (see Color Plates 70 and 71).

›› Heed the signs around you

Whether you're a new info-design student, or a practitioner who continues to learn, you'll benefit from noticing, collecting and evaluating the work of others. One designer took the idea even further, turning his collection of ineffective images into a design project.

A photo of a sign that failed to signal its intention illustrates each week of an appointment calendar called "Distressed Messages." A squashed stop sign leads the parade. It's a parade in which the spectator, not the spectacle, moves through time and space, as is true of wayfinding systems and publications, and not true of (traditional) movies or slide shows.

The stop sign represents one of the calendar's most obvious depictions of a communication failure. Images tend to get subtler as the year progresses. That's deliberate, based on how people use calendars, wrote Designer/Photographer George Tscherny of his work. "Considering that each image is literally 'in your face' for a full week, experience with designing calendars has taught me that the more subtle images may actually communicate more effectively and memorably in the long run."

But because the book you're holding is unlikely to stay open at the same place for days, you're seeing the most obvious images. For example, in the photo that inspired the calendar's theme, contradictory road signs share a pole in Cambridge, Massachusetts. Like much info design, the contradiction probably goes unnoticed by people who don't need guidance, while it frustrates or delays people who do.

Other obviously distressed images include photos of shredded paper, a "pedestrian walk" sign hanging upside-down on an urban telephone pole, and plenty of signs with crumbling, rusting, or absent letters. But the distressed state and the position of at least one photo might seem to add to its intrinsic meaning: Part of a sign advertising "Marriages & Divorces" broke off, taking the *D* with it, while *Marriages* remains intact. And the photo faces the week beginning with April Fool's Day.

Speaking of signs, the "Do Not Enter" sign is so common that we soon learn to recognize it without reading. And it's a good thing, because the design could be misleading. The white bar (looking a little like an opening or slot) separates "do not" from "enter." That's a bad place to break the phrase because if the sign is above eye level, someone who's not familiar with the sign might read it from the bottom up.

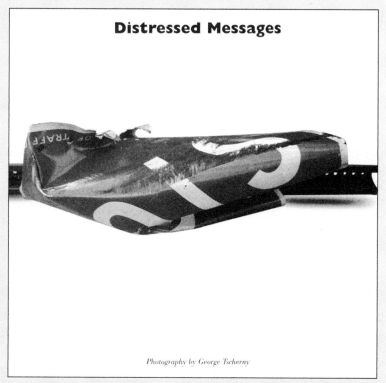

Distressed Messages

Photography by George Tscherny

Disintegrating and misplaced signs and other obviously "distressed messages" illustrate an appointment calender with that title and theme. *Photographer: George Tscherny. Creative director: Silas H. Rhodes. Designers: George Tscherny, Mathew Cocco.*

Photographer: George Tscherny. Creative director: Silas H. Rhodes. Designers: George Tscherny, Matthew Cocco.

Photographer: George Tscherny. Creative director: Silas H. Rhodes. Designers: George Tscherny, Matthew Cocco.

- reorganizing to show what the organization does. Pictures organized by theme, such as health or transportation, represent the organization's activities, and headings emphasize case studies and publications. Those are what many people come to the Web site for, says Renee Anderson of Hot Studio, which redesigned the site. But on the old site, "case studies" didn't exist as a heading, and "publications" was much less prominent.

- strengthening the visual hierarchy and sense of place. Designer Linda Haertling adhered to a strict grid and meaningful type hierarchy. She also added color coding that matches buttons and their destination pages to nonverbally tell users they've arrived where they intended (see Color Plate 71).

- frequently updating a prominent section that gives news about the organization's projects and involvement in world situations, relegating the older information to "archives" on the new site. (Dummy type on the images here means the site hadn't gone live by the time this was written.)

State-of-the-art Web-design guidelines

If you want to base your Web site design on research, *Research-Based Web Design Guidelines,* by Sanjay Koyani and others, is an excellent free resource. Find it on the Usability.gov Web site, by clicking on the "Guidelines & Checklists" section. The *Guidelines* consolidate and rank Web-design research findings by importance and strength. The resource won't replace your own testing, but it can help your team make better pre-testing decisions on key areas, and make the case about designing for function.

"Although we think it's fine to be creative, we always go with functional," Koyani says. So do users, typically. "When you ask users up front to label and organize things, they always go with function." That's true of any kind of site, he adds. "You see from some studies and observing stuff that users get extremely frustrated" when they don't find the facts they want.

Like other forms of information design, Web site information demands a strong contrast between the foreground and background. Koyani mentions the problem of people coming in with "yellow text on a light yellow background, dark yellow text, light yellow background, or magenta on green, or blue and black on a wine background because it matches their branding." Test participants might say they have no problem with it, but you might hear a different story if they have to scan for information across ten or eleven pages or print something, he says.

Other useful research-supported conventions

UPPER-LEFT LOGO TELLS USERS WHERE THEY ARE

Some usability research shows that "when people come to a Web site, the first thing they want to know is where they've landed. Where they look to find out is in the upper-left corner for the logo," Koyani says.

TAGLINE TELLS WHY USERS ARE THERE

Research also endorses using a tagline or a goal statement, rather than only a "wall of words," Koyani says. Web site visitors want to know right away what the site's about and whether anything's in it for them. A good tagline can help.

PUT THE MOST IMPORTANT STUFF FIRST

For the Department of Health and Human Services Web site, surveys and logs showed the links Web visitors search for the most. (See Color Plate 72.) So that's what determines links' order, not "which department had the most information or which agency had the strongest lobbying power, or the alphabet, which the technicians wanted." Audience-favored links also show up "above the fold."

And because testing showed clicking links to be one of the top user behaviors, the design teams added a clickable bullet to each major category link, and non-clickable ones below each link. "We found [that] by adding these bullets and giving people something to get a bird's-eye view of what was behind that link, they could scan the page, understand its relationships, and drill into the one they wanted much faster."

"How to use this book" instructions

Traditionally, how-to books tended simply to present their contents with no "serving suggestion," beyond implicit navigational aids such as a table of contents and maybe an index. Those days are going, inspired by Web sites, and led by information-design-and other how-to-book designers who understand that practical books are more likely to be browsed than read. So they come with instructions for use ("How to Use this Book") and designs that support browsing. Sometimes they also come with diagrams or maps of the contents.

Books might come with multiple or detailed table of contents, or friendly suggestions based on the users' perceived varied needs, job titles, backgrounds, or tasks: "If you're a graphic designer, begin with chapters ___, ___, and ___. If you're a writer, you'll probably benefit the most from chapters ___, ___, ___, and ___." Or "If you want to design stationery, focus on chapters ___ and ___. If you're doing slides, see chapter ___, ___, and ___." Or "If you're new at ___, start at the beginning. If you're experienced, you can skip to chapter ___."

Although readers always have been able to direct themselves by browsing, these suggestions make the book more interactive and customizable, and turn the author into a helpful adviser, seeming to know and understand readers and guide them through the book. Even authors who don't speak to readers that way are still likely to include more details in their tables of contents than those of years past.

But the customized book brings at least two potential risks: getting the user types wrong and being repetitive. Because each section is meant to be freestanding, it might have to repeat information that's meant for dual audiences. And repetition often becomes tedious for any front-to-back reader. But here's another way of looking at it: The repetition might train any remaining front-to-back reader to stop reading that way. (In information design, you'll almost always find at least one other way of looking at it. As always, let your knowledge of the audience—and their questions—lead you.)

Be curious; embrace the question

When Wurman conceived the health care book, his guiding questions were "how to freeze in print a conversation and what is the structure of a conversation." The book, he said, would be like a conversation: "You're asking me a question, I ask some questions back, we amplify it with marginalia, so to speak, and then we take action." And almost every spread in the book is a conversation based on a question.

Not that it's easy to find the question, Wurman says, because a typical education doesn't teach us how to how to analyze the structure of a conversation, organize information, ask questions, or understand the nature of failure. Instead, he says, "we're rewarded for answering a question, not asking one . . . and saying 'I know' (in meetings) rather than 'I don't know.'" In school, we're rewarded for "memorizing things we're not interested in, bulimically put on a piece of paper called a test, and then forgotten. That does not create a body of people who realize that learning is remembering what they're interested in." It doesn't make people *curious*.

To improve your curiosity and ability to find the questions in your projects:

- practice asking questions of clients and the audience
- boil down every project to its essential questions—the problems it needs to solve for the audience

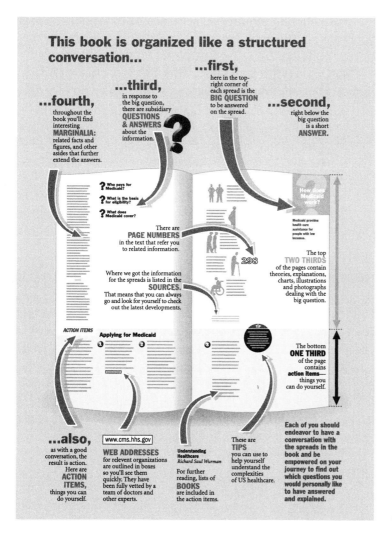

Understanding Healthecare *by Richard Saul Wurman. Designers/Art directors: Richard Saul Warman, Nigel Holmes. Production designer: Loren Barnett Appel.*

• raise your awareness of how you read and comprehend. Develop a practice of noticing things you never did before. See how typography and layout contribute to your ease or difficulty in navigating the info you encounter every day. Notice public messages—such as posters, signs, packaging, and distributed materials—as you drive, park, shop, take public transportation, make and keep appointments, walk around your town, home, office or studio.

Notice what's around you now: An "exit" or "no smoking" sign? Traffic lights? A menu from your local lunch place? The information on your computer monitor? The keypad of your phone? The label on your water bottle, soda can, candy bar? Maybe a memo to the cleaners in your building?

Notice everything and watch the effects of your increased attention on your information design.

Bibliography/resources

Chapter 1: How humans (almost) universally perceive

The Artful Eye, edited by Richard Gregory, John Harris, Priscilla Heard, and David Rose. Oxford University Press, 1995.

Experience Design 1, by Nathan Shedroff. Indianapolis: New Riders Publishing, 2001.

Experiences in Visual Thinking, second edition, by Robert McKim. Wadsworth, 1986.

From Fragments to Objects: Segmentation and Grouping in Vision, edited by Thomas F. Shipley and Philip J. Kellman. Elsevier Science Publishers, 2001.

Fundamentals of Psychology: The Brain, The Person, The World, second edition, by Stephen M. Kosslyn and Robin S. Rosenberg. Allyn & Bacon, 2004.

Human Color Vision, second edition, by Peter K. Kaiser and Robert M. Boynton. Optical Society of America, 1996.

Indirect Perception, edited by Irvin Rock. Cambridge, Mass.: MIT Press, 1997.

Looking at Looking: An Introduction to the Intelligence of Vision, edited by Theodore E. Parks. Sage Publications, 2001.

Memory and Attention: An Introduction to Human Information Processing, second edition, by Donald A. Norman. John Wiley & Sons, 1976.

The Memory Book, by Elizabeth Loftus. Addison-Wesley, 1980.

Perception, by Robert Sekuler and Randolph Blake. Alfred A. Knopf, 1985.

Perception and Imaging, second edition, by Richard Zakia. Focal Press, 2002

Perception of Space and Motion, edited by William Epstein and Sheena Rogers. Academic Press, 1995.

Principles of Gestalt Psychology, by K. Koffka. Harcourt, Brace, 1935.

Semiology of Graphics, by Jacques Bertin. University of Wisconsin Press, 1983.

Symbol Sourcebook, by Henry Dreyfuss. Van Nostrand Reinhold, 1984.

Thinking Visually: A Strategy Manual for Problem Solving, by Robert H. McKim. Lifetime Learning, 1980.

Visual Information for Everyday Use: Design and Research Perspectives, edited by Harm J. G. Zwaga, Theo Boersema, and Henriette C.M. Hoonhout. Taylor & Francis, 1999.

Visual Revelations: Graphical Tales of Fate and Deception from Napoleon Bonaparte to Ross Perot, by Howard Wainer. Copernicus, 1997.

Visual Thinking, by Rudolf Arnheim. University of California Press, 1969.

Chapter 2: Usability and how to achieve it

Contextual Design: Defining Customer-Centered Systems, by Hugh Beyer and Karen Holtzblatt. Morgan Kaufmann, 1998.

The Design of Everyday Things, by Donald Norman. Basic Books, 2002.

Designing Across Cultures, by Ronnie Lipton. How Design Books, 2002.

Dynamics in Document Design, by Karen A. Schriver. John Wiley & Sons, 1997.

Handbook of Usability Testing: How to Plan, Design, and Conduct Effective Tests, by Jeffrey Rubin. John Wiley & Sons, 1994.

Information Anxiety II, by Richard Saul Wurman. Que Publishing, 2000.

Information Architects, by Richard Saul Wurman. Graphis, 1997.

Information Architecture for the World Wide Web, by Louise Rosenfeld and Peter Morville. O'Reilly & Associates, 2002.

Information Design, edited by Robert Jacobson. MIT Press, 1999.

Information Design, by Graziella Tonfoni. Scarecrow Press, 1998.

Information Design: An Introduction, by Rune Pettersson. John Benjamins, 2002.

Open Here: The Art of Instructional Design, by Paul Mijksenaar and Piet Westendorf. Joost Elffers Books, 1999.

Practical Guide to Usability Testing, by Joseph Dumas and Janice C. Redish. Intellect Books, 1999.

Social Life of Information, by John Seely Brown and Paul Duguid. Harvard Business School Press, 2002.

Universal Principles of Design, by William Lidwell, Kritina Holden, and Jill Butler. Rockport Publishers, 2003.

Usability Testing and Research, by Carol Barnum. Longman, 2002
User and Task Analysis for Interface Design, by JoAnn T. Hackos and
    Janice C. Redish. Wiley Computer Publishing, 1998.
Visual Function: An Introduction to Information Design, by Paul
    Mijksenaar. Princeton Architectural Press, 1997.

Chapter 3: How to work with type and layout

Bases for Effective Reading, by Miles A. Tinker. University of Minnesota
    Press, 1965.
Designing Visual Language, by Charles Kostelnick and David D. Roberts.
    Allyn & Bacon, 1998.
Elements of Graphic Design, by Alex White. Allworth Press, 2002.
Editing, by Design, third edition, by Jan V. White. Allworth Press, 2003.
The Elements of Typographic Style, by Robert Bringhurst. Hartley and
    Marks, 2004.
Graphics for Visual Communication, by Craig Denton. Wm. C. Brown,
    1992.
Great Pages: A Common-Sense Approach to Effective Desktop Design, by Jan
    V. White. Serif Publishing, 1990.
The Grid, by Allen Hurlburt. John Wiley & Sons, 1978.
Grid Systems in Graphic Design, by Josef Müller-Brockmann. Hastings
    House, 1981.
"How to Compose a Painting," by Peter Saw. Available at www.petersaw
    .co.uk/ctutor/cmpsitn.htm.
*How to Make Type Readable: A Manual for Typographers, Printers, and
    Advertisers,* by Donald G. Paterson and Miles A. Tinker. Harper &
    Brothers, 1940.
How to Make Type Talk: The Relation of Typography to Voice Modulation,
    by Barnard J. Lewis. Stetson Press, 1914.
Legibility of Print, by Miles A. Tinker. Iowa State University Press, 1963.
Making and Breaking the Grid, by Timothy Samara. Rockport Publishers,
    2002.
The Non-Designer's Type Book, by Robin Williams. Peachpit Press,
    1998.
"The Science of Word Recognition or How I Learned to Stop Worrying
    and Love the Bouma" by Kevin Larson. Available at http://www
    .microsoft.com/typography/ctfonts/WordRecognition.aspx
Stop Stealing Sheep and Find Out How Type Works, second edition, by
    Erik Spiekermann and E. M. Ginger. Adobe Press, 2003.

Type in Use: Effective Typography for Electronic Publishing, second edition, by Alex White. W. W. Norton, 1999.

Typography: How to Make It Most Legible, by Rolf F. Rehe. Design Research Publications, 1974.

Xerox Publishing Standards. Phaidon Press, 1988.

Chapter 4: How to write clearly

Accessibility and Acceptability in Technical Manuals, by Inger Lassen. John Benjamins, 2003.

Guidelines for Document Designers, by the Document Design Center. American Institutes of Research, 1981.

Letting Go of the Words—Writing Web Content That Works, by Janice C. Redish. Morgan Kaufmann, 2006.

Managing Your Documentation Projects, by JoAnn T. Hackos. John Wiley & Sons, 1994.

The New York Public Library Writer's Guide to Style and Usage, edited by Andrea Sutcliffe. HarperCollins, 1994.

On Writing Well, fourth edition, by William Zinsser. Harper Perennial, 1990.

Reporting Technical Information, by Kenneth W. Houp, Thomas E. Pearsall, and Janice C. Redish. Macmillan, 1992

The Elements of Style, by William Strunk Jr. and E. B. White, with revisions, introduction, and a chapter by Roger Angell. Longman, 2004.

Chapter 5: How to use color meaningfully

The Color Compendium, by Augustine Hope and Margaret Walsh. Van Nostrand Reinhold, 1990.

Color for Impact, by Jan V. White. BookSmiths, Inc,: 1994.

The Elements of Color, by Johannes Itten. John Wiley & Sons, 1970.

"How We See Color," from *Color in the 21st Century,* by Helene W. Eckstein. Watson Guptill, 1991.

Interaction of Color, by Josef Albers. Yale University Press, 1975.

The Pantone Book of Color, by Leatrice Eiseman and Lawrence Herbert. Harry N. Abrams, 1990.

Principles of Color, by Faber Birren. Schiffer Publishing Company, 1987.

Principles of Color Design, second edition, by Wucius Wong. John Wiley & Sons, 1997.

Understanding Color, second edition, by Linda Holtzschue. John Wiley & Sons, 2002.

Chapter 6: How to make pictures that inform

Getting It Printed, fourth edition, by Eric Kenly and Mark Beach. How Design Books, 2004.

Chapter 7: Design, label, and caption diagrams clearly

Designers Guide to Creating Charts and Diagrams, by Nigel Holmes. Watson Guptill, 1984.

Designing Infographics, by Eric K. Meyer. Hayden Books, 1997.

Envisioning Information, by Edward R. Tufte. Graphics Press, 1990.

Graph Design for the Eye and Mind, by Stephen M. Kosslyn. Oxford University Press, 2006.

How to Lie with Charts, by Gerald E. Jones. Alameda, CA: Sybex, 1995.

How to Lie with Statistics, by Darrell Huff. W. W. Norton, 1993.

Information Graphics, by Peter Wildbur and Michael Burke. Thames & Hudson, 1998.

Information Graphics and Visual Clues, by Ronnie Lipton. Rockport Publishers, 2002.

Using Charts and Graphics: 1000 Ideas for Visual Persuasion, by Jan V. White. R. R. Bowker, 1984.

The Visual Display of Quantitative Information, second edition, by Edward R. Tufte. Graphics Press, 2001.

Visual Explanations, by Edward R. Tufte. Graphics Press, 1997.

Wordless Diagrams, by Nigel Holmes. Bloomsbury USA, 2005.

Chapter 8: Clear forms improve users' experience

"Forms That Work: The Three-Layer Model of the Form," by Caroline Jarrett. Effortmark, 2000. Available at www.formsthatwork.com/ ftp/DesigningUsableForms.pdf.

"Forms—The Importance of Getting It Right," by Clare Carey and Matt Carey. Lift Creative Communication Design, 2003–2004. Available at www.studiolift.com/resources/forms/index.html.

"Making 1040s A Bit Less Taxing: Form Needs Redesign, but It Would Be Easy Only in Theory, IRS Says," by Avrum D. Lank. *Milwaukee Journal-Sentinel,* April 14, 2004. Available at http://www2.jsonline. com/bym/your/apr04/222255.asp.

"Moving Forms to the Web," by Janice C. Redish. Usability University, 2004. Available at www.redish.net/content/talks/MovingFormstotheWeb.pdf.

Chapter 9: How to help people find their way clearly

Designing & Planning Environmental Graphics Design, edited by Wayne Hunt. Van Nostrand Reinhold, 1998.

Designing the User Interface: Strategies for Effective Human-Computer Interaction, third edition, by Ben Schneiderman. Addison-Wesley Longman, 1998.

Designing Web Usability: The Practice of Simplicity, by Jakob Nielsen. New Riders Press, 1999.

Design Research: Methods and Perspectives, edited by Brenda Laurel. MIT Press, 2003.

Don't Make Me Think: A Common Sense Approach to Web Usability, by Steve Krug. Que, 2000.

Follow the Yellow Brick Road, by Richard Saul Wurman. Bantam Books, 1992.

Making the City Observable, by Richard Saul Wurman. Walker Art Center and MIT Press, 1971.

Research-Based Web Design & Usability Guidelines, by Sanjay J. Koyani, Robert W. Bailey, and Janice R. Nall. National Cancer Institute, 2003. Available at http://www.usability.gov/pdfs/guidelines.html.

The Signage Sourcebook. U.S. Small Business Administration and the Signage Foundation for Communication Excellence, 2003.

Wayfinding: People, Signs and Architecture, by Paul Arthur and Romedi Passini. McGraw-Hill, 1992.

Web Site Usability, by Jared Spool, Tara Scanlon, Carolyn Snyder, and Terri DeAngelo. Morgan Kaufmann, 1998.

Useful information-design web sites, products

Document Design Journal: www.benjamins.nl/jbp/journals/Docd_info-.html

P.O. Box 36224, NL-1020 ME Amsterdam, The Netherlands

www.computeruser.com/resources/dictionary/emoticons.html

www.edwardtufte.com/bboard/q-and-a?topic_id=1

Information Architecture Institute: http://iainstitute.org/

www.InformationDesign.org

http://list.informationdesign.org/mailman/listinfo/infodesign-cafe

Information Design Journal: www.benjamins.nl/idjwww.microsoft.com/-usability

Nathan Shedroff: www.nathan.com/resources

Society for Technical Communicators

- Information Design: www.stcsig.org/id/id_resource_list.htm

- Usability Group: www.stcsig.org/usability/

Mark Barratt: Sue Walker, www.textmatters.com

www.usability.gov/guides.index.html

Jakob Nielsen: www.useit.com

Richard Saul Wurman: www.wurman.com

Index

About the author

As an art major with a smattering of graphic-design courses, Ronnie Lipton's early career spanned graphic design, technical illustration, forms design, and typesetting for ad agencies, publishing companies, and the odd corporation.

Lipton added writing later, with a stint as a copywriter and catalog editor, followed by eight years as the editor, art director, and then also publisher of *In House Graphics* newsletter. At the same time, she organized and presented at conferences and began teaching graphic design and writing at George Washington University, both in Washington, D.C., and at the University of Maryland.

By then, this career's theme had fully emerged: helping designers, clients, and students to effectively combine well-chosen words, pictures, and presentation to deliver a message the audience needs, wants, and can understand; helping them to realize they must start by understanding the audience's needs, skills, frame of reference, and preferences.

Lipton's other books (so far) include *Designing Across Cultures* and *Information Graphics and Visual Clues.*

In addition to working on books, Lipton helps organizations improve their visual and verbal communications, teaches workshops, and speaks at conferences. For help with your information-design projects or for an in-house or conference presentation, contact Ronnie Lipton at ronlipton@aol.com.